*British Social Work
in the Nineteenth Century*

INTERNATIONAL LIBRARY OF SOCIOLOGY

AND SOCIAL RECONSTRUCTION

Founded by Karl Mannheim

Editor W. J. H. Sprott

A catalogue of books available in the INTERNATIONAL LIBRARY OF
SOCIOLOGY AND SOCIAL RECONSTRUCTION and new books in
preparation for the Library will be found at the end of this volume

British Social Work in the Nineteenth Century

by

A. F. Young and E. T. Ashton

ROUTLEDGE & KEGAN PAUL LTD
Broadway House, 68–74 Carter Lane
London, E.C.4

*First published in 1956
by Routledge and Kegan Paul Ltd
Broadway House, 68–74 Carter Lane
London, E.C.4*

*Second impression 1963
Third impression 1967*

*Printed in Great Britain by
Butler and Tanner Ltd
Frome and London*

CONTENTS

Acknowledgments   vii

Introduction   *page* 1

PART ONE

IDEAS WHICH INFLUENCED THE DEVELOPMENT OF SOCIAL WORK

1 Influence of social and economic thought   7
    1 *Conditions*—2 *Economic and Political Theories*

2 Religious thought in the nineteenth century   28
    1 *The Church of England*—2 *The Tractarians*—3 *The Christian Socialists*—4 *The Nonconformists*—5 *The Methodists*—6 *The Unitarians*—7 *The Quakers*—8 *Conclusion*

3 Influence of poor law principles and practice   43
    1 *The problems and principles of poor law administration*—2 *Criticisms by Social Workers and their results*

PART TWO

MAIN BRANCHES OF SOCIAL WORK

4 Family case work—I. Thomas Chalmers   67

5 Family case work—II. Case work societies up to   81
  1869
    1 *Relief*—2 *For local needs*—3 *Jewish poor relief*—4 *Accommodation*—5 *Improvement*—6 *Suppression*—7 *Visiting*

6 Family case work—III. Charity Organization   92
  Society, 1869

7 Octavia Hill   115

CONTENTS

8 Care of deprived children   *page* 126
    1 *Schools*—2 *Orphanages*—3 *Cottage homes*—4 *Boarding-out*—5 *Adoption*—6 *N.S.P.C.C.*

9 The Penal Services   153
    1 *Elizabeth Fry*—2 *Discharged prisoners' aid societies*—3 *The work of Mary Carpenter—reformatory and industrial schools*—4 *Probation*

10 The Handicapped   183
    1 *The Blind*—2 *The Deaf*—3 *Mentally defective, insane and epileptic*—4 *Cripples*—5 *Homes*

11 Moral Welfare   207
    1 *Contagious diseases acts*—2 *White slavery*—3 *White Cross League*—4 *Rescue*—5 *Homes*

12 Group Work—I. Settlements   223

13 Group Work—II. Youth work   235
    1 *Sunday schools*—2 *Ragged Schools*—3 *Modern youth organizations*

Epilogue   259

Index   260

ACKNOWLEDGMENTS

WE wish to express our thanks to those who have helped us in the preparation of this book, and in particular to the Family Welfare Association and its Secretary, Mr. B. E. Astbury, C.B.E., who made some valuable suggestions on the chapters on Family Case Work; Miss E. Steel, B.A., Secretary of the Church of England Moral Welfare Association; Mr. G. J. Morley Jacobs, J.P., Secretary of the London Police Court Missions; the Staff of the Central Council for the Care of Cripples; Mr. R. E. Hughes of the Manchester Boys and Girls Refuges, who himself made some re-searches into the minute books of his Society for our benefit, and to Rev. R. P. McAuliffe, O.B.E., M.A., for his personal memories of the early days of Probation. We wish to say how much we have appreciated the help of Professor and Mrs. Ford, and of the library and clerical staff of the Department of Economics of the University.

A. F. Y.
E. T. A.

University of Southampton.

INTRODUCTION

IN this book we have attempted to fill a serious gap in the literature of British social work. Much has been written about the
social reformers of the nineteenth century and about the social
changes that resulted from their action, but of the methods and
scope of the personal services, whether nationally or locally
organized, that helped the poor and unfortunate nothing really
comprehensive has yet been published. By social work we do not
mean social reform, though some social workers have necessarily
become social reformers. Nor do we mean social services, i.e. the
State or quasi-State organizations for providing a minimum
standard of service as in education or health or for ensuring social
security when circumstances are adverse (Insurances, Old Age
Pensions). We use the term social work as referring to the personal
efforts of individuals who assist those in distress or promote the
welfare of those unsuccessful in promoting their own.

It is important to distinguish, as modern writers have done,
between case work, group work and community organization. The
latter, meaning the mobilization of local or national resources to
meet local or national needs, shades imperceptibly into group
work on the one hand and social reform on the other. In this book
we have commented on the activities in case work and group work
in the last century, even though the distinction between them was
not as clear as it is today. The study of community organization on
the other hand has not so far been developed in this country; and
though it would be untrue to say that the nineteenth century did
not provide interesting examples (e.g. the Jewish Board of
Guardians) the written material is so far very scanty, and with
some reluctance we have decided to omit separate consideration
of it here.

We have examined therefore the main branches of social work
in Great Britain today and tried to trace their development from
their rather confused beginnings to the state they reached by the

end of the century. In disentangling them we have often found ourselves stepping into the sphere of social reform or considering the machinery of the social services, but lines of demarcation are notoriously difficult to draw where human relationships are involved, and as no previous study of this sort has been made we have necessarily been forced to take arbitrary decisions.

The pages that follow are based on such records as exist; but these resources are scanty just when we should have wished them to be plentiful. For although much has been written about poverty, wages, housing and other social and economic conditions of the nineteenth century, too little has been left to us of the records, papers and reports of those who engaged in social work, from which we could glean their principles and study their methods. Had the many unknown social workers of the nineteenth century written about themselves as much as did Chalmers, Loch and Barnett, one wonders if we would now be able to view these giants in quite the same perspective as we do. It was the absence of adequate records that forced us to abandon a much cherished plan to include a section on the social work that working people offered to one another. The Friendly Societies must have done a great deal of personal social work, as must other offshoots of the working-class movement. But we have not been able to discover records which would tell us how and on what principles it was organized. Nor do we claim in any way to have made an exhaustive study, but rather to have included some of the main trends of social work method and policy in the nineteenth century, as far as they can be judged in the light of later twentieth-century standards.

Our studies underlined for us the importance to the development of social work of the general climate of opinion in the nineteenth century. It was no accident that its pace should quicken at the time when social and political events were speeding up. The C.O.S.[1] flowered when political democracy was being established, a national system of education introduced, trade unions enjoying a freedom they had never before experienced, and modern local government developing. In the light of this we felt it important to devote Part I of this study not only to an indication of the material changes in the conditions of life that took place in the century, but also to a brief appraisal of the philosophical and religious ideas

[1] Charity Organization Society.

that influenced men's minds and affected their attitude to the poor and their approach to social work. These, with a discussion of some of the relevant events in Poor Law history, seemed to us a necessary background for a proper understanding of the principles and practice of social work.

PART ONE

IDEAS WHICH INFLUENCED THE DEVELOPMENT OF SOCIAL WORK

CHAPTER 1

INFLUENCE OF SOCIAL AND ECONOMIC THOUGHT

IT is the opinion of Trevelyan that one of the outstanding features of the nineteenth century was the very great advance made in the sentiment and practice of humanity.[1] He claims that our modern love of liberty, justice and humanity comes to us direct from the Victorian age. It is the purpose of this brief survey of the social conditions and mental climate of the early Victorian period to determine why, in view of this growth of human feelings, organized social work took more than half a century to develop from the haphazard charity and philanthropy of earlier times.

Examples of what could have been done had been set by Chalmers. There were well-meaning people of high character, intelligence and ample leisure. Money was available, and was being spent lavishly on charitable enterprises—and not always wisely! Thus the Report on Mendicity in the Metropolis, 1816, mentioned the numerous beggars who had large sums of money in their pockets, gained by a variety of dubious practices.[2] The needs of the people were grave. The necessity for a revolutionary approach to mass misery was proved by the widespread interest in the reform of the Poor Laws. The people themselves, in all kinds of movements, newspapers, pamphlets, protests and violence itself were asking for help in pitiful terms. They had supporters from among all social classes, political parties and religious creeds. Some of the greatest men of the age, Owen, Cobbett, Disraeli, Dickens, Shaftesbury, Carlyle, to mention only a few, were demanding mitigation of the dismal fate of the poor. As early as 1796 Matthew Martin had begun an enquiry into misery in the

---

[1] B.B.C. (Wireless Symposium), *Ideas and Beliefs of the Victorians* (1949), p. 18.
[2] 1816 (396), v. Select Committee on the State of Mendicity in the Metropolis. *Report*, p. 101.

7

metropolis. He had received support from the 'Society for Bettering the Conditions of the Poor' and had indeed received also £500 from the Treasury to pursue his enquiries. His work was fully described before the Committee in 1816.[1] Why was it then that not till much later in the century were large-scale efforts made to deal realistically yet sympathetically with the manifold problems of individual distress?

The answer must undoubtedly be looked for in the climate of the times, in the social and material conditions, and in the habits of thought which moulded men's outlook at that period. There were not many realistic observers such as Colquhoun, whose treatise on Indigence [2] shrewdly examined the cost to the country of widespread poverty. He estimated the burden of poor rates as £4¼ millions. This was for a population of 8,872,980, out of whom over one million were rate-aided in 1803. To the £4¼ millions poor rates had to be added, he claimed, another £3⅓ millions of private charity. Later in another work he estimated that in 1812 the number of paupers had increased to 1½ millions.[3] Their income was £9¼ millions, two-thirds of this coming from parish rates. As Colquhoun estimated the annual national income as £430 millions at that time, it can be seen that about one-eighth of the population was receiving only one-forty-fifth of the increasing national income. His figures also showed that taking the working classes as a whole, they, representing 65 per cent of the population, were receiving 37 per cent of the national income.[4]

I   CONDITIONS

Conditions were altering very quickly in the first half of the nineteenth century. It is arguable that neither before nor after

---

[1] *Report*, p. 5.   [2] P. Colquhoun, *On Indigence* (1806).
[3] P. Colquhoun, *A Treatise on the Wealth, Power and Resources of the British Empire* (1815), p. 125.
[4] As a comparison, and without correcting for the changed value of the pound, note the following figures. In 1934 the National Income was £4,238 millions. According to Constance Braithwaite (*The Voluntary Citizen* (1938), p. 172) £42 millions was spent on charity in that year for a population of 40½ millions. (In the same year the total expenditure on the public social services was £435 millions.) So the amount that Colquhoun estimated was spent on private charity formed nearly 0·75 per cent of the national income at that time, compared with the private charity of 1934, which by Miss Braithwaite's figures, comprised 1 per cent of the current national income.

did social change reach the alarming momentum of 1800-50. It is possible only to outline some of the conditions of life in one arbitrarily chosen period. The year 1832 seems one that can well be chosen from which to survey the England of Wellington, Peel, Jeremy Bentham and Jane Austen. Particularly relevant to our purpose is an estimate of the extent to which the sentiment of humanity showed itself in practice during this period.

Woodward considers there had been an improvement in the attitude of the rich to the poor since the beginning of the century. Yet in 1832 there was still 'a certain callousness, an indifference to suffering and in some respects an invincible blindness'.[1] This was still an aristocratic age, despite the attempts of the middle-class to break into the ranks of aristocracy. It is necessary therefore to understand the attitude of the upper classes to the masses of the poor.

It was not altogether blindness that characterized their attitude, for many forces were at work to open their eyes. It was not so very long since the French Revolution. People in 1832 could well remember 1793, as many of us in mid-twentieth century remember Russia in 1917. Less than twenty years earlier many large country houses had kept cannon ready in case the mob attacked. The claims of the early socialists, the wide public that read Tom Paine, the desperate attempts of the pioneering Trade Unions to survive made the upper classes all too aware of the situation. Their reaction was fear . . . and fear bred repression.

Even the humanitarians of the time feared the poor. Shaftesbury was intensely hostile to any sort of radicalism: Bright was equally opposed to factory reform. Lack of understanding led to contradictions and confused counsels. The French Revolution had come as a shock to complacency and paternalism alike. Fear still reigned where there should have been pity, if not justice. It led to the firm belief that any concession to popular claims would open the floodgates to revolt.

Before passing to examine the actual conditions of the working classes and the protests that they made, it is worth enquiring whether it was revolutionary ideas, or the suspicion that such ideas existed, that had caused such a disastrous gap between governors and governed. The answer is that never before had the upper classes been so directly confronted by the might of the mob.

[1] E. L. Woodward, *The Age of Reform* (1938), p. 18.

The population of the country had doubled between 1801 and 1850. This, as much as the Industrial Revolution, had led to the deplorable conditions of the poor. In a generation great industrial populations grew up; the proletariat that Marx was soon to idealize was coming into existence, and long before Marx, was becoming self-conscious and vocal. The Chartist movement, following the great mass Trade Union movement of 1832–4, was soon to make the aristocrats fancy that their worst foreboding had come to pass. It may be true that 'the key to the Victorian age was the achievement of social peace'.[1] But this was in the future, and after a stormy twenty years. Social peace looked a long way off to the upper classes in 1832.

There were many who did not want a social peace based on the apathy and despair of a servile population. Carlyle thundered against the evils of the time. Cobbett whipped his readers into frenzy by reminding them of the old days when men had minds and souls of their own. The poor felt that everything was conspiring to lower their standards of life and to worsen their condition. The more fortunate of them had tried to gain security through Friendly Society membership. Colquhoun showed that 704,350 people, i.e. one-twelfth of the population, belonged to 9,672 Friendly Societies in 1803. These are striking figures but the mass of the poor nevertheless had not even enough coming in to pay the very moderate Friendly Society dues. The Luddites in 1812 had struck out blindly at new machinery; Peterloo was the culmination of several years of threatened insurrection. In the meantime the Industrial Revolution was developing and extending on all fronts. It is true that the process was by no means completed in 1832. Many parts of England had hardly been touched by the Industrial Revolution. Railways and joint stock companies were in their infancy; the handloom weavers and other remnants of the domestic system still fought a losing battle against inevitable trends.

Already workers in mill and factory, mine and workhouse, felt that overwhelming forces were pushing them ever downwards. As the Hammonds insisted,[2] their protests were not merely against the new machinery, but against the inhumanity of the new order, the new discipline and relentless factory timetable, the fines and

[1] Christopher Dawson in *Ideas and Beliefs of the Victorians*, p. 28.
[2] J. L. and B. Hammond, *The Bleak Age* (1934). *The Town Labourer* (1917).

regulations. Their customs, family ties, dignity as human beings, their very freedom seemed in peril. The main achievement of the industrial progress of which Macaulay boasted seemed to be the organization of the discomforts of poverty into a rigid system. Modern scholars have somewhat modified the picture of the Industrial Revolution given by Toynbee, Marx, Engels and later the Hammonds. Dorothy George, for instance, suggests that the Industrial Revolution was not entirely harmful to the workers.[1] She points out, among other instances, that even in the first years of the nineteenth century, health conditions were improving and machinery already easing many types of hard manual work.

Nevertheless the Industrial Revolution deserves this title on two grounds—(a) because the great manufacturers were daring innovators, (b) because the workers were in revolt against the novel conditions of labour that the factory system necessitated. The factories contained large numbers of workers, among whom two classes were clearly discernible, the small class of highly paid technicians and the larger mass of the unskilled. Conditions were bad enough under the domestic system, but at least no worker was subject to the whips of the overseers, the endless fines, the inhuman discipline.

Particularly had the women and children suffered from the introduction of the factory system. Their fate had been vividly described in the enquiries in 1816, 1832 and 1833.[2] They increasingly took the place of men, particularly in the textile factories of the north, as it was realized that with nimble fingers they could do the work more quickly than men.

The workhouses of the south sent their pauper children north to work in the mills. The factories were often dirty, dangerous, insanitary; the children in all too many cases were treated abominably, flogged, mutilated and degraded. Richard Oastler, in his letters on Yorkshire Slavery, 1833, asked the leaders of the movement for the abolition of Negro slavery what they were going to do about 'the little white slaves of the factories'. The Commissioners

---

[1] M. D. George, *England in Transition* (1931), p. 135).

[2] 1816 (397), iii. Select Committee on the State of Children employed in the Manufactories of the United Kingdom. *Minutes of Evidence.*

1831–32 (706), xv. Select Committee on the Bill to Regulate the Labour of Children in Mills and Factories. *Report.*

1833 (450), xx. Royal Commission on Employment of Children in Factories. *1st Report, Minutes of Evidence.*

of 1833 found that children started work at nine, sometimes eight, and even six or seven years of age; they worked fourteen hours a day, starting at four or five in the morning. By 1833 direct cruelty, according to the Commissioners, was diminishing but overwork all-pervasive. The richer classes of the towns did not choose to concern themselves with the sufferings of the factory children; they were mostly indifferent, for that matter, to the conditions much nearer home of the little climbing boys who swept their chimneys.

The new towns, as the Hammonds showed so vividly, symbolized the helplessness and misery of the masses. Often they were more like filthy barracks than centres of community life. Edwin Chadwick said of them, 'their condition in respect of cleanliness is almost as bad as that of an encamped horde or an undisciplined soldiery'.[1] It must be admitted that efforts were being made in several quarters to improve housing conditions. The housing provision made by some employers such as Owen, Oldknow and Lowther was a decided improvement over many rural homes. Chadwick himself gave instances of five-roomed houses, including three bedrooms, that showed evidence of enlightened thought on the subject. Illustrations are included in his report of new cottages in the Northumberland industrial area. They were clearly a big improvement on the old rural cottages illustrated for contrast. Yet it is obvious that these must have been exceptions. The new wealth was largely going into new factory plant and large-scale communications. As in Russia today, housing had to give place in early nineteenth-century England to the urgent demands of mechanization and industrialism generally.

It is difficult for us to realize quite how barbarous were conditions of life for the poor in many big cities and how uncouth, ignorant and depraved were big sections of the population. In London particularly many of the evil conditions of the age were most evident. It is true that London was not typical of the Industrial Revolution as a whole, for it was in the North that the new industrial towns had sprung up. But London was growing rapidly in size; it was already overpopulated, it had a housing situation that was desperate and sanitary arrangements that were primitive. The submerged tenth of its citizens presented grave

[1] 1842 (HL), xxvi. Sanitary Condition of the Labouring Population. Poor Law Commissioners (Edwin Chadwick). *Report.*

problems of vice, poverty, ill-health and delinquency, particularly in the districts where Irish immigrants lived. The evidence of Montague Burgoyne before the 1816 Committee on Mendicity, for example, vividly described the appalling housing conditions of the Irish in the Marylebone area.

One of the main causes of the deplorable state of the working classes was the neglect of national education. England in the 1830's was far behind several other parts of Europe in elementary education. It is true that in some areas a surprising number could read. Thus the Minutes of Evidence before the Select Committee on *The State of Children in Manufactories* in 1816 showed that in Manchester 529 out of 793 children under ten could read, the figure for those between ten and eighteen being 4,522 out of 5,460.[1] Yet almost alone in Europe, England left the training of her children to Sunday Schools and Charity Schools. Such working-class education as there was remained in the hands of two great religious societies—the 'National Society' and the 'British Society.' The weekday education given at the schools of these societies was a development of the work of Sunday Schools, in which children were taught to read the Bible. The aim of the two societies was not so much to encourage education as such, but to promote religious sentiments among the poor. They were to be trained in Hannah More's words, 'in habits of industry and piety'. It is fair to add that true charity was the motive of the philanthropists who ran the schools, a genuine concern to relieve misery; but a lively fear of a large, ignorant proletariat was never absent from their minds. The education given therefore was to be strictly limited.

Hannah More wanted the poor to read the Bible and her religious tracts, but they should not be taught to write, as that might be dangerous. The subject of working-class education was surrounded with prejudice and indifference. The minority of middle-class and upper-class people who supported the idea yet had no real notion of the value to the community of having at least minimally educated citizens. 'Educational reform was expensive,' says Woodward, 'it brought no immediate results and was concerned with values which could not be expressed in commercial language.' The new manufacturers were enthusiastic about new mechanical contrivances. Their human material was of less interest

[1] *Op. cit.*, p. 374.

13

to them than their expensive machinery. It is true that by mid-century Mechanics' Institutes sprang up in the North country to meet the need for skilled artificers: in 1851 there were 600,000 members of 610 such institutes. But on the whole the masters did not see the advantages of an educated working class until forty years later. Forster, in his speeches for the 1870 Education Act, showed what a lead Germany was beginning to gain in world trade through having higher educational standards in state schools. That any popular education existed at all was due to the rivalry between the Established Church and the Nonconformists. Neither could afford to leave the other alone in the field of educational endeavour; yet their mutual hostility was for many years to be as big an obstacle to educational progress as were prejudice and in-difference on the part of the middle classes. The existence of a large semi-literate mass of town-workers, only too open to emotional appeals from demagogic tub-thumpers, was a menace to industrial progress, as it was a danger to the established order. Few workers approached the standards of civic awareness, and intelligent interest in social matters, that would have justified the democracy that the Chartists claimed for them.

In the heart of early nineteenth-century England, the vast mass of the people were pagans, illiterate, misguided, vicious and prone to emotional outbursts. To preach, as philanthropists did, the gospel of 'self-help' was to overlook the lack of capacity in the poor to understand anything but their own misery. The idea that the working classes needed education not only for work and religion, but for civilized leisure, and in order to fit them for their role in the community, was almost unknown. Were they not thought to be persons incapable of profiting by leisure and fit only for the discipline of long factory hours? Thus arose a vicious circle. The working classes, deprived of the opportunity for decent relaxation, found their pleasure in such amusements as bull-baiting, cock-fighting and heavy drinking. This led to profligacy and crime. Seeing this, the upper classes argued all too often that education would be wasted on such depraved creatures.

This neglect of national education takes us back to the basic and fundamental evil of the age—the widening gap between rich and poor that Disraeli was soon to portray in his novel *Sybil*. Whether it was due to the French Revolution, the Industrial Revolution, growth of population, growth of industrial unions, whatever factor or combination of factors, the result had been that attitudes of rich to poor had become totally indifferent when they were not hostile. Cobbett stated that in his own lifetime people who were once called 'the commons of England' were in the 1830's referred to as 'the lower orders'. In his *Political Register* he maintained that they were spoken of by everyone possessing power to oppress them in the same manner as were animals of the farm. Even the more enlightened of the contemporary middle classes had their blind spots. Flogging in the armed forces, the pitiful conditions of the little chimney sweeps, the vile conditions of lunatics in the madhouses, these things were seldom seen, and seldom thought of, by the wealthy classes of the towns. Likewise their attitude to the 'lower classes' was normally one of detachment and disinterest.

2 ECONOMIC AND POLITICAL THEORIES

Wealth was rapidly increasing, and made life very much more comfortable and spacious for the upper and middle classes. In some ways indeed it helped to make them more kindly and tolerant. This was the age when the slaves were freed and the Catholics emancipated. It seems strange that so much brutal indifference existed where the suffering of the poor were concerned. It is questionable whether fear of the mob by itself explains this indifference. The answer lies more probably in the whole mental outlook of different sections of the well-to-do classes. Idealist historians maintain that to understand a period in history we have to think the thoughts of its leading characters. This is certainly the clue to understanding the social atmosphere of the early nineteenth century. The difficulty is that the leading characters of the age did not think alike by any means. It was an age of intellectual excitement when advances in science and engineering were upsetting traditional ways of thinking. A complete picture of the intellectual life of the time would have to include many diverse currents of thought and opinion. Here we are concerned only with those trends of thought that touched on the conditions of the poor.

Most of the comfortable upper and middle classes were more than satisfied with conditions as they were. They were not philosophers; the facts of industrial progress seemed to speak for themselves. They had not read deeply the work of the real thinkers of the age, the Utilitarian philosophers and economists such as Bentham and Malthus, James Mill and Ricardo. Yet they were apt at quoting from these writers passages which appeared to justify their own increasing prosperity.

Usually they were religious men, and becoming increasingly narrow and bigoted in their conception of religion. They were not generally given, as we shall see later, to deep thought about the social implications of Christianity, being more concerned as a rule with respectable behaviour than with theological niceties. They responded to the sabbatarianism of the Evangelical movement, being thoroughly concerned with its appeal for moral rectitude in themselves and others; but as a body they were not really impressed with the efforts of great Evangelical leaders, such as Shaftesbury, to improve the conditions of the working classes. They were much more concerned with the giant strides that were being made in material progress, with the rapid industrialization of the factories, the vastly more efficient machinery, the greatly increased output and export of British goods to all parts of the world, and of course the profits that made men rich in a generation.

To the wealthy classes 'Progress' was at once the key to the age and the slogan for further endeavour. Physical science was going to solve all human problems; poverty itself, while inevitable at the moment, would be eventually liquidated as the benefits of progress spread even wider. Thus, while complacent about their own major share in the fruits of progress, they genuinely believed that ultimately all would benefit. They were prepared to see a poor man by his thrift and hard work reap his share of the rewards of bounteous progress; but without self-help he did not deserve to prosper. They genuinely did not understand that 'the labouring people are certainly exposed to many casualties from which the higher order of society are shielded' (Colquhoun). Nor did they realize that their own prosperity depended on the efforts of the people, about whose lives they knew so little. Colquhoun had said that 'nothing can exceed on many occasions the sufferings of this useful class upon which the strength, stamina and riches of the country depend.' There is little evidence that they heeded these shrewd words, although Malthus, whose words they were fond of quoting, when it suited them—had himself said, 'I consider the labouring classes as forming the largest part of the nation, and therefore that their general condition is the most important of all.'[1] There did not seem to the middle class any necessity to apply to social matters the scientific ways of thinking that had yielded such golden dividends from industry, for was not a man the master of his own fate! The worst rigours of the Industrial Revolution were slowly passing in the years after 1832. Workers were beginning to enjoy some of the benefits of progress; the standard of life, diet, clothes, and homes of most working men improved considerably in the next few decades. This of course was by no means the work of some blind metaphysical force of inevitable progress, but the results of hard facts such as (from the mid-century) growing state regulation, increasing trade-union activity, more rational organization of industry. But if 'progress was the rule of life, progress in Reform was abominably slow in comparison with the progress in vulgar ostentation of the middle classes'.[2] The well-to-do were blinded by their own new comfort, security and social opportunities. The ideology of progress conditioned their approach to social reform, social work and social problems in general.

The more intellectual, or possibly less complacent, found in the writings of the economists and philosophical radicals moral support for their own wealth and indifference to the plight of the poor. Many an authority has been confounded by the use that disciples have made of his work. The classical economists did not defend reckless economic freedom. Their writings moreover were directed against specific restrictions. 'The system of Economic Freedom', says Professor Robbins, 'was not just a detached recommendation not to interfere; it was an urgent demand that what were thought to be hampering and antisocial impediments should be removed.'[3] This was not always appreciated by contemporaries. They tended to regard the classical economists as apologists for their own social class. Middle-class supporters were not students, in any true sense, of Jeremy Bentham, Malthus, etc., except in so far as they found in their books very comfortable support for their complacency. They misquoted the utilitarians, took passages out of their context and ignored those parts of their writings that did not fit in conveniently with their beliefs.

[1] 1826–7 (550), v. Select Committee on the Expediency of Encouraging Emigration from the United Kingdom. *Report*, p. 317.
[2] C. Dawson, *Ideas and Beliefs of the Victorians*, p. 75.
[3] L. C. Robbins, *The Theory of Economic Policy in English Classical Political Economy* (1952), p. 19.

The term 'Utilitarians' includes men as conservative as Burke and as radical as Godwin, economists such as Ricardo, philosophers like Bentham, and men like James Mill who were both economists and philosophers. It is clearly an omnibus term. But though their detailed views differed considerably, all started from the assumption that men seek pleasure and avoid pain; that pleasure alone is therefore good or desirable for its own sake. The aim of government should be the attainment of the greatest happiness for the greatest number. Much of the confusion, evil consequences and garbled versions of utilitarian teachings came from the habit of accepting Hobbes' account of men's behaviour as essentially self-seeking. The 'greatest good of the greatest number' sounds an altruistic democratic doctrine. But the utilitarians, Bentham and Mill, for instance, often interpreted this to mean that it is undoubtedly right for a man to seek his own pleasure before that of others. This gave rise to the belief in individualism and acceptance of the creed that all men are fundamentally selfish. The greatest good of the greatest number was to be achieved by letting each man seek his own good in his own way. This well represented the intellectual climate of the day. Writers who expressed other views were either tarred with the brush of socialism or dismissed as cranks. Colquhoun had suggested what amounted to a national insurance system. 'We live', he said, referring to Friendly Societies, 'in an age when insurances upon contingencies are ramifying in all directions.' He proposed 'a well-regulated system, judiciously promulgated under the sanctions of government' and outlined a scheme for a 'National Deposit Bank' for local societies. 'Supposing such guidance to exist,' he said, 'and labourers, mechanics and tradesmen were to place in deposit on an average only 3s. 4d per month, the aggregate would amount to £7 million a year.' Such constructive schemes came a century too early. The spirit of the age was represented by the individualism of the utilitarians.

Probably it was the economic theory of the utilitarian thinkers that had most effect on the hardheaded businessmen and industrialists of the age. Adam Smith had taken it as axiomatic that nature's way of securing social welfare consisted in letting each man seek his own good. The individual by trying to better his own condition is 'led by an invisible hand' to promote the public good. State laws only hindered this process; when they are removed, things improved through 'the obvious and simple system of natural liberty'. The limitation that the classical economists put on their own theories was discounted. Professor Robbins mentions the poor view that Adam Smith himself took of the business community as sources of information and advisers on policy. Elsewhere in the *Wealth of Nations* we read, 'those exertions of the natural liberty of a few individuals which might endanger the security of the whole society are and ought to be restrained by the laws of all governments'.[1] Bentham, as Professor Robbins points out, was certainly not in favour of complete abstention from interference by government. He provided in his 'Constitutional Code' for a large cabinet of ministers, a central statistical office, an efficient civil service—none of them signs of lack of governance!

Yet Ricardo maintained that all attempts to raise the standards of real wages by state action were bound to fail. Wages are determined by the laws of supply and demand, there is a 'wage fund' which cannot be increased. Any attempt to improve matters would only make things worse. Colquhoun put it bluntly enough in his *Treatise on Indigence*—'Poverty is therefore a most necessary and indispensable ingredient in society without which nations and communities could not exist in a state of civilization—it is the lot of men, it is the source of wealth, since without poverty there would be no labour.' This theory of wages held the stage until 1869 when it was repudiated by J. S. Mill in a revised edition of his *Principles*.

This wages fund theory seemed to lead to the same conclusion as Malthus' theory of population. His *Essay on Population* caused great controversy at the time, and has done ever since! He considered that there could be no permanent improvement in the conditions of the poor as their number would continually increase, keeping them constantly at subsistence level. Malthus in later editions qualified this statement, but the damage was done! Business men had found academic substantiation of their instinctive belief that the poor were best left alone. If there was to be a constant pressure of population on the means of subsistence it was wiser and more humane to let alone instead of 'striving officiously to keep alive'. Misery and vice, Malthus had demonstrated, were the positive checks that kept the population down to the level of subsistence.

[1] A. Smith, *The Wealth of Nations* (1776), Vol. I, p. 307.

It is only right to reiterate that these economists were not responsible for the biased interpretation of their views by the middle
classes. Yet what has been said about Ricardo could be extended
to all other classical economists of the period. 'We are not discussing Ricardo's economics,' said the Hammonds, 'we are discussing Ricardo's economics as they were interpreted by the
powerful classes.' The doctrines of Malthus and Ricardo fostered
despair in the working classes, complacency in the middle classes,
however careful the economists were to add numerous qualifications to their leading statements. 'The doctrine that poverty was
inevitable and incurable put a soft pillow under the conscience of
the ruling class.'[1]

Turning from economic to political philosophers, some of the
leading utilitarians were radicals, and wanted sweeping changes
in the laws of the land. But the demands of Bentham and James
Mill fell far short of the very left-wing demands of early socialists
such as Godwin. This is not the place to outline the views and
claims of Paine, Godwin, Owen and other writers of the time, who
have their assured position in the history of the development of
socialist thought. Interesting as their views are to the historian,
they had little effect on the vast and wealthy middle class, except
in so far as they increased middle-class fear of the masses. The
political theory of the philosophical radicals accorded well however with the aims of the traders and industrialists. The latter
quoted from James Mill and Bentham, as they had done from the
economists, to justify and indeed glorify the onward surge of
industry. The Benthamites were misquoted as defending laisser-
faire policies in all fields of government. The Benthamites did
indeed want to sweep away many state regulations as being out
of date, but they were not against state regulations as such; one
of the most orthodox followers of Bentham (Chadwick) was a
pioneer in extending the field of state interference, on the gounds
that in some cases the state had to intervene to secure the greatest
happiness of the greatest number. Nevertheless, the limits within
which the philosophical radicals allowed state interference were
very narrow indeed. They endeared themselves to the middle
classes by their attacks on the archaic regulations and privileges
of the old regime. The new commercial and industrial magnates
thoroughly approved of the attacks on the vested interests of the

[1] J. L. and B. Hammond, *The Town Labourer*, p. 195.

aristocracy. They were with the Benthamites all the way when they attacked the corn laws, sinecures, rotten boroughs, political patronage. It was for the good of the working classes too that the laws defending these privileges should be removed; they could only benefit from cheaper food and less wasteful expenditure by the nobility.

The wealthy ignored those parts of Benthamite writings which consisted of qualifications of, and exceptions to, laisser-faire policies. A good example of the current middle-class attitude was the speech of Brougham in the House of Lords defending the new Poor Law of 1834. His attitude was that society should do nothing for its citizens that a prudent man could do for himself. Everything was to be left to personal prudence, thrift and endeavour; these virtues would enable men to provide for sickness, old age and unemployment. Whether this could be done on the 10s. a week and less that many men then earned was not made clear in his speech! On the whole, Benthamism, while aiming at legal reform, positively hindered social reform in the wider sense. It put arguments in the mouths of those who were not interested in alleviating the conditions of the poor, but solely in justifying middle-class prosperity.

A detailed survey of the years between 1832 and 1882 would show a vast difference occurring in the social picture of England. The accumulated miseries of the first half of the century had led to that very confused period in our social history, the 1840's, a period dominated by the Chartist Movement. This was an era in which there was strife between 'Radicals who upheld Factories and Workhouses; Tories and Chartists who abhorred them both; infidel Benthamites leagued with Conservative Anglicans against dissenting manufacturers; landowners denouncing the oppressors of Lancashire; and cotton masters yearning over the sorrows of Dorset'.[1] After the storm of the 1840's a new era dawned for the working classes; it was by no means a paradise on earth in the towns and cities of England in the 1850's, nor did all workers benefit equally; but by the time of the Great Exhibition of 1851 conditions had improved considerably since the dark days of the 1830's.

The chartist movement had apparently failed; but in less than a quarter of a century its main political demands were being

[1] G. M. Young, *Early Victorian England* (1934), p. 48.

satisfied, and Disraeli's leap in the dark in 1867 heralded a big advance towards democracy. The 1870's saw the beginning of free, universal and compulsory elementary education, the early days of political socialism, the legal recognition of trade unionism, all signs of a change in attitude towards the working classes. The part that Chartism played in the gradual development of this new spirit should not be minimized. The philanthropy of the early nineteenth century was a sign of the uneasy conscience of the middle classes. They became increasingly aware of the poverty of the masses as towns spread ever outwards engulfing their pleasant suburbs, and as the new railways carried them past the miles of wretched mean streets.

Chartism had made the upper classes realize for the first time that philanthropy was not enough; more positive measures were formulated to raise the material standards of the workers. Steps had already been taken before the end of the chartist movement to improve the health of the towns. Any improvement of urban conditions helped the poor. Even more important was the fact that state intervention in matters of factory conditions and health opened the door to a limitation in other directions of the laisser-faire attitude that had been responsible for so much mass misery. Public opinion indeed was more receptive to Carlyle's fulminations against laisser-faire in his latter-day pamphlets (1850), and the revolutions of 1848 in Europe had, like the chartist movement itself, made serious-minded middle class men and women think more deeply on social matters. A novel, *Mary Barton*, written by Mrs. Gaskell at this time, was an apology for a crime committed by workers driven to despair during a strike; it could not have been written in earlier times and would not have met with a sympathetic audience. Kingsley and the Christian Socialists asked the middle classes how they could hope to improve the moral standards of the masses if they left them to sink in destitution. Halevy has said of their work, 'we can hardly exaggerate the importance of the part played by Christian Socialists in dispelling the terror of Socialism felt by the middle class'.[1] But the socialism referred to in this quotation was not the political socialism of thirty years later. It was rather an appeal to the middle classes for social justice towards the desperate workers, an appeal for sympathetic co-operation rather than hostility between social classes.

[1] E. Halevy, *Victorian Years* (1951), p. 252.

Already the new spirit had shown itself in legislation. The operation of the Ten Hours Act of 1847 was not as successful as was hoped, but yet it foreshadowed increased leisure for the workers, while their own early efforts to help themselves were rewarded by the 1852 Act legalizing co-operative societies. The repeal of the corn laws and the fillip given to industry by the Bank Charter Act and Limited Liability Acts between 1844 and 1855, these and other causes led to a flowering of mid-Victorian prosperity. At last the lower classes felt more of the beneficial effects of the Industrial Revolution, which up to then had been manifest mainly to the middle and upper classes of society. The labourer of the mid-century was not the desperate and unhappy man of earlier years. Rising wages and cheaper food, more leisure and healthier living conditions had their effect in a surprisingly short time. There was still an underworld later to be known as the 'submerged tenth'; thousands of marginal workers and casual labourers lived in misery on the borderland between destitution and crime; but above this lowest level of poverty big sections of the workers were experiencing a steady rise in their standards of living. Crime and drink figures, highest in 1842, were steadily on the decline ten years later.

The workers themselves deserved a lot of credit for their own efforts. Even in the troubled 'forties a great number of workmen paid into thrift clubs of all kinds. In the cotton districts the Odd-fellows were typical of the rapidly extending thrift movement that meant in effect the acceptance of bourgeois ideals by workers, instead of revolution against them. The middle classes in return admired these efforts and were as a result more willing to tolerate working-class aspirations in other directions. Mr. Tidd-Pratt, Registrar of Friendly Societies, allayed the alarms of the House of Lords committee which heard of the quarter of a million membership of the Manchester Unity of Oddfellows by assuring the Committee of the respectability of the working class thrift movements.[1] Burial clubs were equally strong, particularly in Lancashire; collecting societies such as the Royal Liver and modern-type insurance companies like the Prudential Company had a prosperous future ahead of them. Not only were the friendly societies a means of self-help, but they provided a form of social

---

[1] 1849 (458), xiv. Select Committee on the Friendly Societies Bill. *Report, Minutes of Evidence.*

life in which some colour and pageantry were introduced into an otherwise drab life. Many working men were preparing themselves for democracy by helping in the organization of friendly societies, trade unions, co-operative and temperance societies.

Another sign of a fuller life open to the poor was the changing attitude to working-class education. In the early years of the nineteenth century there was much fear that education of the masses would be a social danger. By 1850 there was no longer the same hostility to public education and the government had set up a new education department; education however was still for another twenty years to be a battleground between the Church of England and the Nonconformists.

The mid-century saw some attempt to bring culture to the working classes in other forms too. There was a successful campaign for libraries and museums. The library movement had been started inside industry itself as more enlightened employers, following the Ashtons, the Strutts and the Gregs, provided libraries for their own work-people. Then under Ewart's Act of 1845 Manchester, Liverpool, Sheffield and other towns started the first public libraries. Nor was the workers' lost heritage of the countryside completely forgotten, and we find towns like Birkenhead, Manchester and Leeds and other large towns providing public parks. 'At Manchester the parks were crowded on Sundays and the Zoological Gardens were well attended by persons who before had spent Sunday dog-fighting or playing at pitch and toss in the beer-houses.'[1]

By the end of the third quarter of the century conditions had improved still further. General wages had risen steadily between 1850 and 1874, as much as 50 per cent for most of the chief occupations. Shorter hours, better education, street paving, lighting and better housing, were gradually improving the manners and general standards of the workers. More leisure meant organized attempts to provide entertainment in new music halls, at the growing seaside resorts like Blackpool, which began catering especially for the working classes. The efforts of temperance movements were having some effect in changing working-class drinking habits, and the change from spirits to beer caused a gradual decline of the squalid 'gin-palaces'. Along with improved standards of living and behaviour, personal thrift among the

[1] J. L. and B. Hammond, *The Bleak Age* (1945), p. 229.

workers continued to develop; the Friendly Societies Act, 1875, had given greater security to personal savings. In the 1880's it was estimated there were nearly four million wage-earners in clubs of one sort or another, and millions more were paying into insurance societies for death benefits. In addition large sums of working-class savings were going into savings banks, building societies and trade-union benefit funds.

It is true that old age, sickness, unemployment, and widowhood were still terrors to the poor and were to continue to be so, but life on the whole was not the grim marginal existence it had been in the 1830's. Further advances had been made since the 1850's. Under conditions of free trade many articles that had been luxuries fifty years before were now generally available, particularly in the field of diet, which was now much more varied and balanced, with the importation of foreign meat and fruit. Clothing and furniture were of better quality. Jobs were also much more varied as the industrial revolution in the basic industries led to a wide increase of new industries with many more opportunities for employment, i.e. when trade was good, though it must be remembered that increasingly during this period slumps and depressions resulted in large-scale unemployment.

By the end of the century the working classes were beginning to feel their strength. Face to face with the employing classes they were no longer in the helpless position they had been fifty years before. Although still confined to a small fraction of the working class, the trade unions had grown in numbers, size, finance, organization and above all in respectability. Up to 1870 trade unions were still to a large extent outside the law, but for some years before 1870 the middle classes had come to recognize the orderly and legitimate nature of collective bargaining. Gladstone's Act of 1870, and Cross' even more favourable Act of 1871, gave a belated legal recognition to a social phenomenon that public opinion had long accepted as just and useful.

This was one symptom of a major change in the outlook of the educated and prosperous classes and in their attitude to state action. Even when the individualistic philosophy of the utilitarians was most influential there were signs of a reaction in favour of restrictions on the economic actions of individuals. Benthamite theory deprecated from one angle any state interference with the actions of entrepreneurs, but another aspect of that philosophy favoured the application of scientific thought to social matters. This led inevitably to the new Poor Law, the Health Board of 1848 and eventually the Local Government Board of 1870. By the 1880's state intervention was firmly established in several spheres of national life.

The state itself had been strengthened by reforms in Parliament, in municipalities and in its own civil service. The latter had grown steadily since the days of Chadwick. A bureaucracy had arisen to carry out the new duties of the state; much of the previous amateurishness and corruption in government had been removed by the institution of the Civil Service Commission in 1855, and the contemporary reforms of Trevelyan and Northcote. The middle class, particularly the lower middle class, was growing rapidly, and prominent in its ranks were the thousands of new civil servants, obvious supporters as well as symbols of state powers. Bureaucracy and democracy in Britain developed together, the extension of state activity being fundamental to each.

Paramount in the progress of state intervention were its registrars and inspectors. The former symbolized the rapid strides being made in the use of official statistics, e.g. births and deaths, and the latter, e.g. poor law, factory, testified to the new importance of government in the life of the nation. Tax revenue had grown from £52 millions in 1841 to £74 millions in 1881 despite Gladstone's desire to keep it to a minimum. The Royal Commission had become a major British institution; the 1880's were a decade of Royal Commissions. Commissions on fever and smallpox, agriculture, economic depression, housing, followed in quick succession.

Likewise by the 1880's municipal enterprise had disturbed many of the cherished beliefs of the earlier Victorians. Under Chamberlain the radical city of Birmingham took the lead in civic reform. As Chamberlain himself said, 'the town was parked, paved, assized, marketed, gas-and-watered, and improved'.[1] The later Victorians were actively concerned about the evils of their big cities, though prone to lapse into inertia and indifference from time to time. Many of the governing classes still retained enough of the older utilitarian point of view to regard with fascinated horror the growth of municipal power, especially in the London County Council, which towards the end of the century was becoming 'that great new sub-state which covets fresh functions every year'.

[1] R. C. K. Ensor, *England 1875–1914* (1949), p. 127.

Not only socialists, but tories such as Randolph Churchill agreed with Jevons that 'the State is justified in passing any law . . . which adds to the sum of human happiness'. It was not a matter of party politics, but an inevitable extension of collectivism made necessary by the growing complexity of social life. The middle classes increasingly had had an uneasy conscience about the poverty that existed to deride their optimistic visions of progress. By the end of the century their dismay at the rapid increase of state intervention was somewhat allayed by the results it was beginning to show in better living conditions, in slum clearance and in the rehousing of the poor. They were moved, too, by pamphlets such as Preston's *The Bitter Cry of Outcast London* (1883), and the great social survey of London, area by area, then being undertaken by Charles Booth was followed with keen interest by the public men of all parties who sought to find the causes and heal the consequences of poverty. There was a popular vogue for the literature of the 'Social Deposits' kind typified by Esther Waters' *All Sorts and Conditions of Men*. The Charity Organization Society, now establishing itself in the forefront of scientific philanthropy, had a large public interested in its activities, yet in a sense it came fifty years too late, for in many sections of the middle class its individualistic notions were already felt to be outdated.

In the early years of the century, the industrial changes had created new problems of poverty. Although a few who were sensitive to such misery tried to alleviate some of the suffering, so new was its impact on the minds of a middle class immersed in the task of developing a new industrial system that, as we have seen, most of them closed their eyes to it. But later generations, less pressed by the need of establishing themselves socially, could be more sensitive to the essential human needs. In spite of the growth of prosperity amongst all classes, it was evident that some were not sharing in the general improvement and were constantly in distress, while a large proportion would regularly fall into poverty in periods of trade depression. The general realization of this, supported by the books of popular writers and the scientific enquiries of Booth and Rowntree, led to a wider acceptance of the need for social work and for its support by private benevolence or state aid.

CHAPTER 2

RELIGIOUS THOUGHT IN THE NINETEENTH CENTURY

IT was not only economic and political theory that shaped the attitude to the poor of the upper and middle classes in the nineteenth century. Religion also played its part in their outlook on social matters. To most of the middle class the economic theories of the utilitarians came at second-hand, but their religious experiences and convictions were personal and real, the product very largely of the Evangelical movement.

THE CHURCH OF ENGLAND

The Church of England in the previous century had been awakened from its apathy by the great evangelical revival in which Wesley was the leading figure. The new enthusiasm was based on the teaching that conversion could rescue all but the most degraded. The clergy, who had become more and more isolated from the common people, were now adjured to rouse people of all classes to the worship of God. Apart from its emphasis on conversion, the Evangelical movement was not unduly rigid on points of Church belief. The Methodists were excluded from the Church of England, not on points of dogma, but as a matter of Church discipline. In their philanthropic activities the evangelicals of the Church of England were prepared to co-operate with Nonconformists, and even at times with liberal freethinkers. The Evangelicals were by far the most active members of the established Church and exercised tremendous influence from the end of the eighteenth to the middle of the nineteenth century. It has been said that more than any other single factor the evangelical movement in the Church of England 'transformed the whole character of English society and imparted to the Victorian Age that moral earnestness which was its distinguishing characteristic'.[1] Evangelicalism moreover, in its broadest sense, united all but the High Churchmen and a few of the Nonconformist sects in a common outlook on religious matters that was basic to the social philosophy of the middle classes.

Evangelicalism meant a way of life, as well as a religious outlook. To understand the humanitarian aspect of the evangelical movement, both within and without the Church of England, one must appreciate the ethical demands it made on its supporters. In most instances the evangelicals, clergy and laymen alike, demanded from the poor who received their charity only such strict modes of conduct as they were themselves prepared to observe.

Public morality had not been of a very high standard in the eighteenth century; the gentry were often loose-living and morally indifferent. The evangelicals, on the other hand, were nicknamed 'the Saints' because they expected the upper and middle classes to set an example of moral behaviour to the lower classes. The effect of evangelicalism was indeed entirely to remodel patterns of conduct among the faithful. Their leaders set an example of strict, abstemious and pious living. The sabbatarian movement, for example, was in full swing at the end of the eighteenth century under Wilberforce's direction. Long before Victoria ascended the throne the middle classes especially had made observance of the Lord's Day a prime article of their creed. The moral fervour and rectitude of the 'Saints' extended to many other aspects of national life. The churchmen, for instance, resembled the philosophical radicals in demanding a less corrupt attitude to public affairs. A good deal of the indignation expressed in the Reform Bill of 1832 and the Municipal Corporations Act was religious in origin. The notorious peculation, patronage and other abuses were felt to be shameful morally as well as politically.

Business morality and religious morality overlapped. Many of the commercial and manufacturing classes, laisser-faire in their economics, were evangelical Christians. Philanthropy was the bridge in many cases between their business dealings and their Christian conscience. They were assured by economic and political thinkers that the pursuit of private profit would lead to the greatest good of the greatest number; but should the profits be

[1] E. Halevy, *Victorian Years* (1951), p. 437.

devoted to charitable purposes any lingering qualms about sharp business deals would be removed. They felt genuinely their duty of private benevolence; what mattered was not how wealth was acquired, but how it was spent.

Nor would it be just to say that it was only their money that the evangelicals gave to charity. Well-to-do evangelical businessmen spared their own time in charitable activities, while their women-folk visited the poor, taught in Sunday Schools and sat on the management committees of philanthropic societies. Evangelical gentry of both sexes showed much enthusiasm for 'slumming', running soup kitchens, night schools and night shelters, distributing tracts and various other forms of benevolent enterprise. But while they were willing to give of themselves they were unwilling to tolerate any major change in social conditions, which might have prevented much of the distress they sought to relieve. It was inevitable, they conceded, that there would be some flaws in the social system, but these could be amended by charity and good will. They would not admit that there were any forms of poverty and distress that could not be alleviated by Christian philanthropy, with the poor laws handy as a last resort. As a result, religious zeal was not as a rule directed to social evils. Newman, for instance, positively disliked to be reminded of problems connected with poverty, while Arnold of Rugby's sympathy with the poor was limited to those who were 'good'!

There were, it is true, individual clergymen, like the Rev. Arthur Wade, who in the early part of the century wanted 'to take the burden from the backs of the industrious and to lay it upon the broad shoulders of the rich',[1] but such clergymen were rare. Often the parson was a magistrate, and as strict an exponent of repressive measures as any on the bench. In the 1830's there were few clerics as brave as the Rev. Osborne who wrote blunt letters to *The Times* on behalf of the Dorset labourers, or as diligent as the Rev. W. Champney of Whitechapel. Champney, one of the finest evangelical clergymen of his time, found a dead parish in Whitechapel when he came there in 1837.[2] In twenty years he had filled the churches of his parish, started Sunday Schools, mothers' meetings, savings banks, a coal club, a shoeblack brigade and a young men's institute. Another example of militant Christianity

[1] E. E. Kellett, *Religion and Life in the Early Victorian Era* (1938), p. 25.
[2] S. C. Carpenter, *Church and People 1789–1889* (1933), p. 47.

in the early part of the century was the Rev. G. S. Bull, who early in his career was noted for standing up for the rights of his parishioners, and ended by becoming a violent demagogue.

In evangelicalism generally however there was often a gap between theological concern for the souls of men and philanthropic care for the bodies of the poor. In some quarters there existed a belief that if only the poor could be persuaded to read their Bible all would be well. The zeal and sincerity of the evangelicals is not doubted; in many ways they were generous, decent, enlightened people. Yet the mass of the working classes were steeped in ignorance and paid little attention to religion. 'The poor, at least in the great towns,' asserts one authority, 'were largely pagan, with a veneer of religious observance.'[1] A contemporary foreign observer remarked that the workers stood on their doorsteps on a Sunday, waiting until service was over, and the public houses were open.

The evangelicals insisted that the trials of this world were to be borne patiently; they were unimportant compared with the joys in store in the world to come. Not many of the working classes accepted this gospel of 'other-worldliness',[2] though later it will be shown that in some parts of the country evangelicalism, especially through Primitive Methodism, had strongholds in important minorities. But for the most part the workers were quick to notice that the middle classes, while belittling this life in comparison with the next, still did their utmost to achieve success and wealth. The new rich looked on others' suffering as 'disciplinary dispensations of Providence', but did not themselves wait for Providence! At the same time it must be conceded that some of the great Christian leaders also declined to wait for Providence, toiling with all their might to remedy abuses, not in the next world, but in this. Oastler the Tory land agent, Stephens the Methodist preacher, above all the great Lord Shaftesbury did not indulge in 'other-worldliness' but campaigned vigorously against evil conditions.

Until 1835-40 the Church of England was still full of abuses. Evangelical appeals for purer personal morality and higher standards of public duty seemed hypocritical while absenteeism was rife in the established Church. In 1838 there were 4,000 livings in which the incumbent was non-resident. 'The Church

[1] E. L. Woodward, *The Age of Reform* (1938), p. 483.
[2] E. Halevy, *op. cit.*, p. 394.

combined in its ranks men with princely incomes for which some of them rendered no service at all and curates who were as badly off as the village labourer'.[1] The Church was also guilty of inconsistency in enthusing over foreign missions while doing nothing about gross abuses at home, such as inhuman flogging in the army.

The evangelicals however waged war against the worst internal abuses of the Church, and drastic reforms followed; as a result the violent radical attacks on pluralism, non-residence and other evils had largely subsided by mid-century. By this time moreover evangelicalism had become mature, and accustomed to setting the moral tone for the Church as a whole. Their essential protestantism had brought the evangelicals nearer to the Nonconformists; in 1846 they had founded together the Evangelical Alliance, which united all Protestants inside and outside the established Church in opposition to Catholic influences.

THE TRACTARIANS

Nevertheless the Church still remained alien to the mass of the workers, who regarded it as indifferent to their needs. Thus while Chartism was occupying the energies of the working classes in the 1840's, the energies of churchmen went into bitter arguments between the evangelicals and Tractarians. The Oxford movement was not a social movement, but the influence of the tractarians had certain social repercussions. Their insistence that the Church was a divine society was a reaction against the extreme individualism of the evangelicals. In many parishes the Oxford movement imbued its rank and file with revived medieval notions of social justice which led to new zeal in the performance of parochial duties. The tractarians however did not really tackle social problems as such. When Newman said that the Church was framed 'for the express purpose of interfering with the world' he was not urging social reform but affirming the claims of religion to rule individual men's lives.[2]

THE CHRISTIAN SOCIALISTS

The Christian Socialists on the other hand sympathized with several of the aims of the Chartist movement. It was a very un-

[1] J. L. and B. Hammond, *The Age of the Chartists* (1930), p. 220.
[2] S. C. Carpenter, *op. cit.*, p. 300.

usual thing for clergymen and religious laymen to side with what most of the middle class regarded as social revolution. Maurice, Kingsley and the other leaders of Christian Socialism had no strictly political ends of their own; their general aim was brotherhood between men and better relations between social classes. In a sense their work for working-class education and trade unionism was more Christian than socialistic in nature. Their efforts were consummated by the foundation of the Working Men's College in Red Lion Square, London.

Both the tractarians and Christian socialists, very different in other respects, had a better understanding of the part that a church should play in the community than had the evangelical majority. It has been said that the established Church at that time did not fully comprehend its functions as an institution.[1] Owing to their failure to understand the social significance of the church as an institution, the evangelicals did not give enough thought to the responsibility of Christians for the economic and social system. The tendency of the Church leaders was to regard matters such as poverty, housing and unjust conditions generally as outside their scope. One historian comments that the Church was merely an ambulance corps in the army of progress, looking after individual casualties instead of being a pillar of fire and cloud at its head.[2]

THE NONCONFORMISTS

The Nonconformists were as little united in a common social policy in the first half of the century as were the different sections of the established Church. Although several Nonconformist churches did much good work for the poor, there was a sad lack of joint effort. Several of the sects, in becoming predominantly lower middle class in membership, had lost touch with the working classes. Thus the annual discussions of the Baptist and Congregationalist Unions during the 1840's showed little interest in efforts to improve working-class conditions by legislation or otherwise. Most of the Nonconformist denominations were thoroughly steeped in current individualistic ideas and stubbornly opposed to interference by the state, whether in labour matters or in popular education.

[1] E. L. Woodward, op. cit., p. 485.
[2] L. Elliott-Binns, *Religion in the Victorian Era* (1936), p. 249.

THE DEVELOPMENT OF SOCIAL WORK

THE METHODISTS

The early Methodists had set out to evangelize the mass of the people. Wesley and his followers had preached in the open air to the weavers and miners who flocked to hear them. Wesley had instituted 'lay preachers' to work with regularly ordained clergy; they were to bridge the gap between Methodist clergy and the mass of their congregations. In the middle of the nineteenth century there were about 20,000 of these lay preachers.

Wesley however was strongly conservative in his social outlook and nineteenth-century development in Methodism saw a conflict between its democratic and its undemocratic elements. Wesley's death in 1791 brought no change in the general social philosophy of Methodism. The apparent connection between terrorism and democracy in the French Revolution strengthened the conservatives in the movement. It convinced them that their leader had been right, especially as revolutionary writers such as Tom Paine were identified by them with irreligion. Furthermore, as the first revivalistic phase passed and Methodism settled down as an important denomination closely linked to the Church of England, the voices of an influential minority of wealthy tended to dictate policy. It was inevitable that they should look with disfavour on popular movements. After the Napoleonic War the government could always rely on the Methodists to use their influence to secure obedience to its decrees.

Thus Methodists, speaking through their two most prominent figures, Jabez Bunting and Robert Newton, opposed the Luddite movement, which was understandable in view of the destructive violence of Ludditism; but they were no more kindly disposed to the very different and much more orderly Reform movement which led to the Act of 1832. In the following year, 1833, their own paper, the *Christian Advocate* was suppressed by the Methodist leaders themselves on the gounds that its editors were permitting articles of too radical a hue to appear in it. Soon afterwards Methodism as a whole turned a stony face when asked to help the Tolpuddle Martyrs. Throughout the 1840's there was strong and steady Methodist opposition to the Chartist movement; later in the same decade their clergy, along with those of other Nonconformists, strenuously opposed the Ten Hours Bill. Methodist preachers, after Wesley, were characterized by an 'other-worldli-

34

ness' that had certainly been foreign to the teaching of Wesley himself, for all his conservatism. This helped to alienate them from the poor, who normally had little use for other-worldly creeds, whether they came from established Church or Nonconformist bodies. Often such creeds had the unfortunate consequence, according to a leading authority on Methodism, that 'holiness very often meant personal goodness without any concern for the problems of contemporary society'.[1]

In some districts, such as the Forest of Dean and North Wales, Methodism was still 'converting' in mid-nineteenth century as in early days, but in most industrial districts Methodism had become one of the settled religions. The *Report of the Religious Census* of 1851 said that most of the new chapels had been built by and for the middle classes. Nevertheless, there were some elements in Methodism throughout the century that favoured democratic developments. The big open-air meetings, the smaller class-meetings in the chapels, amongst other features of Methodist organization, familiarized many working-class leaders with methods of combination, the formulating of rules for self-government, the raising of funds. Likewise the institution of lay preaching gave several workers' leaders their first lessons in public speaking. It has even been said that the story of the Miners' Association in Durham and Northumberland was to a large extent the record of energetic local preachers. Stephens, for example, the great Chartist leader, had been a Wesleyan Minister up to 1834.

Primitive Methodism, especially in the northern counties, was closely connected with agitation for better conditions by the workers; in districts where this branch of Methodism was predominant it more than counterbalanced the more conservative trends of Methodist orthodoxy. In Durham the brand of Methodism current throughout the century was much more working class in sympathy than Methodism itself was in the South. The 'Ranters', as the Primitive Methodists were called, gave the pitmen of the Durham coalfield Bible authority for their demands. It is noteworthy that this branch of Methodism actually doubled its membership in the industrial areas during the course of the Chartist movement.

[1] M. Edwards, *After Wesley* (1935), p. 21.

THE UNITARIANS

One sect that exercised influence out of all proportion to its numbers, particularly in the first half of the nineteenth century, was the Unitarian Church. John Fielden, M.P., the famous humanitarian factory owner, who led the agitation for the Factory Acts with Lord Shaftesbury, was a Unitarian. Himself a Unitarian minister, Fielden insisted that reluctant M.P.'s should face the terrible housing conditions of the big cities. Dickens, a personal friend of his, supported him in the movement to improve the health of the towns. Fielden was only one of the more humane factory owners of the day, who belonged to the Unitarian creed; others were the Gregs, Ashtons and Struts. Unitarians were prominent in the foundation of London, Manchester and Bristol Statistical Societies in the 1830's. Their social interests continued throughout the century. Dr. Southwood Smith, the great pioneer in the field of public health, was a Unitarian. Charles Booth of the London Social Survey, and Jevons, the noted economist, were two of their most prominent representatives at the end of the century.

The Unitarian attitude to reform had been noticeably different from that of the Methodists between 1789-1834. The former were continuously on the side of social progress during this period, perhaps because they themselves had no voice in contemporary government, though mostly out of deep democratic conviction. Unitarian strength derived largely from the many intellectuals who belonged to their sect, and from their greater unity of belief in social and economic theories. 'Their humanitarianism', adds a modern writer,[1] 'was not hampered by a belief in the depravity of man and original sin.' Numerous Unitarians, including ministers, were supporters of the Health of the Towns Association. The Anti-Corn Law League, the efforts of which led to cheaper food for the people, was begun by Manchester Unitarians; one of its chief speakers, along with Cobden and Bright, was the Unitarian minister, the Rev. W. G. Fox.

The Co-operative movement likewise received much encouragement from the sect, as a proved organization for the promotion of self-help and thrift. Unitarian ministers in fact helped to found Co-operative Societies, e.g. at Dewsbury and Lancaster. On the

[1] R. V. Holt, *The Unitarian Contribution to Social Progress* (1952), p. 165.

other hand, it must be admitted that the early trade union movement had little assistance from the Unitarians. Education was a passion with them, and not as with other creeds, a form of sectarian propaganda. They pioneered many schemes for university education, adult education and education for women. They were active in support of mechanics' institutes, supplying all these projects with both money and lectures. They were equally energetic in support of movements for libraries and public parks.

THE QUAKERS

Quakerism as a faith had always included a deep sense of social responsibility. At the beginning of the nineteenth century Quaker beliefs met a strong challenge in the social conditions of the day. The Friends had, since the days of George Fox, developed their own way of life, their own ascetic code of ethics which was central to their movement. The present 'Book of Discipline' had its origin in the first authoritative collection of 'Advice to Friends' issued by the London Yearly Meeting in 1738. It was significant of the Society that its 'Advices' concerned both worship and the actual daily conduct of life. It was characteristic also of Quakerism that, as Elfrida Vipont puts it, 'a renewed search for Truth inevitably involves a fresh dedication of every-day life to service'.[1] The new challenge of industrialism brought many Friends into wider contact with current religious and social movements. 'The days of the Society as a closely-knit fraternity, jealously guarding its ancient traditions and customs, were numbered.' The chaotic physical and moral conditions of early industrial England were offensive to all that was most typical of Quaker ethics. Eager social reformers from among the Friends ventured far beyond the bounds of their own Society, and gained fresh strength from contact with enthusiasts of other creeds. The 'creaturely activity' that the more active Friends undertook during the century was not popular with the more conservative Elders. Many Friends were, however, to emulate the efforts of Elizabeth Fry, Peter Bedford and William Allen to apply Quaker principles to the social problems of the day.

The Quaker approach to social service was consistent with their

[1] E. Vipont, *The Story of Quakerism, 1652–1952* (1954), p. 173.

firm belief that all men are equal in God's eyes. Their creed included a sturdy individualism which maintained that everyone should prove his equality with others by hard work, thrift, upright living and honesty. Thus it was the concern of anyone in difficulties, financial or otherwise, to do all he could to help himself and his family before appealing to others. This had always been the crux of Quaker policy towards their own indigent members.

When however their own members were in need their troubles were discussed at monthly meetings, after investigation had proved they had done all they could to help themselves. Action on their behalf included the finding of work, or grants of clothing or cash; the help they did give was free from the condescension so often attached to charitable giving. It was free also from the not unknown attempt to make charity an easy means of salvation. The Friends, as Jorns has pointed out,[1] 'had repudiated absolutely the theory that the poor should be used as a ladder to heaven'. In other words, the Quaker approach to social work was more akin to modern scientific casework than to the normal charity of their age. While their standpoint was conservative in that they had no thought of changing the social order, the Quakers' social endeavours were full of a humble and truly democratic respect for human dignity.

One point about their social work however must be noted. Assuming that men could normally provide for their own needs, the Friends did not set up permanent relief agencies. Their practice was rather to meet emergencies, group or individual, as they came. Consequently a good deal of their contribution to social work history is of a sporadic nature—but none the less important! Thus the early part of the nineteenth century was remarkable for a wide extension of Quaker service to the needy outside their own community, including help to French prisoners-of-war during the Napoleonic struggle. This of course was the time when Elizabeth Fry was carrying out her great pioneering prison reform. Her fame has tended to obscure other contemporary Quaker social service, which extended into many areas of human need. Most people have however heard of 'The Retreat' at York where the insane were first treated kindly and decently. Opened in 1796 'The Retreat' within a generation produced a revolution in the care and treatment of the insane.

[1] A. Jorns, *The Quakers as Pioneers in Social Work* (1931), p. 69.

Meanwhile in London a Quaker silk manufacturer, Peter Bedford, was working among the poverty stricken silk-weavers of Spitalfields. His closest friend was another Quaker, William Allen. Together they organized relief for the East End poor during the harsh years of the Napoleonic Wars. Their organization included 'the Spitalfields Soup Society', which was concerned not only with providing food, but with family visiting and other help in kind. No case was relieved without personal enquiry, while wasteful relief was avoided. Peter Bedford was equally interested in juvenile delinquency and started a society 'for helping and supporting children who have been released from jail, so as to bring them back to a decent way of life'. It was said that he was on such friendly terms with criminals that if anybody lost a gold watch he needed only to apply to Peter Bedford and it would be returned! William Allen's concern for the distressed extended far outside the London area, for he took an interest in relief schemes all over the country. 'All the letters from different parts of the country', he said in his diary, 'are put into my hands in order to digest the information.' In 1811 Allen had started a journal called *The Philanthropist* which did much to put the benevolent in touch with each other.

This concern with intermittent, rather than with persistent distress, was exemplified later in the century in the Bedford Institute set up in 1867 to commemorate the well-loved Friend. It became a centre for the temporary relief schemes that were devised to meet local crises such as the virulent cholera visitations still attacking the crowded East End slums. Wherever possible the Friends, at the Bedford Institute and elsewhere, tried to avoid pauperizing their applicants; they preferred to give a loan or find employment, but gave outright grants if no other means was suitable.

The Quakers, like Robert Owen, were well aware that many social problems sprang from bad environmental conditions. Consequently much of their energy and good will was directed to preventing poverty, crime and social failure. This was especially evident in the field of education. The Friends had long had schools for their own children; their school at Lancaster was founded at the end of the seventeenth century. A hundred years later, in 1779, the Friends opened a model school at Ackworth, much ahead of the time in educational methods. During the next half-century other schools were opened, using similar enlightened methods, at Sidcot, Islington, Wigton and elsewhere. The Quakers were keenly interested in educational methods and set up their own 'Educational Society' in 1836. Joseph Lancaster was a Quaker who founded a world-famous educational system, based on the teaching of younger children by the older ones who became school monitors. William Allen took a large part in Lancaster's educational work, being for thirty years treasurer of the society set up to promote it. Sunday schools, and adult schools likewise, owed much to Quaker participation. It must be remembered that education in early nineteenth-century England included much that we would term social work. This was notably the case in the Ragged School movement, but it was equally true of Quaker educational experiments. Their schools had originally been intended for members' children, but gradually came to take in non-Friends' children, particularly those who were orphaned or destitute. Likewise in their schemes for older people, who were willing to learn, the Friends included social provisions. Their adult classes for instance incorporated health insurance and savings schemes, while the school in Quaker Street that became the Bedford Institute included a club for working men, among other social experiments. Another example of their educational zeal was an industrial school at Great Ayton. William Allen moreover had founded a home colony at Lingfield, where children were trained in farming and domestic work to make them self-supporting.

Prominent in the attempts of the Friends to apply their ethical principles to everyday life were their efforts to promote good relations between employers and workers. Their views on industrial relations were wise and moderate, in an age when bitter feelings were usual between employers and the growing trade unions. William Allen, for instance, had co-operated for a time with Robert Owen in his attempt to put industrial life on a different and more amicable footing; he had originally been a partner with Owen in the new Lanark mills. In Coalbrookdale the Darby and Reynolds families, pioneers in the iron industry, applied Quaker principles to industry generally, and to their relations with their workpeople in particular. They refused arms contracts, maintained fair prices, observed the Sabbath day. In the same spirit they paid good wages to their workers, housed them adequately and maintained very advanced provisions for their welfare and safety at work. The same example to other industrialists was set by the Quaker Lead Company which had been started at the end of the seventeenth century.

The constant concern of the socially-minded Friends was that the working-man should stand on his own feet through his own efforts. As employers they were good masters, as Carlyle admitted. As business men they acted to the best of their ability as stewards for the poor. Among their most consistent endeavour on behalf of the oppressed was their fight for cheaper food. This it was that inspired John Bright, one of their best-known members, to fight for free trade; it was not remarkable that many Quakers were in the Anti-Corn-Law League that agitated for cheap imported grain.

It was not the whole Quaker body that took an active part in social service and social reform, but those who did apply Quaker ethics and standards of life to practical affairs left a firm mark on the social life of their day. Their efforts, like those of most of their contemporaries, were based on the assumption that help should not be given until self-help had failed. The Friends however were free from the charge often made against other philanthropists and social workers that their aid was tainted with condescension. They came to those they helped literally as 'friends', meeting men face to face on a basis of equality. They were pioneers in their recognition that people's misfortunes and mistakes were often due to bad environment and not always the result of wilful sinfulness. This affected the whole nature of their social work and linked it up logically with their efforts in the field of social reform.

CONCLUSION

The sentiment of human benevolence, and its practical expression, derived directly from religious influence. It came from the quickened knowledge, born of the new religious revivalism, that all men were children of God, and loved by Him. It began to mean, as the century advanced, that all men had equal dignity in the eyes of God, and should therefore be so regarded by other men. And though the doctrine of justice and equality, which the French Revolution had acclaimed, could not be wholly accepted in the Britain of the hundred years that followed, it was gradually affecting men's minds, and above all their feelings. There is no doubt that both the greatest single urge to help the less fortunate, and the change in the approach to social work towards the end of the century, sprang from deep religious experience.

CHAPTER 3

POOR LAW PRINCIPLES AND PRACTICE

I THE PROBLEMS AND PRINCIPLES OF POOR LAW ADMINISTRATION

THE nineteenth-century Poor Law, though the aid it gave was public, and it was operated by statutory authorities, is of great importance in the history of social work. This is so in spite of the gaps it left in the provision for the poor. The predicament ideas which inspired its administration formed part of the intellectual atmosphere in which 'private' social work was carried out. All zealous social workers had necessarily to scrutinize, imitate or reject the methods it used. The full significance of some of the principles and methods of nineteenth-century social workers become apparent only if one calls to mind certain features of the system of public as distinct from private aid, and the way that these methods struck contemporary social workers.

At the beginning of the nineteenth century the future did not look bright for the labouring classes in England. The Napoleonic War had aggravated the difficulties caused by the Enclosure Movement and the Industrial Revolution. Prices had risen substantially in the previous fifty years, particularly the price of wheat which had more than doubled. The family budgets examined in the contemporary surveys of Eden and Davies[1] reveal a grave deterioration in the diet of the poor. The government throughout the period of the Napoleonic Wars sought desperately for ways of preventing widespread starvation. England was still, even up to the middle of the nineteenth century, predominantly an agricultural society. As a result of the Enclosure Movement, which

---

[1] Sir F. M. Eden, *The State of the Poor, 1797* ; D. Davies, *The Case of the Labourers in Husbandry, 1795.*

deprived them of their rights on the common lands, some sections of the agricultural labourers were in as sad a plight as the workers in the new industrial towns.

A large part of the population had constantly to seek help from the rates when they were sick, unemployed, old or otherwise in distress. Relief was given either in workhouse or as 'outdoor' relief in the home. The 15,000 parishes of England varied greatly in the proportions in which they used these two methods of assistance, particularly when able-bodied men were concerned.

Many workhouses had been built since an Act of 1722 permitted parishes to combine for the purpose, although some, like the great Norwich workhouse, had existed long before. In some areas, at the beginning of the nineteenth century, relief was given only in the workhouse, as at Oxford. In other districts Gilbert's Act of 1782 was adopted. In these districts the workhouses were reserved for the old, sick and children and were more in the nature of infirmaries. Some workhouses were well run, but many were not, and as in any case lack of classification meant the sick, the imbecile, the dissolute and the infirm living together, life could not have been pleasant for the inmates, least of all the normal.

The main difficulty was how to deal with the vast number of able-bodied paupers in the areas where they were not admitted to the workhouse. In many areas a deterrent policy was followed by employing men on parish work directly, or indirectly by farming out their labour to ratepapers, especially local farmers. Such methods were often accompanied by brutality and a good deal of corruption. Supervision of the system was by unpaid guardians, helped by paid overseers in the districts which had adopted Gilbert's Act. The hardships of the poor were increased by the vexatious Settlement Acts, degrading in that they made the poor liable to removal from their homes back to previous areas of settlement, inefficient in that they hindered the labour mobility required by expanding industry, and led to endless litigation. Some slight relief was afforded by the Settlement Act of 1795, which provided that a person had to be actually chargeable and not in grave ill-health before action could be taken to remove him. The Settlement Laws continued to be, for a hundred years and more, a bane and an insult to the poor.

The famous Speenhamland system of supplementing low wages out of the rates, on a scale related to the size of the labourer's family and the price of the gallon loaf, spread throughout Southern England. The system served its immediate purpose of preventing distress reaching revolutionary proportions, but it damped out what sparks of initiative and independence remained in the rural working population. It added considerably to the existing confusion between relief and wages. By 1834 the only two counties entirely free from the Speenhamland system were Northumberland and Durham.

The total result of Speenhamland, as we now know, was disastrous, the labourer received in wages less than his share of the product of labour; the balance necessary to maintain him came from the rates. 'The self-respect and self-help of the rural working-class', says Trevelyan, 'were systematically destroyed by magistrates, who, while stern against agitation for higher wages and instinctively disliking real independence, were ready enough to assist the cringing poor.'

The Napoleonic War kept prices up and as long as they stayed high the nation could afford the economic luxury of Speenhamland. With the fall in prices in 1815 the majority of labourers were thrown into complete destitution that led directly to the widespread rioting of 1816. There is no doubt that the Speenhamland system helped to make life even harder for the poor in the long run by keeping wages low, as can be seen by comparison with the few Northern counties where 'Speenhamland' did not reign, although of course in the North a different demand situation existed. It was shown before the Select Committee on the Rate of Agricultural Wages, 1824,[1] that in these 'non-Speenhamland' areas wages were almost double as much per head as in Speenhamland ones.

When the Royal Commission in 1833[2] studied the complicated problems of poor relief, chief among many abuses they put the Speenhamland regime. They recommended the immediate cessation of this system and a return to a much stricter practice of giving assistance. These 'semi-Malthusian Poor Law Commissioners' yet lacking the courage to say with Malthus that the best plan was 'formally to disclaim the right of the poor to support'. They recognized that no great change of policy could be achieved

[1] 1824 (392), vi. Select Committee on the Rate of Agricultural Wages. *Report*, p. 401.
[2] 1834 (44), xxvii. Royal Commission on the Administration and Practical Operation of the Poor Laws. *Report*.

through the parish vestries alone; and therefore proposed a central authority which could combine parishes into unions powerful enough to transform existing conditions, with adequate control and encouragement from the centre. They would not accept the suggestion that had been made to them that poor relief should be a national and not a local charge. They said they could not agree 'to promise, on the part of the government, subsistence to all, to make the government the general insurer against misfortune, idleness, improvidence and vice'.

The report was fundamentally inadequate, as the Commissioners regarded their investigation merely as a study of a particular poor relief system; they did not try to analyse the causes and the nature of the underlying poverty. It was misleading, because condemning Speenhamland it gave a false picture of the function of relief before Speenhamland. Tawney described the Report as 'brilliant, influential and wildly unhistorical'.

A bill was introduced into Parliament in 1834 for which the claim was made that it carried out 'the *spirit* and the *intention* of the Elizabethan Poor Law Act'. A central department was set up consisting of three paid Commissioners with a paid secretary. It was to have the power of making regulations and orders, and to superintend the administration of relief to the poor. From the point of view of administrative history the Act of 1834 was momentous in setting up a powerful central body, having unsurpassed control over local authorities. From the point of view of the poor the Act was equally momentous in its intention of forbidding outdoor relief to the able-bodied; and because of its basic principle of deterrence. The lot of the pauper was to be made so much worse than the lot of even the poorest-paid worker. In other words the demoralizing indulgence of Speenhamland was to be replaced by a sharp new discipline. 'It was at this time that "the House" acquired its sinister meaning,' said G. M. Young. 'The Elizabethan Poor Law which had declared the right to work now degenerated into the Right to Relief without working. But it was the Charter of the Poor. The new Poor Law was the Charter of the Ratepayer.'

If Edwin Chadwick, Secretary to the Commission, had had his way the shock would have been even greater. He wanted at once to prohibit all outdoor relief to the ablebodied. He was, not the only time, overruled by the Commissioners; for the measure was

46

applied piecemeal and at different rates in different parts of the country. The Commissioners turned first to the South, where Speenhamland had had greatest sway. Luckily for them there had been three good harvests and new opportunities for work on railway construction, so the new discipline came into being in the South with only minor disturbances.

The Commissioners acted on the two principles of the workhouse test and 'less eligibility'. An ablebodied man seeking relief had to receive it in the workhouse, or not at all. 'Less eligibility' meant that relief in the workhouse was made as uncomfortable as possible by irksome regulations, few social amenities, poor food and a general and deliberate encouragement of gloom and despondency. Within ten years this policy had cleared up a lot of the stagnation left from Speenhamland in the South of England. The drastic surgery had removed the vicious confusion between wages and relief in the districts most affected by it, but the improvement was partly due to wives and children having to supplement the wages of the men by going out to work, so making up for the lost poor law allowances. Neither in the North nor in the South did wages rise as Chadwick had thought they would when the abolition of allowances gave increased incentive to work harder. In the South family members made up the deficiency, causing thereby a glut in the labour market and still lower wages. By 1846 there were 707 workhouses in the 643 poor law units of England and Wales with an average number of inmates of 270.

In the North the whole background was very different and equally different was the response to the 'New Poor Law'. North of the Trent the workers in effect refused the new system. In many districts the Commissioners had to leave the former system of outdoor relief and allowances untouched. Protests against the Act merged into protests against factory conditions, against restrictions on the trade union development, in short into all the bitter grievances and urgent demands which in 1839 led to the first desperate phase of the Chartist Movement.

Chadwick had misjudged the position in the North. The Speenhamland system was not so prevalent North of the Trent, and where it existed there were good reasons for its continuance. One large body of workers who received allowances in the North were handloom weavers. This craft was declining, yet they were proud and independent by spirit, applying for allowances 'not supinely like southern agricultural labourers', but only because the alternative was starvation. The poor law commissioners recognized their special plight, and speeches in the Commons, e.g. by Sir James Graham, pointed out that relief to them was imperative. A more stubborn problem was the fact of unemployment due to fluctuations in trade, such as the depression of 1838–42. Even strong supporters of the new poor law—Members of Parliament such as Graham and Baines—saw that in this case there was no question of forcing people off long-standing relief lists. Such men normally worked, and worked long hours, but during slumps no work existed for them.

The handloom weaver and the temporarily unemployed factory worker had not previously felt any stigma attached to receiving assistance, when the fault was so obviously not their own. To be faced after 1834 with the workhouse as the only form of relief open to them was a flagrant insult. The Guardians themselves, as at Huddersfield, Rochdale and Todmorden, defied the Commissioners to put the Act into operation. Protest meetings, riots as at Bradford, letters to newspapers, organizations for obstructing the operation of the law, these and other measures showed the fury of the North at the poor law regulations. It led to unheard-of deeds, such as the action of the Fieldens of Todmorden who closed down their mills to make the Guardians resign.

In 1841 not a single Union in Lancashire or the West Riding had discontinued out-relief to able-bodied men. All the Commissioners could do in the industrial areas was to order the Guardians to carry on according to the Act of Elizabeth and leave them to use their discretion. Because of the depression the number of able-bodied receiving outdoor relief had actually increased between 1839–42, from less than a million to over 1,200,000. Protests against the poor law poured in to the government, not only from workers' organizations, but from great editors such as John Walter of *The Times* and public men as Fielden, the factory reformer. A Tory candidate at Bradford, for example, described the new poor law as 'that Bill which separated those whom God had joined together, gave a premium to murder, made poverty a crime, starved the poor man and tried to prove whether he could not live upon bread and water'.[1] The connections of the anti-poor

[1] J. H. Clapham, *Economic History of Modern Britain* (1938), p. 350.

law movement with the Chartist movement would need a chapter in itself. It is enough to point out that the workers thought of themselves as having helped the middle classes in 1832 to obtain political power through the great Reform Act, in return receiving 'the Bastille and the declaration that poverty was the fault of the poor' (Gregg).

It was inevitable that the Act should be regarded as harsh, since it suddenly imposed rigorous administration on men quite unused to any kind of regular government control outside the walls of the factory. It was another aspect of the new discipline from above which exasperated the helpless workers. 'To be numbered, to be visited, to be inspected, to be preached at, whether the visitors were furnished with a poor law order of a religious mission . . . frayed tempers already on edge with mechanical toil.'

In their eighth Report the Commissioners had to admit that more than a fifth of the Unions had not been ordered to stop outdoor relief to able-bodied men. In 1844, 231,000 were relieved in the workhouses of the country—1,247,000 outside them! For 1848 the figures were 306,000 inside, 1,571,000 relieved outside. Nevertheless, although the refusal of outdoor relief to able-bodied could not be strictly applied in all parts of the country, the principle of less eligibility came to be generally accepted. Yet the Act itself, it will be remembered, did not expressly forbid out-relief to able-bodied; it was the set of regulations issued by the Commissioners that enjoined this measure upon local authorities. Nor was a definition of 'able-bodied' given in the Act. Was it for instance to include able-bodied women as well as able-bodied men? There was consequently a good deal of flexibility and varia-tion in the administration of the poor law, despite its central principle of national uniformity.

Nor were the intentions of the Commissioners deliberately in-human, as judged by the standards of those days. For example, in the workhouses employment was to be of a useful nature. Fictitious or artificial tasks were 'pernicious' and 'ought to be carefully prevented'. In the Report which led to the 1834 Act it was said 'We deem everything mischievous which unnecessarily gives to it a repulsive aspect.'[1] The authors of the Act moreover

[1] 1834 (44), xxvii. Royal Commission on the Administration and Practical Operation of the Poor Laws. *Report*.

allowed a place for charity over and above the minimum requirements of the law. 'Where cases of real hardship occur,' the Report said, 'the remedy must be applied by individual charity, a virtue for which no system of compulsory relief can or ought to be a substitute.'

Unfortunately, until the Goschen Minute of 1869, no attempt was made to encourage a fruitful and sensible co-operation between poor law and private charity, and some social thinkers, following Chalmers, felt that private charity and public relief could not live side by side, and that the State system should be abolished. The Act contained no direct incentives to philanthropic effort. Its whole spirit, despite the disclaimers against repression made by its authors, was in fact a spirit not of charity but of repression. The new administration was more efficient and uniform, but it meant that 'instead of the pious Christian washing the feet of beggars, whom he would meet in Paradise, a public official was required, at the least cost, to suppress a common nuisance'.[1] The parish officer became so obsessed with the idea of economy that his main interest was not to do constructive charitable work for the poor of his district, but to get rid of the nuisance at the least possible cost to the rates.

After the turmoil of the Chartist Movement and the poverty and unrest of the 1840's, there came for England a short period of prosperity of which the Great Exhibition of 1851 was the symbol. England led the world in industry, and workers shared the fruits of industrial progress for the first time. Consequently, though conditions of great poverty abounded in our cities, the mass of the working class was very much better off than in the 1830's or 1840's. This fairly general prosperity shifted the focus of public interest for a time from the operation of the new poor laws. In the 1860's, however, came a recession, due to increasing German and American competition, in the general conditions of prosperity. This decline brought not only increased numbers of unemployed, and increased applications for relief, but a recognition that the new poor law Act had by no means solved the problem of pauperism.

The Act of 1834 had been based on logical utilitarian principles. Changing social conditions however had their own logic, so had

[1] S. and B. Webb, *English Poor Law History in the Last Hundred Years* (1929), Part I.

the weaknesses of human nature, the idleness, officiousness or misplaced zeal of Union guardians or officials, and the hard facts of regional differences which made uniformity difficult to achieve. A contemporary writer (E. Barlee, author of *Friendless and Helpless*, 1863) describing the rapid increase in the annual figures of destitute poor, quoted numerous newspaper headlines of death from exposure and starvation, and suicide through want, which were only a tiny fraction of the tragedies of poverty. The headlines, while rousing public indignation for a day or two, were soon forgotten, she said, leaving undisturbed the unsatisfactory poor law system, ultimately responsible for so much tragedy and despair. In London alone a third of a million received relief of one sort or another in 1863, not counting 70,000 vagrants helped in 'Refuges'. Nor was the sum raised by poor rates insufficient, she thought, the £5½ million in 1861 being ample, had it been wisely expended.

2 CRITICISMS BY SOCIAL WORKERS AND THEIR RESULTS

In the 1860's many voices were raised against the abuses that had grown up in the poor law system, hidden by the national prosperity of the 1850's from all but the suffering paupers. It is convenient to summarize these criticisms under two headings; the complaints brought against the whole administration of out-relief, and those made against the workhouses.

(*a*) *Out-Relief.* Attempts were continually being made to refuse this form of assistance to the able-bodied, in pursuance of the Commissioners' set policy. During the 1850's considerable success was achieved in this policy, particularly in the south. Where outdoor relief was granted to the able-bodied it was usually on the 'labour test', the performance of set tasks such as parish road-repair jobs outside the workhouse. Various experiments were made in this direction such as the 'municipal task schemes' for cotton workers unemployed in Lancashire during 1863-6. In other respects out-relief was to be administered with strict attention to thrift and the drastic penalizing of improvidence. This was clearly understood in every Union. In some ways however there was considerable variation. This was one of the complaints made to the *Royal Commission on Friendly Societies*. Society members, it was said, never knew how they would be dealt with—some Boards did not recognize club benefits in assessing the amount of out-relief;

other Boards took half and yet others the whole of friendly society sick-pay into account.[1]

There was just as much variation in investigation as in assessment. Sir Baldwyn Leighton claimed that when an applicant came to a Board a minute investigation was made into his circumstances, his home visited and his family and relatives noted. He admitted however that in London 'where applicants are many and relieving officers few' such investigation was not very thorough. Nevertheless the earnings of the applicant and his family were checked, as well as his rent, the state of his home, the name of his employer, his membership of sick club, etc. A further variation in practice, according to Leighton, affected the recipients of outdoor relief. In his area it was not given to illegitimate children, nor to deserted wives 'whom experience shows to be generally in collusion with their husbands'! In his district, if the rent were high, relief was given only for a short time in order to make the applicant find a cheaper place.[2] In these two respects, as in many others, local interpretation of regulations varied, so the harshness of the poor law pressed more rigorously in one district than in another.

Another complaint was that no out-relief would be granted until an applicant had exhausted his small savings and was accordingly destitute, thus deterring many of the poor from trying to save at all. The Settlement Laws were as onerous as in pre-1834 days and were still among the chief targets of critics of the poor laws: Pashley's *Pauperism and Poor Laws* (1852) was largely a condemnation of them. A further allegation was that the poor law guardians and officers were brutal and inconsiderate; one contemporary writer called them 'some of the roughest and harshest members of humanity'. Many really necessitous and deserving persons dared not face the treatment they could expect to receive from officials more concerned with the rates than with humane feelings. Relief might be given by the relieving officers in money or in bread, flour, food-tickets. There was some corruption in the system of food-tickets, and the poor in any case hated them as pauperizing and humiliating forms of assistance. 'Distress of the truest kind', said the author quoted above, 'is deterred and its

[1] 1871 C.452, xxv. Royal Commission on the Friendly and Benefit Building Societies. *1st Report, Minutes of Evidence.*
[2] National Association for the Promotion of the Social Sciences (1871). *Transactions.*

victims starve and die.' Professional paupers on the other hand were not afraid or ashamed to cringe, and robbed both the poor laws and the voluntary charities, sometimes defrauding the friendly societies into the bargain.

Some contemporary observers were disappointed that out-relief had still survived as the main system of relief in many districts. They were often humane and kindly disposed persons who were convinced in their own minds that the fundamental principles of the 1834 Act were sound, that as far as possible workhouse assistance was to be preferred to out-relief, especially of course to able-bodied men. Only by cutting down what they considered the lavish expenditure on out-relief could pauperism as a national social problem be kept in bounds. Thus G. W. Hastings, President of the 'Association for the Promotion of the Social Sciences', claimed that had the new poor law regulations been unflinchingly applied 'pauperism would have been crushed out with a stern and wholesome hand'. He gave examples to prove that several districts were defeating the intention of the Act by giving more in out-relief than in indoor relief; e.g. in 1870 Woodbridge in Suffolk spent £1,476 for indoor and £6,099 for outdoor relief.

Canon Barnett considered out-relief more demoralizing than workhouse admission for several reasons. He complained that treatment by relieving officers was harsh, their attitude to recipients being suspicious and grudging. Out-relief was nearly always inadequate, a few shillings a week being merely an incentive to begging to supplement the relief allowance. Poor standards of investigation, he said, led to fraud and imposition. Adequate outdoor relief would not only bankrupt the union, but would undermine habits of self-reliance in applicants. He described out-relief as a sort of monster which destroyed its own parent, the local rates from which it was drawn.

Octavia Hill, giving evidence before the *Royal Commission on Housing*, expressed much the same point of view, agreeing that she would prefer to see 10s. per head being spent to keep the poor in the workhouse rather than 2s. or 3s. per head granted in out-relief.[1]

It is evident that highminded and public-spirited observers such as these had an ideal picture in their minds of what the poor law

[1] 1884–5 C.4402, xxx. Royal Commission on the Housing of the Working Classes. Vol. II. *Minutes of Evidence.* Q.9160.

ought to be, not dissimilar from the original Benthamite dreams of the framers of the 1834 Act. The criticisms made in the 1870's were repeated throughout the century, organized labour increasingly taking up the protests of earlier independent critics, but with very different intentions from those of Barnett and Octavia Hill.

(b) *Workhouse.* Criticisms of the workhouse were as common as criticisms of out-relief. Barnett indeed who criticized out-relief on the grounds, among others, of extravagant expense, did not seem to realize that the workhouse system was an even more expensive means of assistance. Guardians tried to uphold the principle of less eligibility by maintaining workhouses big enough to accommodate the able-bodied unemployed as well as the sick and the old, but this was in many cases a good deal more expensive than giving the very small amounts of out-relief of which Barnett complained. In 1863 it was claimed that it cost 6s. per head weekly to maintain the poor in workhouses at a time when families of six or seven people were living on 12s. to 14s. per week outside. Thus Guardians were forced in many cases to follow the injunctions of the central authority in the matter of workhouses but longed, as Professor Finer says, for the days of out-relief, which were so much cheaper.[1]

It was largely the attempt to cut down the expense of workhouses that led to another much-criticized development. It had been the intention of Edwin Chadwick that the new system should include careful classification of types of inmates, with separate accommodation for aged, sick, children, lunatics and other classes of pauper. In the endeavour to keep down expenses, little was actually done to carry out this policy; the administration of a large, all-purpose workhouse, though costly, was at least cheaper than the provision of separate blocks and staff for different sorts of poor.

A feature of the workhouse system that sorely distressed the poor themselves was the break-up of the family unit. There was little attempt at classification of inmates, but sex segregation was rigidly enforced, so man and wife separated if both were admitted. Likewise outdoor relief might be given to a man's family only on condition that he himself should enter the workhouse; or a widow might be permitted to retain two of her children with her at home, while her other children were forced into the workhouse. Distress-

---

[1] S. E. Finer, *Edwin Chadwick* (1952), p. 83.

ing to the poor, it was equally distressing to many middle-class Victorians concerned with the sanctity of the family. It was strongly alleged that a family broken up by residence in the workhouse seldom regained its unity and self-respect. Admission often entailed selling the home furniture, with very little prospect of being able to refurnish a new home at a later date. Decent standards within the family were often debased by contact with the idleness, shiftlessness and corruption of many of the regular workhouse inmates. Chadwick himself on one occasion admitted that a large proportion of criminals sprang from the idlers whose background was the workhouse.

As for its grim and prison-like atmosphere, its deliberately deterrent gloom, one example alone will suffice. A typical paragraph in the regulations quoted in the *Report of the Poor Law Commissioners for 1835* reads:

All paupers except sick, aged, infirm and young children shall rise (6 a.m. in summer, 7 a.m. in winter) be set to work (7 a.m. and 8 a.m. respectively) leave off work (6 p.m.) and go to bed (8 p.m.) and shall be allowed such intervals for meals as are stated, and these several times shall be notified by the ringing of a bell.

'They were to be kept constantly occupied in toil, persistent and monotonous, with every element of encouragement, stimulus, responsibility, initiative and skill *deliberately* eliminated,' as the Webbs so aptly put it. To the honest workman, struggling to keep a home and family to return to after long hours at work, the workhouse bell matched the factory bell, both equally harsh and repellent symbols; in the factory he could at least preserve his human dignity; the workhouse seemed contrived to undermine all dignity and self-respect.

It was not the poor man alone who deplored the state of the workhouses. One of their greatest antagonists was the social worker and reformer, Louisa Twining. There were two aspects that excited her passionate opposition. The first was the isolation of the workhouse from the outside world. The workhouse world existed behind closed doors which hid from outsiders the grim reality of the pauper's monotonous routine. As Miss Twining commented in her memoirs, public interest in the matter had declined since the publication of Dickens' Oliver Twist. Only the people directly concerned, the paupers, the Guardians and the officials, knew how dreary and prison-like workhouse life really was. She criticized the authorities' determination to maintain this 'closed door' policy.[1] Her second criticism concerned the poor quality of poor law officers. Officials put every obstacle in the way of inspection by outsiders. When she sought permission from a Board of Guardians to visit an old lady who had entered the workhouse, permission was refused. When she applied over the heads of the Guardians to the central Board, she was told bluntly that such visits might encroach on the work of the chaplain and other officials; permission was refused. It was not for some years that general permission was given for such visits.

There were many incompetent officials, masters and matrons, quite unfitted for their posts by any training, or knowledge of, or sympathy with, the poor. In the sick wards there were generally untrained and insufficiently supervised nurses, drawn from the ranks of the paupers themselves. Altogether there was too much petty officiousness and abuse of power, making workhouse life quite unnecessarily austere and regimented.

The work of Louisa Twining and the 'Workhouse Visiting Society' was directed partly to improving conditions of adult paupers. Miss Twining's efforts first took the form of workhouse visiting in London. Her example stimulated Miss Frances Power Cobbe to organize similar visits in the Bristol area. The work was mainly performed by 'wives and daughters of men of high position and influence'. In 1859 the 'Workhouse Visiting Society' was formed, putting the work on a more regular footing and encouraging the setting up of district committees to further their efforts. In every case it was necessary to obtain both the permission of Guardians and the co-operation of the workhouse master and chaplain. In many instances this was by no means easy, and called for constant persuasion, patience and vigilance. The general aims of the movement were (a) the improvement of the material conditions of the institutions; (b) the moral and spiritual improvement of the inmates; (c) publicity in every form for the dangers, abuses and misery of workhouse life.

The first aim was to be achieved by regular visiting, directed not only at the comfort of individual inmates, but constantly surveying cleanliness, diet, furniture, etc., and discouraging unnecessary austerity on the part of master and matron. Efforts were made

[1] L. Twining, *Recollections of Life and Work* (1893).

to encourage increased classification of inmates, one of the original intentions of the 1834 reforms. Some progress had been already made in this direction by the central authority, as from 1848 onwards the Lunacy Commissioners took over increasing numbers of lunatics from the poor law. A big step was made in London in 1867, when it was arranged that the sick were to be treated separately from the rest of the inmates, and pauper nurses were abolished. It was a long time however before the provinces followed suit. Directly due to Louisa Twining was the effort made for destitute incurables in ordinary wards. She succeeded in getting them placed in separate wards where outsiders could bring in special food and comforts.

In Liverpool, Agnes Elizabeth Jones, who was a Nightingale nurse, pioneered a nursing service within the workhouse. She demonstrated the necessity of appointing a trained nurse as Matron, convinced her Guardians that to neglect sick paupers was no way to reduce pauperism, and introduced decent discipline and order into one of the most disorderly and scandalous workhouses in the country. She formed a small, efficient loyal staff and established an example of high nursing standards in her workhouse which materially helped the work of Wm. Rathbone and others for a regular service of trained nurses in workhouse wards.

Miss Twining and her Association were likewise determined to improve the qualifications of those in charge of workhouses, especially those in charge of infirmaries. On the type of master and matron employed depended the whole atmosphere of the institution. With this purpose in mind she tried to get women elected as members of Boards of Guardians. In this capacity they could help to realize the general aims of the association, and could be particularly useful in seeing that suitable appointments were made to poor law posts. Their first success was the appointment of Miss Martha Merrington to Kensington Board of Guardians in 1875. In 1880 a society was formed for the express purpose of electing women as Guardians. The efforts of Louisa Twining and her colleagues to achieve reforms by using influence at higher and lower levels of administration was matched by personal service for the workhouse inmates. Visiting was directed towards comforting and instructing the sick, and to instructing and raising from a state of complete ignorance the mass of the depraved and pathetic paupers. Constant efforts were made to encourage useful occupations during their hours of leisure, and workhouse libraries were set up for the minority who knew how to read.

The third purpose of Miss Twining's Association was to gain publicity for any abuses within the workhouses. This she did by ensuring that official enquiries into workhouse conditions were given adequate coverage in newspapers, and by inaugurating in 1858 a campaign of letters to newspapers, urging reform. Likewise she addressed herself to bodies likely to be interested in workhouse reform; for example, she contributed papers to the 1857 Social Science Congress in Birmingham. Her agitation brought a more regular circle of active supporters such as the 'Ladies Diocesian Association', founded in 1864 to help the cause of workhouse visiting. One result of the increased publicity was the initiation of an enquiry by the 'Lancet' in 1866.

From 1870 onwards the results of pioneering efforts began to show themselves. Public-spirited men and women increasingly demonstrated their dissatisfaction with workhouse conditions and the administration of out-relief. They were spurred on by the famous Goschen Minute from the government, and by the foundation of the Charity Organization Society to reconsider the relations of the public bodies and voluntary societies. The Goschen Minute of 1869[1] suggested that voluntary societies should limit themselves to supplementing incomes, granting bedding and clothing to those on out-relief, and providing services legally prohibited to the Guardians, e.g. purchase of tools. The destitute were to be left to the poor law. Particularly suggestive was the injunction that complete information should be passed between voluntary societies and Boards of Guardians in order to prevent overlapping and duplication of assistance. Though the Minute was sent by the Local Government Board to the Metropolitan Board of Guardians, as an expression of the official view it was influential throughout the country. The Stepney Board of Guardians stated that the Minute had been read with great satisfaction, and that they were determined to 'put an end to the evils attendant upon indiscriminate alms-giving'. They declared their intention to publish immediately lists of those in receipt of relief, so that charity organisers could be better informed. It is clear that contemporary concern

[1] 1870 C.123, xxxv. Poor Law Board. *22nd Annual Report*, 1869–70. Goschen, *Minute* dated 20 November 1869.

with the state of the poor law was not going to be an unmixed blessing to the poor themselves! By the Metropolitan Poor Amendment Act 1870 the maintenance of indoor paupers over sixteen years of age became a charge on the Metropolitan Common Poor Fund to the extent of 5*d*. per day per person. Part of the intention of the legislature was to encourage the local administration to use indoor rather than outdoor relief measures, by putting some of the cost of indoor maintenance on the whole metropolis, rather than on purely local finances. In 1871 an out-relief circular to local authorities definitely advocated the reduction of the proportion of out-relief granted. Policy after 1870 was clearly in the direction of substituting workhouse instead of out-relief as the principal form of assistance. Several boards began to limit their operations to the provision of institutional relief, leaving domiciliary relief to be provided from voluntary sources. In Whitechapel outdoor relief was almost entirely abolished. Between 1869 and 1879 the numbers of those relieved 'outdoors' had fallen from 5,339 to a mere 143! An equally rigorous system produced similar results in the Stepney and St. George districts.

This attempt to bring to fruition the original intentions of Chadwick and Nassau Senior involved steady pressure from Inspectors appointed by the central authority. As a result of detailed enquiries they made into the administration of outdoor relief throughout the country, a series of reports were drawn up, all of which condemned the lax practices of the Guardians in the matter of out-relief. The first report of the Local Government Board, 1871–2 declared, for instance, that 'outdoor relief is in many cases granted by the Guardians too readily and without sufficient inquiry'.[1] The Inspectors advised that (1) outdoor relief should not be granted to single able-bodied men or women, (2) that it should not be granted, except in special cases, to a deserted woman during the first twelve months after her desertion, (3) that in the case of able-bodied widows with children, they should consider taking the children into the workhouse so that widows could then earn their own living rather than receive out-relief. Relief, the Board advocated, should be given for shorter periods, relieving officers should visit more frequently, and contributions from relatives should be more strictly exacted. Reports of the Local Government Board for the ensuing years were mainly concerned

[1] 1872 C.516, xxviii. Local Government Board. *1st Report*, 1871–2.

with the efforts of the Inspectors to enforce this sterner policy. For example, the model byelaws drawn up by the Manchester Board of Guardians in 1875 were highly praised by the Inspectors, who urged other Boards to adopt them as a means of tightening up the out-relief system.

Where co-operation between poor law guardians and charity organizations existed, as advocated by the Goschen Minute, the Local Government Board generally received the support of private agencies. Thus the Charity Organization Society in their third Annual Report (1872) drew attention to various meetings between interested parties at Malvern, Reading and London. 'All these meetings', it was stated 'declared themselves in favour of restricting outdoor relief in accordance with the spirit of 1834.' They urged 'the expediency of treating out-relief as an exceptional privilege to be allowed only to persons of good character under special circumstances.'

One aim of the new policy was deliberately to force the hands of relatives by making them take into their homes old or sick relatives to prevent their having to enter the workhouse. Where this was not possible 'hard cases' should be helped by private charity, said Mr. Longley, government inspector, in the 1873-4 report. Illogically enough, the Inspector hoped that such private charity would be forthcoming when absolutely necessary, but that it would not be a stable institution too readily accessible to the poor. He wished charitable provision from voluntary sources to remain 'precarious' and 'intermittent'.

Constant attempts were made to maintain this stricter regime, but many influences towards the end of the century tended towards more lenient administration. In any case, despite the efforts of the central administration, there were very wide divergences in local relief practices, as was admitted by the *Select Committee of the House of Lords on Poor Law Relief (1888)*. Elsewhere it has been shown how public opinion was changing on the matter of working-class conditions. No longer was it unanimously agreed that the poor should forever bear their lot in patience. The Electoral Act of 1867, the Education Act of 1870, the legal recognition of trade unions, were signs that the scope of democracy was being enlarged. Political change was in the air; new socialist movements such as Hyndman's 'Social Democratic Federation' and the 'Fabian Society' were followed by more popular labour movements. The classical survey of London conditions by Booth and his assistants had drawn the attention of social thinkers from all parties to the claims of the poor. The University Settlement movement had given an opportunity for the future leaders of the country to obtain some experience of slum conditions.

During the last quarter of the century there was a strong public feeling that the old and the chronic sick should not be penalized by harsh poor law conditions, and in more radical circles it was urged that the old at least should be removed from the field of poor law altogether. During the 1880's there was much discussion of schemes for old age pensions. Best known was the plan of Canon Blackley for a small pension to all wage-earners on reaching the age of seventy; his scheme also included provisions for sick payments during working life. Considerable interest was taken in Bismarck's 'Sickness and Accident Insurance' laws of 1883–5 which gave Germany the lead in social insurance. In 1891 Joseph Chamberlain added his very strong support to proposals for old age pensions, and there followed a decade of official examination into outlined schemes, the highlight being the *Royal Commission on the Aged Poor of 1895.*

Part of the new humanitarian feeling, towards some sections of the poor, was directed towards workhouse sick-wards. Formerly sick paupers were housed in wards in the ordinary workhouse building. Between 1867–1888 London gave a lead by establishing separate infirmaries in nearly all its workhouses. Sir H. Owen, permanent secretary to the Local Government Board, in the latter year spoke of the big increase in the number of infirmary beds, the provision of many more trained nurses and of resident medical officers.[1] In the London area too, all kinds of specialized institutions had been initiated out of the Metropolitan Common Poor Fund. The larger cities of the country emulated, and in some cases excelled, the efforts in this direction made in the metropolis, but there was an inevitable time-lag before the effects of the new spirit reached the smaller towns and country districts.

The personnel of the Boards of Guardians was changing somewhat in composition during this period. Social reformers from all parties were increasingly seeking a seat on Boards as an entry into local politics, and as a means of studying conditions of poverty at

[1] 1888 (363), xv. H. L. Select Committee on Poor Law Relief. *Report, Minutes of Evidence.*

first-hand. The composition of the Guardians was further widened after 1894, when the property qualification for membership was abolished. This trend was important in giving public spirited citizens a chance of seeing and doing something about life behind the workhouse walls.

By the time of the *Royal Commission on the Aged Poor* in the last years of the century, it was clear that much progress had been made in social thought since the mid-century; and public opinion had affected official practice. In the case of the aged, it became the usual practice to give outdoor relief unless there were special reasons which made this clearly undesirable. The Royal Commission Report gave the conditions under which old people could be best helped in workhouse wards, especially infirm and helpless folks without relatives. An exception to the general trend was London, where it was admitted that for financial reasons most aged were still relieved 'indoors'. The Commission stressed the evils of the inadequate grant of outdoor relief. Mr. Davy, one of the Local Government Board inspectors declared roundly that 'guardians ought to see a man on outdoor relief properly clothed, housed and fed . . . they have no business to send him 2s. a week and wash their hands of him'.

The Boer War probably prevented the Report of this Commission from being as effective as it might have been, but the more lenient spirit was evident in Local Government Board circulars in following years. A circular of 1896 urged guardians to offer 'respectable aged' out-relief, rather than admission to the workhouse. A circular of 1900 stated that out-relief for the deserving poor generally was a definite policy of the Board, and furthermore, added that relief so given should be adequate. Boards of Guardians were to see that 'in every way deserving paupers should be treated differently from those whose previous habits and character have been unsatisfactory'.

This survey of the poor law in the nineteenth century reveals what an essential role it played in the social scene. When social work in the proper sense was in its infancy and the welfare state an impossible dream in the minds of a very small minority, poor law loomed very large in the lives of the poor. It featured as an inescapable background to the great movements of the day, such as Chartism. All pioneers in social work had to make up their minds on their attitude to the state provision for paupers, especially about the need for out-relief and the classes to which it should be granted. It is not surprising that some of the vast social changes sketched out by the legislation of the first decade in the twentieth century were based on reports of the *Royal Commission on the Poor Law*.

PART TWO

MAIN BRANCHES OF SOCIAL WORK

CHAPTER 4

FAMILY CASE WORK—I

THOMAS CHALMERS

IN 1913 Professor Tawney made clear that to him 'the problem of poverty was not a problem of individual character and its waywardness, but a problem of economic and industrial organization'. If this were the view of 1913, it was not generally held at the beginning of the nineteenth century. The common belief then was that many of the poor were afflicted because of their own perversity. Even widows and orphans, the handicapped or sufferers from bad health who were in poverty were not in every case regarded as deserving; for were there not many in like pass who did not become parasites on the community, but whose guardians had foreseen and provided against such an emergency; or who through their own strength of character and resourcefulness had overcome the dangers of poverty and dependence? Denied the resources of modern psychological and genetical research, those with a social conscience who wished to ameliorate the lot of the under-privileged were obliged to accept facts as they saw them, and the motives and methods of social work they performed were similarly unillumined. To them the greatest social problem was the fact of poverty, and the researches of Eden in his *State of the Poor*, 1795, had not only described the conditions in which the poor found themselves in the early years of what proved to be a long and expensive war, but had also investigated the various hypotheses then current about the causes of poverty. This, though in no sense a scientific document in the modern meaning of the phrase, did indicate how widespread were poverty and misery.

Some years later in 1806, Colquhoun, the Metropolitan Magistrate, produced his treatise on *Indigence*, quoting widely from previous authors on the subject, like Eden, Daniel Defoe, Adam Smith, Jeremy Bentham, Malthus, Sir Thomas Bernard and others. Colquhoun's exposition on the causes of poverty was as clear as any available at that time, and had a wide circulation. But as with the writings of Malthus certain sections only were generally accepted, and the rest ignored by all but the few. Thus Colquhoun pleaded for greater productivity so that the national income could be increased. He advocated a centralized system of education and an extended use of apprenticeship so that the working classes could achieve the dual purpose of solving their own individual difficulties and increasing the national prosperity. Yet those who felt concern for the condition of their fellow citizens in want or distress tended to be less influenced by these larger considerations, and more by his division of the poor into the deserving and the undeserving.

It was not 'poverty',[1] he had said, that was the evil. For a man was in poverty when he had no property, no surplus upon which to live, but must depend upon his own labour for subsistence. Poverty so defined, he declared, was an indispensable ingredient in society, as unless man was obliged to labour, no work would be done, and our civilization would fall. It was the state of 'indigence' that was the real danger. For indigence could be defined as the state of anyone destitute of the means of subsistence who either could not or would not work to procure it. It was obvious that between poverty and indigence there were many gradations. Circumstances might arise in which a person was permanently or temporarily forced out of employment, whether through handicap or bad trade. This he called 'innocent indigence'. When a danger like this threatened, he argued, it was necessary to 'prop up poverty'. In other words he wanted social relief or social work among the 'deserving'. But in others, indigence was 'culpable', through waste, drunkenness, or immorality; in these cases relief should be absent and punitive methods used instead. He admitted that 'innocent indigence was often confounded with the culpable', a confusion that was bound to occur so long as members of one class drew moral distinctions about how members of another class should behave, but on the general principle of the division between the culpable and the innocent he was quite clear. The way was therefore open for the humane and sensitive to give what help they could to those in poverty and trouble from causes outside their own control. It is in the work they did that the origins of

[1] P. Colquhoun, *Treatise on Indigence* (1815).

family case work are to be found. Theirs was the simple response to a given situation, theirs the friendly acts of good neighbourliness which when organized and developed have become the skilled and sophisticated relationship of social worker and client that is implied by the modern connotation of case work.

It is not easy to find a common pattern in the work of the innumerable societies, temporary or permanent, that were in existence when the century opened or were formed in the early part of it; nor much that could be thought of as a coherent policy or an established method of work. Most societies were *ad hoc*, with little idea of what others were doing, and if co-operation were fostered, it was on a local basis, seldom on a national. The one centre of thought and influence that did stand out in the seven decades before the foundation of the C.O.S. was that of Thomas Chalmers, whose ideas on poverty and visiting had an effect far beyond the confines of Glasgow. If there were any unity in family case work then, it was due to him, and to his basic philosophy about social work and the rights and duties of the poor.

More than a century after his death it is difficult to tell whether Chalmers will be remembered most for his influence on social work, or the part he played in the disruption of the Scottish Church. Born in East Anstruther, Fife, in 1780, the sixth child of a prosperous merchant, he was educated at St. Andrews University and in 1802 was called to a church in Roxburgh. From this vantage point he was able to observe the working of the English Poor Law and became so critical, that his opposition to it became the foundation of his later social work experiments. He was transferred to Glasgow, and from 1819 to 1823 took charge of the newly created Glasgow parish of St. John's, where his charitable work became famous. He left to take up again University work, and by 1828 became Professor of Divinity at Edinburgh. His profound interest in Church government brought him, four years later, to the position of Moderator of the Scottish Established Church, and in 1843, after years of difficulty as leader of the Disruption Movement, he became the first Moderator of the Free Church. He died suddenly in 1847 at a meeting of the Free Church Assembly, and was buried 'amid the tears of a nation and with more than kingly honours'. A mathematician by training, an economist from interest, and a Church scholar by calling, Chalmers was not only a man of outstanding ability and an orator of a high order, but also a humanitarian with a wide social experience. He was known and honoured wherever English was read and spoken, and was the intimate friend of leading men and women throughout the United Kingdom.

He was a prolific writer on all the subjects that interested him, but though he wrote about and discussed his theories on 'Charity' for most of his life, the actual years spent in trying them out were limited to his four years in the parish of St. John's. For the purpose of this study, therefore, we must confine ourselves to an analysis of his work during those four years, and an assessment of the legacy of social work theory he bequeathed to the nineteenth century.

Chalmers' Scheme for Poor Relief

Before his remarkable experiment was launched in 1819, he undertook and completed the monumental task of visiting and noting the circumstances of every family in the Tron Parish of Glasgow, containing about 11,000 people. To those of us accustomed to the work of the social surveys, the completion of such an enterprise, along with his parish work, in under four years, gives some indication oi the vigour and pertinacity of the man. He found that while two-thirds of his parishioners had cast off every form and practice of religion, a surprising state of affairs for the early days of the nineteenth century, a large proportion were living a hand to mouth existence on poor relief, demoralized and friendless, and likely to remain so he thought as long as relief was administered legally. It was this conviction that led him to persuade Glasgow Town Council to create the new Parish of St. John's in one of the poorest parts of the town, where he could try out his scheme of voluntary relief for the poor.

He was obliged to dovetail his new plan into the existing town scheme for the indoor and outdoor relief of the poor, which was administered by the 'Town Hospital' out of compulsory contributions from the citizens, in much the same way as English Poor Law operated. There was a further relief fund in Glasgow, contributed voluntarily through the Churches and administered by the General Session (consisting of Clergy and Elders). There were therefore already in the parish a number of 'Sessional' and 'Hospital' poor who, if able-bodied, were receiving temporary *ex gratia* payments, or if not in that category were being 'relieved' in the same way as their English compatriots. With these he did not interfere, only stipulating that no new claimants should be relieved that way. Instead, he proposed the institution of an 'Evening Collection' fund, which would become the sole source of relief for the poor of the whole parish. The fund was deliberately kept small (it was provided by the evening collections at his church, attended mainly by local residents, and not by those at his morning service, which was largely attended by the rich of Glasgow, who flocked to hear him preach) and seldom reached more than £80 per annum, so that the deacons, who administered the fund, would not be tempted to give money too readily, and the human frailty of generosity with other people's money would be restricted.

He divided the parish into twenty-five units, each under the care of a deacon, and each having some fifty families or about four hundred population under his care. It was the duty of the deacon to investigate and understand the circumstances of each individual who came to him for help. Having done this, each deacon must seek out what 'natural resources',[1] as Chalmers called them, could be mobilized to solve the problem of those who came for help. First the applicant must be stimulated to industry to see if he could earn his own livelihood. Then his economy should be investigated to see if he could save more, or spend more wisely. If these two were insufficient, the relatives should be sought to see if they had anything to spare; and if help from this source also were not available or were insufficient, the case should be made known to the neighbours in the hope that by their joint effort over a short or a long time, the stigma of 'pauperism' might be kept from their friend and neighbour. Only if all this failed should the parish fund be used to succour those in need. Thus the deacon's task was to encourage an *esprit de corps* among the families in his neighbourhood, so that it became a matter of honour and distinction to see that none should fall by the wayside. A deacon could also measure his success by having the least number of cases to bring before the Court of Deacons. These regular meetings of the deacons had three purposes: to exchange information and advice, that is to act in some ways like a Case Conference; to be a yardstick of the success of the scheme; and to administer a deterrent to incorrigible characters with whom other methods had failed. A 'Paupers' Roll' was kept, and to have his name inscribed there was the worst stigma that could befall a person. To prevent this the Deacons' Court was

[1] T. Chalmers, *On Charity* (1900), p. 300. Ed. N. Marston.

prepared to treat cases as 'casualties', almost as 'first offenders', and by giving a donation, and perhaps the help and advice of other deacons, would strive to set a man on his feet.[1] Even so, crude gifts of money 'without any meaning' were discouraged, instead, they were designed to create that state of mind and body in which the individual would seek to fend for himself. Help was to have a moral and educational end, not a demoralizing one.

It is clear that the working of a project of this kind would depend greatly on the nature of the visitors chosen for the work, and here Chalmers was not without his notions of the characteristics of a good social worker—thus, in a letter from him to Mr. Campbell Nasmyth in December 1819, he wrote:[2]

Be kind and courteous to the people, while firm in your investigations about them; and in proportion to the care with which you investigate will be the rarity of the applications that are made to you. . . . If drunkenness be a habit with the applicants, this in itself is an evidence of means, and the most firm discouragement should be put upon every application in these circumstances. Many applications will end in your refusal of them in the first instance; because till they have had experience of your vigilance, the most undeserving are apt to obtrude themselves; but even with them shew goodwill, maintain calmness, take every way of promoting the interest of their families, and gain, if possible, their confidence and regard by your friendly advice and the cordial interest you take in all that belongs to them.

On the whole he found the less well-off deacons did best, not because of any want of will on the part of the wealthy, but because, as he said,[3]

the sight or knowledge of wealth inspires avarice in the mind of a poor man, and causes him, by a little more profligacy or a little more destitution, so to excite pity, that a permanent pension may be available. Moreover the possession of riches makes the wealthy more slothful in the carrying out of their principles.

Almsgivers were warned by Chalmers not to be promiscuous in their giving.

Better far, when giving, either to give personally and secretly having ascertained the nature of the need, and the justification of the request,

[1] T. Chalmers, *On Charity*, Cap. V.
[2] T. Chalmers, *On Poverty* (1912), p. 345.   [3] *Ibid.*, p. 321.

shewing that it means personal sacrifice to them; or that giving to one may mean giving less to another who may be in sorer straits.[1]

Chalmers' Principles

It has been suggested earlier that the greatest single factor influencing Chalmers to propound this new method of social work was his observation, during his formative years, of English Poor Law in action. He saw in the system something that was not only demoralizing to the individuals who participated, but completely illogical in principle; and all his writings hark back to the dangers and folly of a legal system of poor relief. For such was the nature of man, he said, that given the sight of a bottomless pocket in the public fund, he would lose all incentive to strive for himself and his family, and would be encouraged to lie back and wait for public charity to support him. His experience had proved this to be so. Officials in England, according to him, cared little about the adequate investigation of the resources available, and were prone to accept too readily the misery in which a person lived, and to give relief accordingly. His view of officials was soured by what he saw, and he felt that officialdom dried up the springs of initiative and adventure in those who exercised it. As for the lack of logic, he argued that if a man had the right to a relief of his wants, why should this right not be fully, openly and cheerfully conceded to him. Yet in England the 'almshouses approximate to a gaol and the house of charity to a house of correction'. The argument made to him by many that a rigorous style of administration kept down the expenses of poor relief made no appeal to him either. For, as he said, the restraints and humiliations hardened the finer and better spirits of the English peasantry, and led to an increased demand for this type of expenditure, with the additional burden of a moral injury done to the applicants who would be 'more blunted in all their delicacies, more insensible to all their feelings, whether of honour or of natural affection, than heretofore'.[2]

Though in some ways Chalmers was a leader of his generation, he was also a child of his time. Many of his assumptions were typical of his day. He accepted without question the rightness and inevitability of the existing class structure: He spoke of the 'upper and gentle' class and the 'lower orders',[3] whom he described as of

---

[1] T. Chalmers, *On Charity*, Cap. V.
[2] T. Chalmers, *On Poverty*, pp. 201–7. [3] *Ibid.*, p. 291.

humbler condition to whom 'Providence has assigned an inferior place in the scale of income and society', and said that 'the inequalities of life are often spoken of as artificial, but in truth they are most thoroughly natural'.[1] Not that Chalmers wished to see the working man exploited. Indeed his whole aim was to create an 'erect, sturdy, well-paid and well principled peasantry'[2] and to this end he encouraged any movement, such as Savings Banks, which would bolster up the moral fibre and proud independence of the lower orders. It was to character-building, rather than to material aid, he looked for the solution of an individual's problem, and this was achieved only through Christian education. It might be logical, perhaps, to argue from this that man's character could easily be undermined, and that this danger was particularly present among the poor. In his view the poor could be easily corrupted by almsgiving, and it was the responsibility of the rich not to part with their gifts too easily.

While he had most likely read Eden's work on *The State of the Poor*, and Colquhoun on *Indigence*, nothing comparable to the scientific investigations into poverty, made by Charles Booth and his successors were available to him, so that his notions of the nature of the poor were the orthodox ones of his time. Poverty to him meant 'when a man is in want of adequate means for his own subsistence'. It was relative, being different for a nobleman from a labourer. He accepted without question the divine saying, 'The poor are always with you', declaring that 'no-one knows where poverty comes from',[3] but because it was there it must be accepted. Yet to argue from this, he said, that the State ought to step in and relieve poverty would be quite erroneous, the resources of 'nature' being sufficient. From this came his condemnation of the idea that every man has the right to a basic minimum.

Whatever the calls be which the poverty of a human being may have upon the compassion of his fellows, it has no claims whatever upon their justice—the proper remedy, or the remedy of nature for the wretchedness of the few, is the kindness of the many—but when a 'right' is introduced into this department of human affairs, then one of two things must follow: either an indefinite encroachment on property, or the disappointment of the people.[4]

[1] T. Chalmers, *On Poverty*, p. 164.   [2] *Ibid.*, p. 170.
[3] *Ibid.*, p. 225.   [4] T. Chalmers, *On Charity*, p. 57.

Principles of Chalmers' Social Work

Though many of the principles and methods underlying Chalmers' work are generally unacceptable today, they followed inevitably from his assumptions. His main aims were twofold; to abolish 'pauperism' and to promote 'charity'. By 'pauperism' he meant the reliance in whole or in part on poor relief or the discreditable tendency of some to live on the gifts of others in preference to honest work. By 'charity' he meant that benevolence which moved the giver to sift each case, even at the cost of self-sacrifice in time and energy, so that the relief forthcoming was the most likely to promote the moral character and the sturdy independence that was his chief aim. The benevolent were to be guided by what he called the 'Four Fountains'. With the abolition of the Poor Law, Chalmers thought,[1] 'little rills of sustenance', far more effective than any legal system, would flow over the land. The first and most important of these was 'Self-help'. Without the demoralizing influence of doles, the individual would bestir himself to fend for his own. Self-reliance thus encouraged would soon raise a man out of his poverty and wretchedness and the whole community would be the better, for instance,[2] in one district two young children were deserted by their parents. Had the children been taken at once upon the parochial funds, the 'unnatural purpose of the parents' would have been promoted. The helpless infants were therefore left to the neighbourhood, the deacon meanwhile making every endeavour to detect the fugitives. One of the parents was discovered and brought back; and the other, finding his object frustrated, voluntarily returned. If self-help were impossible or insufficient, the second line of defence was the 'Help of Relatives', whose hearts would be opened and help stimulated if they saw their nearest kin in need. For example, an old and altogether helpless man sought parish aid. It was ascertained that he had very near relatives living in affluence to whom his circumstances were represented, and into whose unwilling hands, compelled to do their proper work, he was summarily committed. One wonders how both sides supported this propinquity! If this second method also failed, 'the Help of the Poor for Each Other' was the best third possibility. It was not the 'amount of each gift that matters, but the number of gifts which, when added together gives a far more

[1] T. Chalmers, *On Poverty*, pp. 213–20.   [2] *Ibid.*, pp. 350–1.

plenteous dispensation than from any other source'. A mother and daughter, sole occupiers of a single room, were both afflicted with cancer, for which one had to undergo an operation while the other was incurable. Nothing would have been easier than to have brought the liberalities of the rich to bear upon such a case; but this was rendered unnecessary by the willing contributions of food and service and cordials by those living round this habitation of distress. 'Were it right', asked Dr. Chalmers, 'that any legal charity should arrest a process so beautiful?' Only if these three had been tried and found wanting would Chalmers fall back on the fourth 'Fountain'—'Help from the Rich'.[1] He was convinced that a legal poor relief put a barrier between the rich and the poor, and that its removal would open springs of spontaneous help from the rich.

One must remember that he clearly differentiated between 'indigence' and 'affliction'. The former should be treated as described, but affliction such as blindness, insanity, etc., should be treated for what it was, and in many cases he thought an institution was the best solution. Nor was he opposed to the use of public money for the upkeep of such places, believing that adequate care should not be jeopardised through lack of funds. He was not even opposed to the use of public money in the home if it had a constructive purpose, as the following example showed. The father and mother of a family of six children both died. Three of the children were earning wages, three were unable to work. The three elder applied to have the three younger admitted to the Town Hospital. They were remonstrated with about the evil of breaking up the family. The offer was made of a small quarterly allowance if they would continue together. They yielded to the suggestion 'kindly but firmly urged'.[2]

Chalmers was always hostile to panaceas and to what he called 'systems'[3] such as 'the potato system or the cow system or the village system of Mr. Owen'. The scheme he fathered was certainly systematic and carefully planned, and was one of the first in this country to be so. It lasted for eighteen years, and at the first stocktaking, four years after the start, he recorded with pride some of its success. The average number of applicants in receipt of financial relief was one per district, ten had none at all. Each deacon

[1] T. Chalmers, *On Poverty*, p. 12.
[2] W. Hanna, *Memoirs of Thos. Chalmers* (1849).
[3] T. Chalmers, *On Charity*, p. 223.

received an average of five applications per annum, and spent about three hours per month investigating them. Thus was it proved, he said, that the springs of private charity,[1] 'so beautiful a part of man's relations with man' reduced pauperism almost to nothing. Evidence was not forthcoming on what the poor thought of the scheme, nor to what straits relatives and neighbours were put in caring for the less successful or healthy among them, nor on how many would have applied if there had been any hope of getting anything. Nor was there evidence of the rich accepting responsibility for the miseries of the poor in this typically working class area, except when individuals were asked for help in individual cases, so one may perhaps have some doubts about the success of his scheme, at any rate in human terms. On the other hand, Chalmers claimed that his poor did not migrate to other parishes where poor relief might have been available, but rather that his parish suffered an accession of poor from outlying districts. Whether his evidence was strictly accurate is not so certain. For the register he kept was of proved paupers, and while he knew of their movements, he knew nothing of those not on the register, who might well have moved out of the parish seeking help less rigorously administered.

The scheme collapsed in 1837 for several reasons. The first was financial, because though the Parish of St. John's claimed not a penny piece from the Municipal assessment, it had to continue paying to the General Fund; secondly, the scheme aroused intense opposition and dislike from sources outside the parish; and thirdly, the influence of its founder was by then so far removed.

His Contribution to Social Work

It would be idle to say that the Glasgow scheme of charitable endeavour either proved or disproved Chalmers' theories about the nature of the poor, or the way to overcome poverty, but he started a school of thought, later developed by Octavia Hill, Denison and Loch, which led to the C.O.S. movement and the technique of social work for which they stood. His main contributions to the new thinking included:

1 Individual interest on a small scale, as in a village, will work and be effective. He demonstrated this by dividing up a large urban parish, each under the care of a voluntary visitor, so that all

[1] T. Chalmers, *On Poverty*, p. 250.

the poor or potentially poor, their family circumstances, their history and even their personalities could be known. His example was followed by numerous imitators, from social workers in mid-nineteenth century Elberfeld, and twentieth-century workers among the aged, to wartime Civil Defence teams. It was essentially the device of voluntary work.

2   He taught the evils of promiscuous and sentimental giving. By arguing that man was weak and likely to succumb to the thought of reaping unearned riches from the generous, so that he was encouraged to exaggerate his misery to obtain largesse from those whose emotions he could move; and by prophesying that he would not in the long run be any better off for such aid, Chalmers anticipated by many decades the arguments of Charles Loch and his associates.

3   He pleaded for adequate understanding of all applications for relief. As he said:[1]

> It is not enough that you give money, you must give it with judgment. You must give your time and attention. You must descend to the trouble of examination: for instance, will charity corrupt him into slothfulness? What is his particular necessity? Is it the want of health or the want of employment? Is it the pressure of a numerous family? You must go to the poor man's sick-bed. You must lend your hand to the work of assistance. You must examine his accounts. You must try to recover those wages which are detained by the injustice or the rapacity of the master. You must employ your mediation with his superiors, and represent to them the necessities of the situation.

Thus did he teach one of the fundamental tenets of all modern case-work.

4   He preached the necessity of exhausting all possible avenues of help (as in his 'four fountains') before having recourse to public funds. Though this appealed to a century of Chadwicks and Lochs, and was the foundation of C.O.S. policy up to the twentieth century, it is a principle not quite so firmly held by the advocates of the Welfare State.

5   Finally, he paid attention to the selection and training of his social workers. Nearly a century before organized formalized training began, Chalmers was thinking out what would be the best kind of people to supervise the districts, and what advice on principle and method he could give them.

[1] T. Chalmers, *On Charity*, pp. 221–2.

The Elberfeld System of Poor Relief

Of all the schemes to be influenced by Chalmers' teaching and example, the one most closely approximating to his was the 'Elberfeld system'. Though it was not a British invention it is appropriate to examine it in some detail, because it not only derived from British thought, but later came to influence it.

It was in 1853, sixteen years after Chalmers' system of charitable relief came to an end in Glasgow, that a poor relief system organized on similar lines was begun in the city of Elberfeld on the German Rhine, and the idea spread to many other towns in Germany during the nineteenth century. The C.O.S. itself, through its secretary Charles Loch, who visited Elberfeld, owed some of its inspiration to the methods he saw in practice there. William Rathbone also visited Germany on several occasions in 1869 and later; and much of his work in Liverpool was fertilized by what he learnt.

In 1853, Herr von der Heydt, divided the town into a number of districts, each under the care of an 'overseer' or almoner. The districts were sub-divided and placed under 'Visitors', who were responsible for a small number of cases, perhaps four or even fewer. The general principles of relief were laid down by a body known as the 'Town Administration of the Poor', consisting of a few Councillors and other leading citizens, and any relief given came from public funds. The visitors met fortnightly, under their overseers, to discuss the cases and to decide what should be done. They undertook to visit regularly, and by kindness and through educational methods, to help a man to his feet again. All the resources of his family and friends were called upon to the full, and relief was given only when other means failed. These methods, along with what must have been a fairly crude kind of case conference, were what so interested British observers.

The principles of the scheme had in them a novelty that appealed to many. In the first place, the visitors were legally obliged to undertake this 'voluntary' work if they were chosen. In practice, such was the dignity and importance attaching to the office of visitor and overseer, that there was never any lack of suitable men willing and anxious to fill the posts; the small case load made the task possible even for the busiest. The essence of the system was that it was disciplinary and educational, seeking to prevent pauperism rather than merely to relieve the poverty of the moment, and it was based on the principle that 'everything can be done by personal intercourse with the poor, nothing without it'.[1] There was no workhouse. The able-bodied received relief in return for labour given (and could be compulsorily detained if idle or dissolute), but in circumstances of need relief was always given out of public funds for basic necessities.

The scheme differed in many ways from that of Chalmers, yet there were important likenesses in the sub-division of the town under personal voluntary visitors, the care in choosing the visitors for their competence and kindliness, the careful inquiry and investigation of each case, the regular supervision and friendly advice, and in the use of what Chalmers called the 'natural' resources of the family and neighbourhood.

In its turn the Elberfeld experiment influenced English developments in social work. William Rathbone, through the Liverpool Central Relief Society, was by 1887 dividing the city into sections under voluntary 'friendly visitors' each with a small case load, and each charged with the task of avoiding 'the hard suspicious tone, which those who make a profession of relief work are apt to acquire as they become inured to the sight of poverty and soured by the recurrence of imposture'. If the scheme was not as successful as he had hoped, it was generally acknowledged to be an improvement on what went before.

While these were examples of the direct impact of Chalmers on social work method, instances of the indirect effects of his work were not hard to find, as will be seen in the following chapter, which sets out to examine the main streams of endeavour in family case-work up to the second half of the century.

[1] E. Rathbone, *William Rathbone* (1905), p. 371 *et seq.*

CHAPTER 5

FAMILY CASE WORK—II

1 *The Relief Society*

BROADLY there were seven types of organizations concerned with social case work during the early part of the century. Each of them was influenced in some degree by Chalmers' philosophy, though none of them followed his precepts as closely as did the citizens of Elberfeld.

Most of the early organizations had in them an element of relief, but some set out to offer nothing else, and if they were Quaker in origin frequently did so out of principle (see Chapter 2). Admittedly most of them were temporary, being inaugurated to meet a sudden emergency, such as a hard winter, a severe recession in trade, or some other visitation, which caused poverty and distress. It would be idle to cite examples, as those which remained solely relief bodies of the soup kitchen, clothes-distribution variety usually faded out when the emergency receded. Those that had any permanence, such as the Bedford Institute in London, or the Mildmay Deaconesses' Home, had some characteristic other than temporary relief work to ensure them a long and useful career. This was particularly true of the organizations set up by churches and chapels, who when need arose, often established relief centres.

2 *Societies to meet a Local Need*

It might be said that all charitable organizations in the nineteenth century were started to meet a local need, even if they were extended later to meet a wider one. But some needs did arise locally, for which only a local answer could be given. Such were the 'Strangers' Friend Societies', of which one was started as far back as 1785 in London, and another in 1789 in Liverpool. It is understandable that into both these growing centres of population strangers were flocking from the rural hinterland, and from Ireland or Europe. Many arrived destitute, most without friends, and soon the local inhabitants realized that a serious problem was in their midst. The Jews also, especially in London, were conscious of the influx of their brethren from abroad, and Dr. Stallard writing in 1867,[1] commented on the care being taken of the immigrants who, however, were 'on the whole more clean and tidy and their houses more comfortable than those of the English poor'! The Liverpool Society had been originally started by the Methodists, but had later widened to include members of other religious communities. It appears that emphasis was put on the need for investigation to ensure that only the deserving might receive help; and the committee met weekly to discuss the cases and allot relief. Thus a rudimentary 'case committee' method began to appear.

3 Jewish Poor Relief

The Jews are of particular interest in the history of social work, for the spirit and methods of their endeavours were in marked contrast to those of many other agencies who all too often took their cue from the Poor Law. By the middle of the century over 50,000 Jews had settled in London alone, and many needed help after arrival. On the whole, the men and women who required assistance were of a reasonably good type, little given to excesses of behaviour such as heavy drinking, tending to be fairly considerate of one another and loving domesticity. As it is unlikely that the less efficient members of their religion migrated, it is probable the Jewish community in London had on the whole to deal with a ' helpable' clientele. Various societies concerned with the education and apprenticeship of the young, the care of the aged, and with the protection and in many cases the boarding out of orphans, were formed. No less than six societies made themselves responsible for the burial of the dead—the fact of application to them being taken as the sole test of poverty. 'The act of burial is looked upon as a privilege by the rich, rather than as a bounty to the poor.' Hospital accommodation for the sick, soup kitchens in time of emergency, and general relief for poverty in both cash and kind were prevalent.

As there had been a certain amount of overlapping between the work of these various agencies, and a tendency for the rich to move

[1] J. H. Stallard, *London Pauperism. Amongst Jews and Christians* (1867).

to the West End, where they lost touch with the poor, in 1859 it was decided to form a Metropolitan Board of Guardians to raise money by assessment on all Jews and to administer a 'Poor Fund'. The Board was assisted by various Committees, such as the Relief Committee, the Visiting Committee, the Medical Committee and so on, and met once a month for general business. The Relief Committee, meeting twice a week, heard all cases reported by investigating officers, and gave help on the advice of the voluntary visitors and the clergy. The visiting committee, made up of men and women, worked on a plan similar to that of Dr. Chalmers in Glasgow. Each member made himself responsible for a number of poor families, visiting them, examining their resources, seeking to find out how they could help themselves, or be helped by their relatives or friends, and only if this failed, bringing the case to the 'Guardians' for help. Such help as was given was then distributed by the visitors.

The principles upon which the whole system worked were enlightened and remarkably generous. Instead of regarding every applicant as a potential swindler, the guardians accepted the genuineness of every case, until the opposite was proved. They argued that the repressive policy of many English relief agencies, and of boards of guardians prevented people asking for help until it was too late to do any good. Their attitude of almost inviting applications was more constructive, they thought, in that people came to them when descending the path of pauperism, but before reaching the depths of demoralization in which a helping hand could do little good. The Jewish board advocated the complete investigation of every case, not just to prevent the conscienceless and undeserving from getting relief, but to give the most efficient form of relief for the particular case. The guardians kept a complete record of all cases helped, and declared that impositions were virtually impossible. Refusals of help were as few as five per cent of the cases. Two other principles should be mentioned to show how constructive they were. No relief was given to a family at all unless an undertaking were obtained that the children went to school, and no relief was given unless it were adequate, both in amount and in length of time. Thus, in the case of a hawker whose wife and son had died of fever, the guardians removed the father, himself ill, and his remaining six children from the infected premises and placed them in lodgings, for which £4 4s. per week was paid until the father's health was restored. Meanwhile, the furniture and clothes were destroyed, the premises whitewashed and cleansed, and when the family went back again, they had been given new furniture and clothes and a grant of £3 towards re-starting the business.

The Jewish Guardians were very critical of the administration of the English poor law, whose costs were so much higher than their own, and whose overheads, in the building and upkeep of work-houses, seemed to them a misuse of public money. They were critical of some of the Christian Church social work, in which the minister had, they suggested, no alternative but to spend half his time raising money for relief and giving it away to the poor, when the poor law itself should have performed this function. 'The physical and moral condition of the poor is not to be raised by visits, tracts and soup tickets, but by a systematic acknowledgment of social duty.' It is doubtful if in any other town the Jews developed so articulate a scheme as they did in London. In Liverpool they founded a Jewish Ladies' Benevolent Institution in 1849, which gave personal service to those in need, especially medical care to the sick in their homes. But they could not persuade their members to adopt the punctillious investigation that characterized the London plan.

4 Accommodation Societies

Though most of the general societies of the early nineteenth century were established to deal with the poor wherever they were found, some had as their chief object the provision of beds for the homeless, and a crop of Refuges and Asylums made their appearance, especially in the London area, though other parts of the country had them too. Indeed Liverpool, whose 'Night Asylum for the Houseless Poor' was founded in 1830, claimed to have been the first town in the country to institute such a scheme. In London a large number of these hostels or lodging houses had been set up by 1846, when a Select Committee reported on them.[1] A few, copying some of the religious houses in the Middle Ages, set out to give bread and soup, with a bed for the night. Others tried to go further, and to provide a house for certain classes of the poor, such as young women and girls of good character, until their histories were in-

[1] 1846 (388), vii. District Asylums for the Houseless Poor in the Metropolis. Select Committee. *Report, Minutes of Evidence*, etc.

vestigated, and they were found a situation. The 'West End Refuge' developed a scheme of this sort in 1861, and had to deal with no fewer than 124 destitute girls in the first year. It sent some to be trained, others back to their parents, and others were found employment.[1] The idea of free dormitories was later to be criticized by the C.O.S., which declared that the casual wards existed for this purpose, and that such schemes encouraged mendicancy. But those who worked in them claimed that many of the people sheltered had been refused admittance at the workhouse[2] and in any case it was a pity to subject some of the girls of tenderer age to the depravities of the workhouse. One interesting aspect of these schemes was the ticket system familiar to pre-1948 hospitals, whereby a subscriber would have perhaps two tickets to distribute for every shilling he contributed.

5 *Improvement Societies*

Some societies set out to implement a theory of social rehabilitation advocated by their founders. Though not strictly concerned with family case work, they are perhaps worth mentioning here as contributing to the philanthropic effort of the century. One example was connected with the New Lanark Cotton Mills, founded in 1814 by Robert Owen and William Allen, who hoped to remove temptations to vice and immorality from their workers by improving their living conditions and forming in them habits of morality and virtue through education, savings banks and other methods of self help. Another was the 'Labourers' Friend Society', founded in 1830, which in 1850 became the 'Society for Improving the condition of the Labouring Classes'. The original purpose of this society was to provide allotments and small holdings for labourers to use as part-time occupation, or full-time in periods of unemployment. The society subsequently decided to concentrate on the provision of more and better houses for the labouring classes, believing with Owen, that the provision of a decent environment was the main solution of the distress of mankind.

6 *Suppression Societies*

It is typical that many of the voluntary societies, which later became constructive case work organizations, started life in an

---

[1] E. Barlee, *Friendless and Helpless* (1863).
[2] H. Bosanquet, *Social Work in London* (1914), Cap. I.

effort to suppress social evils or to protect 'decent citizens' from those who would prey upon them. A few examples will suffice to illustrate this category.[1] In 1801 Sir Thomas Bernard founded the 'Society for the Suppression of Vice'. The 'Metropolitan Mendicity Society' was founded in 1818, with the object of giving food or money to out-of-works, and helping them to find a job. Mendicity societies began to appear all over the United Kingdom and were initially to suppress vagrancy by introducing the vagrant to a more settled way of life. In 1813 Edinburgh had started one to suppress beggars.[2] This Mendicity Society had four committees, one for investigation, because they thought this must be the foundation of every act of real benevolence, one for the supply of food, which could be given without enquiry if the case were obviously urgent, a third for education, because they believed in the good Scottish tradition that the way to moral integrity was through the mind, and the fourth for employment, as this was the best way to achieve permanent rehabilitation.

A notable example was the Bath Society for the 'Suppression of Common Vagrants and Imposters, the relief of occasional distress and the encouragement of the Industrious Poor',[3] a title which indicates the progression of thought common to many of these early case work agencies. It appears that in 1805 a meeting was held in the drawing-room of Lady Isabella King to find out what could be done for the town of Bath, which was then infested by a swarm of beggars. These beggars came to Bath for the season, 'to attend in the train of wealth and fashion wherever it assembles, and forsake all industrious occupation and prey on the profusion of benevolence'. During the previous season pedestrians had been 'obstructed by wretches sprawling on the pavement, exhibiting mangled limbs, fictitious sores and counterfeiting convulsions in order to extort alms'. The result of this meeting was the foundation of a society to deal with the 'Bath Beggars', a title well-known for the most shameless of mendicants. The members began by appointing and paying a Beadle to ascertain and apprehend these vagrants, and offered a further five shillings to the ten shillings the city already offered for the arrest of these persons. For a time, it was

[1] 1846 (388), vii. District Asylums for the Houseless Poor in the Metropolis. Select Committee. *Report, Minutes of Evidence*, etc.

[2] C. S. Loch, *Papers and Addresses*. 'A great Ideal and its Champion' (1923), p. 185.

[3] P. V. Turner, *Charity for a Hundred Years*.

said, the number decreased, but owing to war and post-war conditions in 1812 and again in 1817, the number increased.

The policy of the society was not wholly repressive, as the committee made it their business to inform beggars where help could be got, and even went to the length of creating employment for respectable men out of work. This enlightened plan for the encouragement of industry had two sides to it. One was the award of loans to individuals in order to set up their own businesses and, according to the accounts, up to £1,000 per annum was lent in this way, most of which seems to have been repaid. The other was the subsidizing of business men provided they would employ more labour. In 1817, for instance, a Mr. Moore, shoemaker, was granted £100 'to enable him to employ thirty respectable men who were out of work'.

A further aspect of the Society's work which became most important as the years went on, was the relief of the needy. The society determined to confine its benefactions to the 'deserving', and at times must have been greatly exercised about where the dividing line should be drawn. For instance there was considerable difficulty in the case of Ellen Eades,[1] second wife of Richard Eades, said to be the daughter of his first wife, and therefore his stepdaughter as well as his wife. Relief was finally approved on the grounds that as they had gone through a form of marriage, perhaps not legally, they had done what they could to make the situation respectable. On the other hand, those who had been drunk the night before were not relieved, nor were those already on poor relief. Exceptions to this might be made in the case of the sick poor, since it was argued that supplementation might prevent serious distress and the sick person be helped to return to work more quickly.

Relief at first took the form of bread, soup and grocery tickets, but by 1871, owing partly to the influence of the C.O.S. and partly to lack of funds, this practice was restricted in favour of more constructive case work, although some kinds of relief continued for certain classes of the needy. For instance, after a thorough investigation of their character and resources, the aged were given pensions, but only if they could prove 'purity of character'. One lady who died,[2] at the age of ninety-three, had been a pensioner for twenty years, during which time she had received a total of £52

[1] Ibid., p. 29.   [2] Ibid., p. 41.

from the society—hardly the height of munificence! Another class of relief, which had been started as early as 1805, was the provision of layettes for 'female objects of distress'. They were limited however to those 'actually married, of good character and in need'.

The work of the society hinged on the investigation carried out by a 'Voluntary Board of Visitors', and though temporary relief of a small sum could be given in an emergency, the normal method involved bringing the case to the weekly committee meeting for full discussion before authorization was given. The history of the Bath Society is a good example of what happened to others, such as the 'District Provident Society' in Liverpool (1830). These societies started as repressive and self-protective, but with time and a greater understanding of the evil they had set out to abolish they became constructive because they aimed at helping people to achieve independence. What is so interesting is that some of the techniques they used were in many respects similar to those of the modern case-worker.

7   Visiting Societies

Probably the strongest link between Thomas Chalmers and the C.O.S. was what could be regarded as the case work of the visiting societies. At their best these societies' visitors set out to befriend the poor and through actual visits to understand the precise nature of their difficulties. Most of the visiting societies were associated with the Churches, who even before Chalmers had begun to develop this service. Later, after about 1820, they multiplied and received new impetus due, no doubt, to his teaching.[1] Thus by 1835 in London alone, the Church of England, the Congregationalists, and the Presbyterians each had visiting societies. The Rev. John Blackburn, the Congregational Secretary to the 'Christian Instruction Society', frankly admitted that his society, founded in 1825, had been greatly impressed by the statements of Dr. Chalmers on the[2] 'necessity of aggressive movements upon the lowest classes of the population in order to accomplish their moral reformation'. For this purpose nearly two thousand voluntary visitors were visiting over 40,000 families. The visitors usually called twice a month, and

---

[1] 1835 (465), vii. Education in England and Wales. Select Committee. *Report, Minutes of Evidence*, etc.

[2] *Ibid.*, para. 607.

besides inquiring whether the family attended a place of worship, possessed a Bible, or if the children went to school, they were also concerned with the families' material condition, their savings bank resources, their membership of a benefit society, their need for hospital treatment and the like. To help the visitors, local visiting committees were formed to which the visitors reported, and from which financial aid might be obtained, though it was a cardinal principle of the society to refrain from allowing the visitors to go round with money in their pockets to relieve distress. Instead, should specific need arise for which some other charity existed, the society preferred, through its visitors, to be almoners for this charity.

We have seen that visiting societies connected with the Church of England parishes in London were in existence by the beginning of the nineteenth century, but it was not until 1843 that the 'Metropolitan Visiting and Relief Association' came to be formed. This was due to the action of Church and Lay dignitaries,[1] among whom were Bishop Blomfield (Bishop of London), Sir Walter Farquhar and Mr. W. E. Gladstone, who had known and admired Dr. Chalmers for many years. The purpose of the association was to recruit as many voluntary visitors as possible, and to ensure that they would get to know and help every parishioner in need. Furthermore, the association set out to bridge the gulf between those who relieved distress and those who were relieved, by animating all alike with a conception of the 'high destiny of the human soul, whether incarnate in the body of a riverside labourer or of a duchess', and by abstinence from any action which savoured of largesse being thrown by the wealthy to the ignorant and destitute.

The incumbent of every Metropolitan parish was in the scheme, and a parish visiting society was set up to help and encourage the joint efforts of priest and lay visitors. Within a few months over a thousand voluntary visitors were recruited to visit parishioners likely to need help. Keeping records of cases seems to have been a prominent part of this scheme, each visitor being expected to keep two documents. One was his own journal, where he noted the facts of a family's situation, his impressions, and the general help given, and the other was the report to the local committee. It was clear,

---

[1] J. C. Pringle, *Social Work of the London Churches* (1937), p. 179.

said Pringle (at one time the Rev. J. C. Pringle was general secretary of the C.O.S.),[1] that this was family case work. Each family was thought of as a whole, and every side of its welfare was considered by the visitors. If financial help were needed, the association made itself responsible, but none was forthcoming without the strong support of the visitor who had investigated the case. Prevention was a strong plank in the whole edifice. Thus the association encouraged payment into savings banks, and itself formed clothing clubs which had voluntary collectors and paid interest on the money so deposited. In 1853, for instance, no fewer than 30,451 persons in London deposited £14,665 in the 'Penny Bank' of the association. Closely associated with this in later years was the 'Society for the Relief of Distress' founded in 1860 by Mr. Gladstone and Sir Walter Farquhar. This also was based on the visiting principle, and it was as a voluntary visitor for this society that Edward Denison worked when he went to Stepney in 1867. Many of the people concerned with these two societies were instrumental in founding the Charity Organization Society in 1869, and by 1881 the three had amalgamated.

Visiting societies of one sort or another seem to have made their sporadic appearance in most religious connexions and in many parts of the country. Sometimes the visiting was the preserve of lay workers, and sometimes, as in the Mildmay Deaconesses' Home, of the Clergy. The value of the work varied greatly, and some of it doubtless richly deserved the criticisms that were levelled at it by the C.O.S. and others. An example may be cited from a report to the City Council of Edinburgh prepared by Dr. A. Ward in 1868. In this, he advocated more and better visiting, but argued that it should be freed from religious bodies, because sectarianism prevented co-operation among like-minded public citizens who would join to improve the lot of the poor if they were not separated by religious dogma. Moreover, the Church Visiting Societies, he said, led to hyprocrisy. How could the visitors be single-minded if they wished to advance the interests of their Church on the one hand and yet had to relieve distress before they could do so? And how could the poor be honest in their conversion to the Faith, if that was the only way to obtain bread? His conclusion was that the poor would be more receptive to religious teaching, if some of their distresses had first been removed by lay agencies.

[1] J. C. Pringle, *Social Work of the London Churches*, p. 184.

CONCLUSION

Long before the inauguration of the C.O.S. in 1869, some of the elements of its teaching had been both propounded and practised. The principle of no relief without thorough investigation was evident in the work of many of these pioneers. The notion of kindness and courtesy (said to be so lamentably absent in many of the officers of the poor law) was strongly supported. The elements of case work method—the interview, the visit, the case committee, the sifting of evidence and consideration of the needs of the whole family before deciding on what to do—can be traced throughout the century. But though much of the machinery was there, the workers to man it were not always as carefully selected as Chalmers would have had them. For the principle that workers should be trained made little progress until the advent of the C.O.S.

Two other considerations might be mentioned in this assessment of case work up to 1869. One was the almost universal decision to confine help to the 'deserving', that is to those considered worthy of help by those who had help to give (a very different conception from the notion of 'helpability', a modern criterion). The other was that agencies did not persist very long if they confined themselves to the giving of material aid of the soup-kitchen grocery-ticket variety. Without case work of a deeper kind, involving social or physical rehabilitation or spiritual care, 'charity' had no future.

CHAPTER 6

FAMILY CASE WORK—III

THE CHARITY ORGANIZATION SOCIETY, 1869

IF there is mystery surrounding the birth of the C.O.S.—and the conflicting claims of many people to have been the originators suggest this—the circumstances that brought it into being are not in doubt. For to some extent it was the variety of organizations that resulted from Chalmers' teaching that precipitated action. Their overlapping, their competition, the human weaknesses of those who served them, led many thinking people to sigh for a coherent policy and some organization among the Charities.

Some examination of these defects gives us the clue not only to the reason for the establishment of the C.O.S., but to the principles on which it was based, and which it has preached so passionately ever since. Overlapping has been mentioned. Although the original motives which led to the establishment of social work organizations in an area may have been quite diverse, it required self-discipline and self-denial on the part of each of them not to extend their scope until overlapping occurred. As self-discipline in the form of refusing help to someone in distress was so difficult, the only way to prevent the evils was seen to be co-operation between the organizations, and the external discipline of a co-ordinated plan. That there was insufficient co-operation between organizations was abundantly clear not only from C.O.S. writers and sympathizers in London, but from many other parts of the Kingdom. Thus in Liverpool[1] in 1855 there were three main relief societies, the 'District Provident', the 'Strangers' Friend' and the 'Charitable Society'. There was no co-operation between them, but almost open competition resulting in much abuse. In Edinburgh Dr. Wood[2] in 1868 complained bitterly of the multiplicity of relief

---

[1] M. Simey, *Charitable Effort in Liverpool* (1951), p. 91.
[2] A. Wood, *Report on the Condition of the Poorer Classes of Edinburgh* (1868).

societies, each going on its own way without thought of what the others were doing; and he looked longingly at the example of New York, where in 1844 an association had been set up for relief work for the whole city, and to Paris, where organized relief had been practised for many years.

This lack of co-operation led to a further abuse which was if anything an even more powerful stimulus to reform—indiscriminate giving. Had each society made adequate investigation of each case before giving relief, the worst evils due to the lack of co-ordination might have been avoided. But it was sometimes difficult to reach the truth of a client's statement without some reference to other organizations, and where relief appeared to be a matter of urgency, the professional scrounger could go profitably round from agency to agency. It was the human weakness of the social workers that was often to blame. Without training, and often without adequate preparation regarding the aims and purposes of the society they served, these good-hearted, somewhat sentimental workers all too often were so taken in by apparent distress that they tended to give relief as a matter of course. This was to put the best view on lack of discrimination, but less worthy motives were sometimes ascribed to them. It was said, for instance, that some churches competed with each other in gifts of soup and food tickets, in order to increase their congregations; that such was the competition among the relief societies working with the homeless, that John Burns decided to clear the Thames Embankment of all charitable societies distributing relief there. It was said that 'charity' had become a fashion, and that joining a charitable organization was a step in social climbing. Even the Social Science Association (1857) could not be absolved from this tendency. There was, moreover, the human but dangerous tendency that benevolence might be simply a relief to the feelings of compassion in the giver, the sort of feeling that made Captain Parker Snow at the second annual meeting of the St. Pancras district committee of the C.O.S.[1] declare it 'to be the Christian duty and according to the manly and generous character of an Englishman if he saw a poor person in the gutter to give him a penny out of his own twopence without asking whether he was deserving or not'. A further objection to indiscriminate giving was the tendency for the worker to give what he thought the client ought to need, irrespective of the actual needs

[1] H. Bosanquet, *Social Work in London* (1914), p. 121.

or desires of the client himself. An extreme, but fortunately innocuous example of this was quoted by Miss Jennings;[1] a Wesleyan Minister of Deptford insisted on giving to underfed children free breakfasts of a mug of coffee and a piece of cheese, the latter because he himself was particularly partial to cheese! But more serious examples were quoted of positive harm being done by lack of discrimination.

It was not just giving that was so much condemned by the C.O.S. as the effect the practice had on the receivers. Canon Barnett,[2] for instance, felt that it made those of the poor who were ready to down tools do so at the slightest hint that easy money was available, that they were encouraged not to support themselves, but to work up their case as an applicant, and to exaggerate their distress and poverty for the purpose of gaining public sympathy. Other writers[3] of the period echoed these sentiments, and pointed to further demoralization, in that if the relief took the form of food tickets it encouraged the poor to sell them for what they would fetch; or the shop-keeper would be tempted to supply goods other than those specified on the ticket. It was noted by many that the public houses seemed to flourish best when relief money was about. Moreover, indiscriminate giving came in fits and starts. There would be much of it during the winter, and people came to rely on it, then when it was withdrawn, many of the recipients were in a worse plight than before, as their moral fibre and independence had been sapped. The C.O.S. complained about the injustice of some of these charities; for instance, coal charities first inspected coal bins and coal sheds, and if these were empty coal was given, but if the provident had joined the C.O.S. coal clubs, they got nothing, no matter how much they needed it. The effect on the honest hard-working man must not be forgotten either. For what encouragement was there to him when his neighbour, who had not tried to keep his job, was receiving such easy money?

Nor was the effect on the giver forgotten: When he saw his gifts being squandered on the undeserving, or used for luxury and perhaps vice, his heart was hardened. The press would give publicity to heart-rending accounts of distress and money would pour in, but subsequent appeals had to be accompanied by even

---

[1] H. Jennings, *Private Citizen in Public Work* (1930), Cap. IV.
[2] H. Barnett, *Life of Canon Barnett* (1918), p. 230.
[3] C.O.S. occasional papers. Octavia Hill, *The C.O.S.*

more spectacular stories of misery to make the public respond. This was known by the professional poor, who deliberately set out to manufacture sores and other distresses.

A factor which influenced some, but by no means all, was the inadequate out-relief given by some Boards of Guardians, since this encouraged the recipient to go round from charity to charity for supplementation. For instance, the guardians of some parishes would grant a widow with several children 1s. 6d. per week with 3d. a week for each dependent child. The widow would then often be left to supplement this sum from whatever charitable agencies she could find. Inadequate relief was not confined to the poor law, but was also the habit of many charitable organizations which, having a limited amount to spend, spread it over as large a number of recipients as possible, with the result, the C.O.S. said, that none of them was helped back to independence, but all were encouraged to sink still further into dependence.

In some of the large towns, but particularly in London, it had become fashionable to try to regenerate some of the most degraded members of society by making a special approach to them. There had thus developed 'Thieves' Suppers' and 'Prostitutes' Meetings'. These the forerunners of the C.O.S. greatly condemned. As Sir Charles Trevelyan said:[1] 'We are doing all we can to form the thieves and prostitutes into a class.' The truth of his remarks seems to have been generally accepted, but for a time this form of philanthropy was popular.

It must not be thought that the C.O.S. was the first to react against the abuses and mistakes of the various social work organizations. As far back as 1863, under the influence of William Rathbone and others, the leading charities of Liverpool had formed themselves into the 'Central Relief Society', whose object was to help the deserving poor over sudden emergencies, so that they need not have recourse to the poor law. The secretary of the society was paid, and careful investigation of each case was the bulwark of the scheme. It advised individual donors to divert all their gifts and to refer all their cases to the society. In Edinburgh, as we have seen, a case was being made out for more co-ordination and less indiscriminate giving either by societies or individuals.

So much had opinion been influenced by some of these arguments that in the year of the formation of the C.O.S., a

[1] H. Bosanquet, *op. cit.*, p. 7.

Government department was moved to express an opinion which undoubtedly gave a fillip to the new organization. This was the famous Goschen Minute of the Poor Law Board 1869 on 'The Relief to the Poor in the Metropolis'. This Minute, which was in no sense a Regulation, and was addressed to the Boards of Guardians in the Metropolis only, set out the official view about the sphere of 'Poor Law' and of 'Charity'. It stated that poor relief should be confined to those actually destitute, that in no case should it be given to those with insufficient wages, as it would negative the necessity for self-reliance and thrift. Where relief was given it should be adequate. 'Charity' on the other hand could be given where means were insufficient to prevent a person becoming a pauper. 'Charity' should not be given to those on relief, except to do what the poor law could not do, such as redeeming tools from pawn, or helping a pauper to travel to another town where he might find work. Cash supplementation of relief, which had occasionally been practised, was not appropriate. For if it were given openly it must be taken into account by the official in making the determination, while if it were given clandestinely, it led to abuse.

The Goschen Minute helped to build a point of view shared by the C.O.S., though it was not a factor in bringing the new organization into being. How this happened no one really knows. It is possible that the precipitating element in the situation, which had been growing clearer to the clergy and others in the 'Metropolitan and Relief Association', was the reading of two papers. The first was read in June 1868, when the Rev. Henry Solly, a Unitarian Minister, opened a discussion before the British Association and the Society of Arts on *How to deal with the Unemployed Poor of London, and with its 'Roughs' and Criminal Classes*.[1] This resulted in the creation of a committee of influential men, who formed themselves into an association and drew up a series of prospectuses. There appear to have been some differences of opinion among them, and at one time, according to John Ruskin, there were two associations. However, by December, a second paper was read by Dr. Hawksley on *The Charities of London, and some errors of their administration, with suggestions for an improved system of Private and Official Charitable Relief*, in which he suggested a scheme for the central organization of all charities in London, and their administration through

[1] H. Bosanquet, *op. cit*, pp. 17–20.

district offices, to be financed by a tax of one per cent on the annual income of each charity. It is true that the charities refused this plan, particularly the financial proposals, but by April 1869, at the instigation of Lord Lichfield, offices had been found at 15, Buckingham Street, and a 'Society for Organizing Charitable Relief and Repressing Mendicity' came into being. A year later the simpler title 'Charity Organization Society' was substituted.

Two of its paid and full-time secretaries were so important that they deserve mention by name. Of these Mr. C. B. P. Bosanquet[1] was the first in time. He took over the organization in July 1870, when its funds were low and its whole existence in jeopardy. Between that date and 1875 when he became an active landlord in the north of England, he was instrumental in opening several offices, and in bringing others into close co-ordination, while at the same time furthering the propaganda which was characteristic of the movement. He thus laid a firm foundation upon which his successors could build. The other was Charles Stewart Loch who at the remarkable age of twenty-six took over the secretaryship when Bosanquet resigned. He remained until 1914 when he resigned through illness. It was undoubtedly to the ability, the singleness of purpose and enthusiasm of these two men, particularly the latter, that the C.O.S. owes its profound influence on nineteenth and twentieth century social work throughout the world. A simple summary of their teaching may be found in some verses quoted from an anonymous American writer.[2]

> *I gave a beggar from my little store*
> *Of well-earned gold. He spent the shining ore*
> *And came again, and yet again, still cold*
> *And hungry as before.*
>
> *I gave a thought, and through that thought of mine*
> *He found himself, the man, supreme, divine,*
> *Fed, clothed, and crowned with blessings manifold,*
> *And now he begs no more.*

Principles

We have suggested that a clue to the principles of the C.O.S. may be found in the mistakes and abuses of the past. These

---

[1] *Ibid.*, p. 150.   [2] C.O.S. *Conference Reports* (Kendal).

principles included organization and co-operation in charity; help for deserving cases only; the limited scope of charity; the help to be sufficient to promote regeneration.

1 *Co-operation and Organization*

In order to present a coherent front for the achievement of this ideal in London, the central organization proceeded to set up district committees, coinciding as far as possible with the poor law areas, to do the field work, to act as focal points for the local charities, and to work in close touch with the poor law officials. The central organization would meanwhile concern itself with the general oversight of the districts, and the promotion of this and other purposes for which it had come into existence. The C.O.S. were at pains to make clear that by 'Organization of Charity' they did not mean amalgamation and unification. 'Our object', they said,[1] 'is not to relieve existing societies of their appropriate work, but rather to supply them and private individuals with a machinery which will enable them to dispense relief more wisely and more effectively.' Organization was not an object in itself. It was a means to an end, and the end they worked for was to raise the standard of charity, or 'case work' as it began to be called (*circa* 1885), so that mere giving should no longer be confused with charity, and that haphazard almsgiving should give place to assistance skilfully given after taking into consideration all circumstances, including the services offered by other charitable organizations.

Co-operation had another meaning to these pioneers. It meant not only co-operation between givers, so that overlapping and waste were prevented and standards raised, but also co-operation between giver and receiver. As Loch said,[2]

without the giver giving to good purpose, and the receiver taking and turning to account with as good a purpose, both fail. Both can be deceived. The giver deceives himself into thinking any gift is better than none, and the receiver is deceived because he thinks good will come of the gift, which it will not, unless he consciously puts it to good purpose.

2 *The Deserving*

The second principle concerned the types of people needing

---

[1] C.O.S. *Annual Report* (1875).
[2] C. S. Loch, *A great Ideal and its Champion* (1923), p. 141.

help, and the purpose of any help given. The C.O.S. was never tired of saying that the purpose of good social work could not be achieved unless it was recognized as remedial, as concerned with the causes of poverty or ineffectiveness in the individual, and not simply with palliatives that would relieve a situation temporarily. The exponents were very clear about the responsibility everyone had for himself. It was good for the poor, they declared,[1] to meet all the ordinary contingencies of life, such as occasional sickness, or unemployment, the expenses of a large family, and the impotence of old age. For the poverty stricken to know that there was state provision against these misfortunes, or that private charity would absolve them from the thrift needed to make provision for themselves, would undermine the spirit of independence. It would moreover open the road to idleness and drunkenness, and the last state would be worse than the first. But should a poor person be overtaken by some sudden and unexpected misfortune, or if sickness or special infirmity were protracted, then let him be assured, it was said, that there were those at hand who would gladly help him in his misfortune. Help was therefore to be limited to the deserving, by which was meant those who had made every effort to provide against the rainy day, but who had had more than their normal share of bad luck.

Any definition of this kind necessarily involved problems of interpretation. An abnormally hard winter, as in Stepney in 1878, led to giving relief to the unemployed bricklayers who had used up their savings and required help. But there were other occasions when such a decision was not so easily reached. For instance in 1878 Mr. Peek gave a certain sum of money for the relief of necessitous children. For the administration of this the C.O.S. drew up certain rules. First, an enquiry into each case should be made to find out if it required charity or the sterner treatment of the poor law. Then care should be taken not to give aid in a way which would aggravate the necessity for it, or would precipitate an emergency because the family had become demoralized by unconsidered aid. Finally, the neighbours should be considered; would they be demoralized by the sight of easy money, and themselves deteriorate into pauperism? The prevention of such deterioration was a prime object of C.O.S. policy. The members felt a thorough understanding of this principle implied the education of

[1] C.O.S. *Annual Report* (1876).

the rich as well as the poor. For the rich, knowing little of the poor, but hearing of some need, tended to[1]

forget charity and rely on charitable relief. By a hasty misapplication of charitable resources they would save the children, and ignore the parents, the children's natural instructors, whom it were worth all the gold and silver of charitable relief if they could live near and reclaim from idleness, intemperance, unthrift and squalor. They would feed the destitute and clothe the ragged, forgetful of those larger moral and social laws, which rich and poor must alike obey, if craftsmen and labourer are to have regularity in employment, and if the day's toil is to bring with it a recompense sufficient for support.

3 Limit to Scope

The principle of selecting cases to be helped so that only those who had shewn signs of being willing to help themselves came within the list of 'assisted cases', was followed by a third principle which the C.O.S. of those days preached with vigour, but not always with success. This was the principle of 'limited scope'. As Edward Denison had said 'it is necessary for philanthropists to do what they can do, well'. As we have seen one of the difficulties of the past had been that an agency started with a certain purpose would then be led to give help not quite within its scope, until gradually it was dealing with all types and conditions of people, undertaking far more than it had the resources to cover, and seriously overlapping the work of other bodies. It was to prevent this that the C.O.S. begged for discipline, resistance to the temptation to attempt too much, and a limitation in the work of each agency. 'Our business is not with the poor as such', said Loch,[2] 'but with those who are in distress, providing the distress is not preventible.' An analysis of assistance given and refused in the first decade and a half of C.O.S. work illuminates the working of this principle (see C.O.S. annual reports 1870 onwards). For in no year were more than half the applicants assisted, and in one (1879) the proportion fell to only one-fifth. Many of those refused help were referred to other agencies, sometimes (1875) even one-third being dealt with in this way. In these ways was the principle of dealing only with those cases that came within the strict scope of the C.O.S. implemented, and the policy of friendly co-operation with other charities pursued.

[1] C.O.S. *Annual Report*, 1883.   [2] C. S. Loch, *Charity Organisation* (1890).

4 *Adequate Help*

A fourth principle was that help given should be adequate, or as Lord Beveridge years later and in another context pleaded 'adequate in amount and in time'. The object was to regenerate the individual and his family and to promote independence. To achieve this end all cases were carefully sifted, and if no evidence of helpability, i.e. of willingness to help themselves, existed, the application was refused or passed to the poor law. If assistance were to be given, the case was passed to another agency when this was appropriate. But by the 1880's this practice had been modified owing to the inability of any one agency to do all that was needed in the assistance of a family. In its place, the method of appealing to as many agencies as seemed appropriate to the particular case was adopted, and the committee was thus able to concentrate on each assisted case the amount of help adequate to its needs. Failing support from other charities, the relief fund available to the C.O.S. was used. An examination of C.O.S. records shews how the principle worked in the early years. Not all help was in cash, though seldom fewer than half the assisted cases were given money. Each year several hundreds were found employment, and some were given loans to help them over a difficulty, while others, sometimes as many as one-third, were given letters to the hospital. Canon Barnett, who had been intimately concerned in the C.O.S. in its early years, and who thoroughly believed in its principles, was adamant about this one. His wife, writing years later, described how difficult it was to put into practice in the parish of St. Judes, Whitechapel, where he resided. Accustomed as the people were to receiving an occasional few coppers[1] 'they were astounded and very angry when money was refused. So much so, that many times threatening crowds gathered outside the Vicarage —sometimes throwing stones through the windows—and were often dispersed only by the advent of the police'. Yet for all this Canon Barnett persisted in refusal, and concentrated on those cases where constructive work could be done. For example, a certain James Stuart came for help.

When asked if he could lime-wash cellars, he agreed readily. So a job was made for him at the Church, and his wages were earned. His wife at the time being pregnant was helped and later sent to a convalescent

[1] H. Barnett, *op. cit.*, vol. I, pp. 84 *et seq.*

home. Later they were given a loan to buy furniture and move into a better house. This was repaid and the family, which had been destitute and anti-social, were helped in their rehabilitation to a sturdy independence.

Following on the principle of reserving help for the 'deserving', the C.O.S., especially in its early years, was vigorous in uncovering and, if necessary, prosecuting persons and institutions found to be dishonest. 'It found London infested by hordes of fraudulent societies, impostors and begging-letter writers, and to clear the field of these was essential to the cultivation of genuine Charity.'[1] It therefore set up an 'Inquiry Committee' whose purpose was to sift the bona fides of every person or institution about whom there was the slightest suspicion. Thereafter it compiled a cautionary list and published warning after warning 'against giving money to persons who go from house to house presenting circulars and collecting in a speculative way for vague metropolitan or national objects',[2] and urged the public of the need for inquiry as much into the nature of charities as into the truth of beggars' stories. The list was kept at the office, and the public told they could consult it as often as they wished. In certain cases the society initiated prosecutions, the 'Free Dormitory Association' and the 'National Bible and Clothing Society' being cases in point. There is no doubt that much fraud and dishonesty were both abolished and avoided in this way, and if the society was sometimes over-zealous in its investigation, as when it placed Dr. Barnardo's Homes on its list for a short time in 1877, the purification of charitable effort in London, and indirectly elsewhere, justified any mistakes that might have been made. Its activity made enemies, and as the vested interests were smoked out they turned and stung their tormentors. By 1890, as the annual report showed, no fewer than 1,087 institutions had been investigated.

Methods

The several methods advocated and practised by the C.O.S. marked no new chapter in the development of social work, but it was due to the society that they were drawn together into something coherent and articulate. While the machinery it used was not new, its emphasis was different. For these reasons we tend to date modern case work from its activities. The machinery by which

---

[1] H. Bosanquet, *op. cit.*, p. 116.   [2] C.O.S. *Annual Report* (1872).

its principles were applied was the committee system. We have seen how district committees were set up to undertake the field work. These committees had several purposes. On the one hand they were a meeting ground for members of other charitable organizations, thus promoting understanding and ensuring co-operation. On the other, their regular meetings were intended as executive gatherings, where cases presented by the visitors and other workers could be discussed in the light of all the knowledge available, and appropriate action decided upon. A third, though incidental purpose, was to spread C.O.S aims and methods through committee discussion of actual cases. In the C.O.S., action was the result not of the unaided judgment of a single social worker, but the combined knowledge and wisdom of the group.

The essence of the method was thorough investigation. 'Investigation', the society remarked in the Annual Report of 1895, 'has four-fold value. It enables us to decide whether a case is one for help or not. It helps us to decide the form that assistance should take to give the most permanent results. It enables us to find means of assistance apart from cash, and it helps us to give the best advice for the future welfare of the client.' Their spokesmen were determined to rid themselves of vague generalizations and opinions not based on evidence, and to substitute careful enquiry into the facts of the economic and social life of the family, its previous history, its friends and relations, and above all a clear understanding of the way the client himself thought he could be helped. They believed firmly in cross-checking, so that wages, debts and other facts could be discovered as accurately as possible, and in cross-references, so that the opinions of friends, neighbours and relatives could be obtained. They admitted that making such enquiries was troublesome, and none would take less than a week to make, but they felt that any social work, worthy of the name, justified the trouble taken. Nor did they fear resentment from those investigated. 'After all,' they said, 'no one in real need or who is honest can resent it!'[1]

A natural corollary of investigation was the case-paper. They had early produced a format containing space for details of the number and size of the family, the income from whatever source, necessary expenditure, and the nature of the request, along with

[1] C.O.S. *Conference Reports.*

103

the name of the employer(s) and two or more references. Loch thought such a case-paper should be[1] 'kept at a Central Office, where it will be accessible to those who need it, but not available to any person who happens to be in the office. The accumulation of knowledge in this way' he went on 'gives us knowledge of the individuals—those who are systematic alms-seekers, and those who go only in moments of stress. This information not only prevents duplication in labour, but provides a clue as to what should be done, if anything.'

On the question of visiting, the C.O.S. did have something new to say. It was, naturally, a necessary part of the system of investigation, and it should be skilled and thorough. But visiting should be undertaken only for a specific purpose, and at the invitation or with the consent of the client. The society denigrated the wholesale 'house to house' visitation as practised by the visiting societies. By the end of the century the members were becoming even clearer in their minds about this difficult question; as Barnett said in 1908,[2] 'visitors have to justify their place in the modern world. They can no longer claim that wealth and education gives them the right to obtrude their relief. The old world of neighbourliness has changed, and visitors in many ways are out of date.' The place of the visitor, they suggested, was to provide a human touch to the official instrument. A visit undertaken without an object undermined the self-respect of the visitor and those whom he visited. Visitors were necessary as personal links between guardians, the C.O.S. and other organizations. Nor did the society deny the value of cross-visiting, whereby a client received an occasional visit from a different person, who might get a fresh view of the case, and might be able to offer valuable advice.

A further link in the chain of case work method on which they insisted was the 'follow through'. Not only was this important for the satisfaction of seeing a case successfully completed, but because valuable lessons could be learnt about which methods were likely to succeed, and which had led to failure. Finally, the stages through which help should pass were discussed and taught as part of the method. They were an echo of Chalmers' 'Four Fountains' —self-help, help of relatives, help of neighbours and friends, and only if these failed should charitable funds be considered.

[1] C. S. Loch, *A Great Ideal and its Champion*, p. 141.
[2] *Social Service Handbook for 1908.*

In this way case-work methods, developed haphazardly through the nineteenth century, were gathered together, considered in their relation to the declared purpose of the C.O.S., developed into a coherent plan and taught to succeeding generations of case workers. Little that the C.O.S. taught was new. But it developed a body of transmissible knowledge, and lost no opportunity to pass it on, not only to its own workers, but to social workers and philanthropists wherever they were to be found. This is a main source of the fame which is justifiably its own. It is not, however, the whole picture. For it learnt from its own experience, and in learning inaugurated developments which were to have far reaching effects in the succeeding century.

Training of Social Workers

Of these developments, the training of prospective social workers may ultimately be seen to have been the most fundamental. Its history belongs more properly to the twentieth century, but by the end of the nineteenth century experiments were being tried out, and talks and discussions on the subject held, so that by 1903 a School of Sociology had been instituted by the society. An early mention of training is to be found in the C.O.S. annual report for 1879 (1880) which referred to a special conference of Honorary secretaries and Delegates to teach one another the elements of office management, case recording and methods of presenting cases to committee. This was followed by lectures on the aims and purposes of the C.O.S., and on case-work method. By the 1890's training was becoming more important every year, and was taking the form not only of lectures and discussions, but of practical training with the district secretaries. In 1899[1] the society was beginning to distinguish four grades of learners: those who came out of curiosity, but finding the work too difficult soon left; those who were willing to learn the handling of straightforward cases only; those who belonged to other organizations, who were being trained in C.O.S. methods through close co-operation; and those who would become the leaders of the C.O.S. in the future—the chairmen, the hon. secretaries and the committee members.

By the last decade of the century considerable controversy existed in the C.O.S. about the nature and methods of the training.

[1] C.O.S. *Annual Report* (1895).

Some thought, for instance, that living in a residential settlement was best, others suggested that close co-operation with the workers in the C.O.S. district office gave more direct experience. The question of the relative importance of theory and practice also exercised them. Some feared 'learning by experience' as a method of training, because of the harm done to the poor when mistakes were made. Others felt that the responsibility of knowing that suffering might be caused to others by failure was both educational in itself, and an indispensable part of the training. All seemed to agree that some study was necessary; that every worker needed to know the facts about local conditions; the statutory and voluntary agencies; the organizations in which self-help could be developed such as friendly societies and savings banks; the level of wages in the neighbourhood, and the cost of living. Some suggested that the worker should have insight into the outlook of her clients, and should be at pains to understand his thought processes and behaviour mechanisms, so that help given would be as constructive as possible. For all this, adequate library facilities were, they thought, indispensable, and the C.O.S., considering this important, has housed at its headquarters today, one of the best libraries of books on social work. Besides general but relevant knowledge of this kind, the early case workers believed in precise instruction on methods of case recording, visiting, inquiring, letter writing and accounts.

Agreement on the exact balance of theory and practice in training was not found, though all accepted the need for both. But though some would throw the new recruit into the maelstrom of practical case work on the 'sink or swim' principle, others advocated a more careful and gradual introduction. They feared, for instance, to introduce her at once to the most degraded slums, for apart from the undesirability of sensationalism, they thought she might tend to lose perspective. Instead, they suggested, she should work with and carefully observe the methods of a competent case-worker, followed by individual work on her own with selected cases, and only after passing through these stages should she take on a varied case load.

While these controversies were going on, district secretaries, settlement wardens, almoners and others imbued with C.O.S. principles were struggling to meet the claims of the multifarious duties in the office and at committee and to give what time they could to training the newcomers. It was admitted, even as late as 1910, that though a C.O.S. committee had been set up in 1897 to examine the methods of training adopted by the London district committees, more progress had probably been made in convincing public opinion that training was necessary, than in rendering instruction as effective as it might be.[1]

Paid Workers

The problem of salaries for social workers was also widely discussed towards the end of the century. The appointment of paid, full-time social workers was not the result of the movement for training, but it was felt, even then, that a salaried professional service was impossible without training. As early as 1870 the C.O.S. appointed its first paid General Secretary (Mr. Bosanquet), and in 1879 a motion to introduce paid secretaries into each district was proposed. This aroused vehement opposition, both on grounds of expense, and the fear that voluntary work would be killed by it. One committee had tried a paid secretary and found they got on better without him. Others were quite satisfied with their work as it was. So the matter had to be shelved for a few years. However, by 1883 five paid officers were appointed by head-quarters, to be attached to the districts for 'local work and organizing charity'. Apparently this system worked well, and the level of case work was raised. Towards the end of the century paid workers were appointed to advise the districts and help to train volunteers. The relationship of paid and voluntary workers has never been an easy one. It is difficult to find cases which will give volunteers work suitable to their temperament, hold their interest, give them some measure of responsibility and yet which will not suffer from the 'occasional nature' of their services. There was then, as there is now, a greater tendency for those who undertook serious training for social work to take up a paid appointment, and there grew up the dichotomy with which we are all too familiar, between the voluntary worker and the paid, possibly more experienced and perhaps trained one. All the same, until well into the twentieth century the C.O.S. had a number of fully trained, unpaid staff prepared to take full responsibility for the work of the office during holidays or emergencies.

Whilst the C.O.S. was facing problems of internal growth, its

[1] C.O.S. *Conference Reports.*

influence was being spread over the whole United Kingdom, and into other parts of the world. In this country, by 1894, no fewer than eighty-five organizations in various towns had embraced the principles of the C.O.S. Some were so much in sympathy that they actually affiliated to it (seventeen did so in 1879). By the early 'nineties annual conferences to discuss aims and methods of case work had been inaugurated, and were found immensely useful to the participants. Meanwhile close co-operation by correspondence and interchange of visits was being maintained with other countries. The 1882 annual report mentioned contact with no fewer than one hundred and eleven towns in twenty-four different countries. Dr. Devine, writing of the New York C.O.S., stated frankly that it was founded in 1882 on the principles and methods of the London C.O.S.

While it was involved in organizing and educating, the C.O.S. was not backward in promoting social reform and suggesting new ways in which case work methods could with advantage be extended. Thus, in its first annual report, it stated its intentions of considering, with a view to action, the 'great question of Sanitary Improvement, Emigration, Education, Provident Societies, Improved Dwellings for the Poor and other collateral subjects', and this it did with energy and some enlightenment, as Mrs. Bosanquet has told in Part II of her book. It is appropriate to dwell here on two of the matters that arose out of this attention to major questions. (1) One was the creation of an entirely new branch of social work, that of hospital almoning, (2) and the other was the proposal to start a 'mutual register'.

1 *Hospital almoning* arose directly out of C.O.S. action in the closing years of the nineteenth century. After some years of discussion, one of the society's most capable Secretaries, Miss M. Stewart, was lent in 1894 to the out-patient department of the Royal Free Hospital, her salary being met jointly by the two voluntary organizations. Her work was to secure for the [1] 'patients such care, assistance and attention outside the hospital as should enable them to profit to the full by the medical treatment received; the hospitals being thus linked up with public authorities and charitable organizations to secure the improvement of the condition of the poor.' In the despatch of these duties she was in an excellent position to detect fraud, and to know whether patients

[1] *Report of King Edward VII Hospital Fund 1912.*

were able to contribute to the cost of their treatment at the hospital. It is unfortunate that this least constructive aspect of her work should have seized the imagination of so many people, particularly the hospital collecting societies, who advised that enquiry agents should be attached to all hospitals to prevent the abuse of hospital charity. Many have deplored the appointment of these agents since, being quite untrained in case work, they did harm to the growth of almoning proper. But it has to be recognized that in this way embryo almoners' departments did make their appearance in hospitals, which would not otherwise have thought them necessary, while constructive case work was still being pursued by Miss Stewart at the Royal Free, where a small training school for future almoners was gradually being developed. By 1898 St. George's Hospital had appointed an almoner trained in this way, and by 1902 the Westminster had followed suit, while Leeds was the first north country hospital to try the scheme. Until 1907 the task of finding and training almoners remained in the hands of a special committee of the C.O.S., but in that year it was thought advisable to form an independent body, the Hospital Almoners' Council, consisting of almoners, members of the C.O.S. and other interested people. Meanwhile the C.O.S. both in its private meetings and at its conferences was examining the work and watching the growth of its child. Papers were written or read giving advice on different aspects of the almoner's work (cf. C.O.S. Occasional Papers), but always stressing those fundamental principles for which the C.O.S. had become famous.

2 A '*Mutual Register*' in which the agencies co-operate to enter the names of all applicants, and details of help given, has always appealed to the logically minded as a way of improving the efficiency of all the associated agencies, since each has access to the register and can check whether or in what way applicants have been helped before. It prevents overlapping or fraud, enables a social worker, interested in a family, to take counsel with other agencies similarly interested, and helps to concentrate all available forces on them. Early attempts by the C.O.S. to establish such a register failed. This was lamented even in the second annual report (1871), but was regarded as due to the small size of the doles then given, and the labour of keeping the register. Even up to the end of the century little progress had been made, and if later there were periods of success, it was usually due to the

enthusiasm and indefatigable energy of the person keeping the register, who by tact and perseverance was able to encourage other agencies to send in their returns promptly. On the whole, however, what would appear on the surface to be a sensible and efficient arrangement, did not always work well in practice, as the early C.O.S. workers discovered.

We cannot leave this survey of the C.O.S. contribution to social work without reflecting on some of the opposition it had to meet in the first thirty years of its existence. For much as it was supported by its adherents, and passionately as it was defended by its friends and workers, it was forced to meet criticism which some times descended to compaigns of vilification. The most vicious attacks, though not the most serious, came from the vested interests whose habits of thought, or even whose personal position (e.g. the secretary of the 'Free Dormitory Association') had been challenged by the C.O.S. Willing to stoop to any method to gain their ends, these critics produced pamphlets, incited press compaigns even in papers as reputable as the Westminster Gazette, and on one occasion tried to break up the society's annual meeting. Their attacks ranged from heart-rending accounts of individual cases which they declared the C.O.S. had refused to help, through innuendoes that all was not as it should be with the society, as certain officials or well-placed persons such as Lord Shaftesbury had withdrawn their support, to the suggestion that the benevolent were being fraudulently deprived of the money they contributed to charity, as so much of their contributions was being swallowed up by the enormous salaries the officials paid themselves. Most of these statements were palpably untrue, and could easily be refuted by the C.O.S., though the jibe that costs of administration were the major part of expenditure was readily admitted, since the society never had been a relief agency, but an organizing and investigating one. These attacks, though wounding when they came, did little permanent harm with the supporting public and often did good, as the excesses drove many to sympathise more actively with the Society's aims and methods.

Where these criticisms were to be regretted was in the harm they did in the minds of the poor, their clients. At the same time it would seem, from the scanty evidence there is, that the poor were themselves critical of the way in which some of the investigation was done in those early years. The 1888 annual report from the Hackney district set out to refute certain criticisms that investigation meant delay, and a genuinely urgent case was sometimes made worse by it; that employers and friends were catechized; and that some inquiries were harsh and unkind. Mr. Clement Attlee, himself a social worker in the East End for many years and able from personal experience among the poor to sense their attitude, condemned the tone of suspicion that ran through C.O.S. work—'a general assumption that all applicants are frauds unless they prove themselves otherwise'.[1] He commented on the lack of tact shewn by some of the workers in dealing with people's intimate problems. But failures of this sort, apart from the natural resentment felt by people whose requests for help were refused, were superficial defects due to the failure of the human agent to be as patient and sympathetic in all circumstances as he might have been. No amount of training, or having the right personality, or being 'called' to the work can obviate occasional lapses, and when they do happen their effect is magnified sometimes beyond recognition. At the same time the principles of the C.O.S., distinguishing as they did between the 'deserving' and the 'undeserving' must give some substance to the charge that the onus of proof that they were 'deserving', lay with the clients, and one cannot explain the criticism all away by blaming the human element.

More fundamental opposition to the C.O.S. lay in the changing philosophy of the last decade of the century. Poverty was no longer regarded as the natural state of the mass of the people. Many were arguing that it was as much an accident that some were born into poverty as that others were born into riches, and that being so, the accident of a person's birth should not affect his opportunities in life. With the growth of egalitarianism came the plea that the community should in some way guarantee a basic standard of life, and an equal opportunity for all, irrespective of the status in society the individual found himself. This led to the growth in the demand for social services which would provide education, school feeding, old age pensions, unemployment and sickness schemes, as a right for every citizen. Sufficient has been said already to shew how completely opposite this was to all for which the C.O.S. stood. Their adherents had argued from the beginning that an individual was responsible for himself, that it was his duty to provide against the ordinary risks of life for himself and his

[1] C. Attlee, *The Social Worker* (1920).

family. The purpose of social work was to find out how each family in distress had got that way, and if there were any hope of lifting it to independence again. But anything that was likely to undermine a man's desire to fend for himself was to be eschewed, so they opposed schemes of state or municipal relief, which[1] 'will make labourers less self-reliant, and will encourage loafers to increase and multiply'. They opposed old age pensions, the municipalization of hospitals, and free or cheap meals for school children ('an insufficient and pauperizing system of relief'). And by opposing them, they drew upon the C.O.S. the obloquy of the reforming spirits advocating such schemes.

The opposition of the 'Socialists', as they regarded the heterogeneous collection of people who held these views, unfortunate though it might be, was one thing, but the opposition of Canon Barnett, one of their oldest and staunchest supporters, was quite another. He had been feeling out of step with them for some time as a letter to his brother in 1888 shewed:[2] 'Wednesday I went to meet a lot of C.O.S. folk re a proposed training farm. They were just impossible—refusing to do anything except clothe themselves in their own righteousness.' But matters did not come to a head until July 1895, when he read a paper in which he said that though the district committees had been doing excellent work, and had had much influence, the C.O.S. itself had lost touch with the trends of thought, and instead of leading public opinion on social questions they had become 'idolaters of former dogmas', and out of sympathy 'with the forces that are shaping our times'. This attack coming as it did from Barnett, was a severe blow to Mr. Loch and the C.O.S., for though some of Barnett's arguments may have been founded on a misconception of the relationship between the centre and the district committees, he was voicing a fundamental criticism that was being made by many.

A further criticism, associated neither with the dispossessed nor the 'new thinkers', attacked one of the fundamental doctrines of the C.O.S., and sprang from the deep concern felt by some of the charitable for the degenerate and the degraded. This concern had expressed itself before the beginning of the C.O.S. in the 'Thieves' Suppers' and 'Prostitutes' Meetings,' and was to appear later in the work of such organizations as the Salvation Army. It derived

[1] C.O.S. *Annual Report* (1893).
[2] H. Barnett, *op. cit.*, vol. II, pp. 265–6.

in part from the Christian doctrine that all men are brothers and that no matter how low a man has fallen, he can still be helped. This now seemed inconsistent with the C.O.S. teaching that only the 'deserving' should be helped, and was to have a profound influence in modifying that teaching as the years passed.

Conclusion

It is not our purpose to follow the fortunes of the C.O.S. into the twentieth century or to see what modifications in its principles, its methods and its name have come with the years. It is left therefore for us to note the chief contributions of the C.O.S. It is clear that it was in the direct line of descent from Chalmers, that its philosophy resembled his in every particular but two. For while Chalmers would have abolished state relief of poverty as an encouragement to pauperism, the C.O.S. recognized the need for a poor law to relieve complete destitution and to deter those who without the menace of its rigours might be tempted to fall into destitution. Further than that they refused to go, but it is significant that in the half century that divided them from Chalmers they should have accepted so much. The other difference was in their attitude to visiting. Chalmers contemplated with equanimity the thought of wholesale house-to-house visiting: it was fundamental to his scheme that the deacons should get to know all the families in their districts. The C.O.S., on the other hand, doubted the wisdom of this paternalism, and preferred instead to visit only if asked, and to see friends and relatives only with the clients' express consent. In other ways, however, the connection is apparent. In their views on the need for independence, thrift and preparation for misfortune on the part of the working man, on the resources that should be tapped in case of a breakdown, they were at one. If Chalmers placed less emphasis on the need for cooperation in charity it was because the scale of rival charities in his day had not reached the proportion it did later.

The C.O.S. did not contribute anything new to the methods of social work. We have seen in a previous Chapter (Chapter 5) how all the techniques of case work had been advocated and experimented with by the many organizations that grew up during the century. The C.O.S. made its mark because it believed in these techniques, codified them and passed them on indefatigably from worker to worker, from charity to charity. It laid the foundation for a profession of social work, with its own discipline and its own code of ethics. In its *raison d'être*, the organization of charity, its reach exceeded its grasp. For though a great deal of overlapping and competition between charities were brought to an end, and though many consented to unite in 'Guilds of Help', 'Central Relief Funds' and the like, the proliferation of charitable organizations continued.

Two other contributions may be mentioned. First, the C.O.S. insisted that in their diagnosis of distress and prescription for treatment it was the welfare and regeneration of the whole family they sought. It is significant that through the late nineteenth and twentieth centuries, when the legal responsibilities of members of the family for one another have been gradually abolished, when greater specialization in social work has made different workers interested in different members or aspects of the family, the C.O.S. has clung firmly to its original principle, that it is the interests of the family as a whole that should be paramount.

Secondly, it insisted on a scientific approach. It was determined to stamp out, as far as possible, the undiscriminating emotional responses to poverty, and to substitute for them decisions upon action following the careful collection of the relevant facts. At a time when Darwin and Huxley dominated men's minds, and Booth and his Social Surveyors were developing fresh techniques in ascertaining social facts, it is not surprising that the C.O.S., an eminently educated coterie, should have sought a scientific method of social work. For being rescued from the sentimentality of some of the Victorians, those of us who come after should be grateful.

A quotation from Mary Richmond's Memoir of Sir Charles Loch might well conclude this chapter.

In March 1905 Loch was made a D.C.L. by Oxford. The Oxford Magazine in congratulating the University upon its recognition of a service so unique, and for which year by year the public debt had been rolling up, declared that the C.O.S. was 'widely disliked and universally trusted'—a better reputation to have than if the 'dis' were removed from before the 'liked' and placed in front of the 'trusted'.

CHAPTER 7

OCTAVIA HILL

OCTAVIA HILL has sometimes been called the grandmother of modern social work, because her influence and her principles permeated all the later nineteenth-century thought, as those of Thomas Chalmers had done earlier. Her special concern had been the development of decent well-managed dwellings for the underprivileged, on the assumption that no one could be a self-respecting citizen in the humiliating and degrading slums of her day. This work interacted with other charitable enterprises so that by 1875 she was an indispensable link between progressive people in most fields of social work. But, while her work and her ideas were important in themselves, her personality and influence were equally so, though she was too modest to realize it. To quote only two of the many philanthropists with whom she co-operated, Ruskin was early impressed with her zeal and varied talents, and later Canon Barnett was greatly influenced by her.

Born in 1838, she knew considerable hardship and poverty in her early years. Her father had been an energetic and capable business man, but successive financial misadventures, ill-health and a large family had reduced him to a state of compulsory retirement. Octavia Hill's mother, daughter of the famous Dr. Southwood Smith who had, with Edwin Chadwick, been a pioneer in public health, was his second wife. Through her mother, Octavia thus had a direct link with one of the social reformers of the day; and her grandfather was a continual source of inspiration, and actively influential in her personal life. When her mother, Caroline Hill, became a widow and was left to bear the main burden of caring for her large family of daughters, it was the great public health pioneer who often stepped in with practical help. It was through her mother that Octavia came under the influence of the Christian Socialist movement. At the time of the

115

Great Exhibition of 1851, the Christian Socialists, led by Frederick Denison Maurice, were founding associations for co-operative production. One of these was intended for distressed people of the middle class. It was this Ladies' Co-operative Guild that gave Octavia Hill her first introduction to social work, for her mother was asked to become its secretary. The Guild office was in Fitzroy Square and there the family moved from their little cottage in the then rural surrounds of Finchley. Not only did Octavia come in contact for the first time with social work, but it was her first encounter with the mass poverty of a big city, an impression heightened still further by reading Mayhew's *London Labour and the London Poor*. 'At Fitzroy Square', she said, 'the first real knowledge of misery and poverty came to me'[1]—at the age of thirteen!

The Christian Socialist movement, besides having this indirect effect on her future, had a direct one too. 'It remains true', she wrote later, 'that it was my early connection with the body of Christian Socialists to which much of my present work must owe its spirit.' It was this movement that first gave her experience of personal responsibility, a toy furniture business started for the employment of Ragged School children. She worked hard to make the enterprise pay, and it gave scope at once for three of her leading drives—altruism, artistic interest and business proficiency. Though she was still only fourteen, she took charge of the whole business, design, manufacture, packing, pricing and accounting, as well as paying the children for their work! Besides being a valuable business apprenticeship, this gave her direct introduction to personal casework. The youngsters were desperately poor, very rough and often vicious. Yet she managed to keep order in the little workshop, mainly by getting to know each one of the children personally as a friend and co-worker. 'I have to study how to interest each,' she said at the time. 'I connect all they say, do, or look, into one whole, I get to know the thing they really care for.' She also made it her business to know their homes and thus began her knowledge of the houses and the family life of the poor. She superintended their meals from the point of view of cost, diet and table manners, took them on outings to the country on Saturdays and organized parties for them.

Meanwhile Octavia was trying to find time for her chief interest, her painting. Ironically enough, the hobby that was

[1] Moberley Bell, *Octavia Hill* (1951), p. 19.

meant to be a relief from her pressing social work duties led her into the path of her true life's work. For it was through her art that she met John Ruskin, and through him that she took up, purely fortuitously, the management of housing property. One day in the 1850's when Ruskin called to see the work of her mother's Co-operative Guild, he met Octavia, was impressed by her and, to the delight of a hero-worshipping young girl, invited her to visit him at his house. Thus began a friendship that was to last for many years, and out of which came a new kind of social work. Meanwhile he sent her copying work and in other ways encouraged her artistic propensities. Still occupied with her ragged children and their toy-making, additionally burdened with the artistic duties that Ruskin continued to put upon her, in 1856 she undertook yet another task. One of the main Christian Socialist experiments was the Working Men's College. Octavia Hill became its secretary at £25 per annum. She found it interesting, and inspiring to her idealism, but she did not get on well at first with 'the ladies', voluntary teachers who ran the classes. 'As I am thrown among "ladies" I hope I may discover good in them,' she charitably declared! Impatient with them at first, she did eventually warm to some of these social workers and made friends with them.

As if the young Octavia had not enough on her shoulders she found herself becoming more and more the financial prop of her family. Her mother's work with the Guild had ended, or rather the Guild itself had failed; Mrs. Hill was writing articles and Octavia's sister Miranda was teaching. Her father had left many debts which had to be cleared. So Octavia took on classes at the school where Miranda taught. The result was inevitable; her health was undermined and in 1857 she had the first of several breakdowns and she was obliged to give up most of her work with the little toy-makers. By 1860-1, the family fortunes had improved; her mother had published a book, her sisters were teaching, while she herself was taking several classes, besides drawing for Ruskin and acting as secretary to the Working Women's classes attached to the Working Men's College. At this time the family decided to pool their efforts and start their own school at Nottingham Place, where they now lived. Typically, Octavia made the school serve her wider purposes by encouraging the pupils to take an interest in social conditions; several of them later became her assistants. It was characteristic of her that she made each of her interests the handmaid of the other.

Despite her social activities, Octavia still thought that art was her true vocation, and that her social work was an occupation for her spare time. She kept in close touch with Ruskin. It was not surprising therefore that in 1864 he consulted her on how to use an inheritance he had just received, for a worthy social purpose. Her response was to suggest 'a small lodging-house where I may know everyone and do something towards making their lives healthier and happier'. By the next year she had acquired on Ruskin's behalf three houses in a Court near Nottingham Place. He insisted that the scheme should yield 5 per cent return on investment, so that others should be induced to follow suit. In the next year he bought 'a row of cottages facing a bit of desolate ground, occupied with wretched dilapidated cowsheds, manure heaps, old timber, and rubbish of every description'. This was the kind of property she hoped to improve so that both tenants and landlords would benefit. The tenants she found were equally un-promising. They had large families of dirty, undisciplined children, while the adults were given all too often to drunkenness and fighting. When she took over some property in Deptford some years later, on her first visit she found a woman lying at the foot of the stairs, badly beaten by her husband. She had been there from Saturday night to Monday morning, too injured to move, and left alone by the other tenants through fear of the husband. Her first task on taking over the property was to put it into reasonable repair with decent sanitation, adequate water supply, new windows and whitewashed passages and hallways. Her job with the tenants was to establish friendly relationships while in-sisting on regular rent-paying and decent standards of living. At first they were uniformly hostile to her and it took considerable physical courage to face the drunken, brawling inmates of the broken-down courts and alleys. But from this small beginning, with a few groups of derelict property, sprang the elaborate system of social improvement which has influenced social work and social action ever since.

In the early years of her housing experiment her work was private, intensely personal and free from publicity. From 1870 onwards, however, her efforts became increasingly publicized by her admirers, and her name became well-known in progressive circles. This development had its ironical side, as in principle Octavia Hill detested both publicity and large-scale social endeavours. 'She believed', said her brother-in-law, Maurice, 'in personal and sympathetic intercourse with the poor as far more important than any organization.' Her work was, however, so novel and effective that she found herself a public figure, quoted, respected, sometimes insulted, for her efforts on behalf of working-class housing. Depite her dislike of large-scale relief schemes she became in 1869 a member of the newly formed Central Council of the Charity Organization Society. The Council was more of a federal body than an executive one, so she was able to preserve some of her principles on observing that the local district committees retained a good deal of autonomy. At one of the early meetings of the C.O.S. she read a paper on 'The Importance of Aiding the Poor without Almsgiving', which explained clearly why she was prepared to add C.O.S. activities to her already wide range of social work.

She did more than take a place on the Central Council, in order to put her special knowledge at their disposal; she took charge of the impoverished Walmer St. district of Marylebone, and in that area put her principles into operation. She abolished coal tickets, free meals and cash assistance, insisting instead on detailed investigation and careful case-work, employment being offered wherever possible. This was something not previously experienced by the poor of that area and was at first resented bitterly. But she persevered, and in her own words 'there has been some very happy intercourse during the last year, we have come to know each other better and sometimes the bitterness of feeling has seemed to me wholly gone.' As Moberley Bell puts it, 'her knowledge of the people, of the charitable agencies, of laws affecting the poor, as well as her power of getting on happy terms with fellow workers made her invaluable'.

During this period (1870-5) she found time and energy to take a very active part in the Open Space movement, which aimed at saving some of London from the builders. Maurice asserted that this movement was as important to her personally as her housing work. It was, indeed, part of her central purpose of promoting beauty in urban surroundings. Through the efforts of the Open Space enthusiasts many areas, such as Parliament Hill, were saved to become later part of London's Green Belt. Meanwhile her fame was spreading, and she began to be consulted by statesmen and others anxious to put important housing reforms before Parliament. In 1873, for instance, the C.O.S. appointed a special committee on working-class housing, and here Octavia Hill co-operated with Lord Shuttleworth who later, in 1874, introduced the matter in the Commons. The result was the important Artizans Dwelling Act of 1875, which was in great part her work, for it was based on the C.O.S. report, at every stage in the preparation of which her advice had been sought and her amendments accepted.

At the same time her own housing work was growing. The few houses purchased with Ruskin's money had expanded into a huge management undertaking, involving in 1877 as many as 3,500 tenants, and as much as £35,000 in invested funds. She was still trying desperately to keep touch with the tenants of her earlier houses, while supervising the social workers whose training she now undertook so that they could help in both her housing and C.O.S. work. The pressure of this, as well as a long and bitter argument with a hostile medical officer of health, a fierce controversy over the Open Spaces movement, a most painful breach with Ruskin, an unhappy love affair ending in a broken engagement, and the death of a very dear friend and fellow-worker, together proved too much for her, and in 1877 she again broke down and was forced to go abroad for several years to recover. She did not, however, lose touch with all her friends and activities in London, and during her convalescence she was rewarded with the good tidings that her housing measures were being imitated in Liverpool, Manchester, Dublin and Leeds.

On her return to duty in 1882, she was appointed by the Ecclesiastical Commission to manage a large part of their property in Southwark. This involved some reorganization of her plans, and, to cope with this special task, she had to depute more and more of her supervision in other districts, as in Deptford, to her assistants. Shortly afterwards the Ecclesiastical Commissioners were sufficiently impressed by her methods to entrust to her care another 160 houses in the Lambeth area. Nor was she any less in demand for the advice she could give to those in authority. She was asked to give evidence before a Select Committee on housing, presided over by Sir Richard Cross, who had introduced the Bill of 1875, and later to the Royal Commission on Housing of 1884, from which much can be learned about the general principles which governed her social work, in housing as in other spheres.

Principles

1 The first of these principles was the necessity for businesslike dealings. It was novel to the men of her day that a woman should become expert at business techniques, particularly in the very complicated field of working-class housing. Octavia Hill was no sentimental idealist, but an extremely hard-headed and capable business woman. She explained to the Royal Commission[1] that she divided bad dwellings into three classes; (a) those so bad as to require demolition; (b) those improvable but in the hands of unsuitable landlords; (c) those in the hands of owners who wished to improve their property. Having decided which property it was possible to acquire and what repairs would make it more habitable she learned how to put into operation a whole scheme of improvement which involved owners, tenants and her body of assistants. The experiments of the early years justified themselves and became the foundation of a uniform plan of management. Management, whatever it may have conveyed to the landlords, was to her far more than mere rent-collecting. In one of her papers to the C.O.S. she said,

It means full knowledge of the rights and duties of both landlords and tenants—repairs promptly and efficiently attended to, references carefully taken up, cleaning sedulously supervised, overcrowding put an end to, the blessing of ready-money payments enforced, accounts strictly kept, and above all, tenants so sorted to be helpful to one another.

2 Her second principle is contained in the last phrase of this quotation, for she held that all the business acumen in the world would not achieve results, if constructive social work with the tenants were neglected. As she said when referring to destructive drunken tenants, 'the only way of dealing with them is to buy up their homes and then to make improvements in them conditional on their own care and good behaviour. . . . When we buy up these old houses,' she told the Royal Commission in 1884,[2] 'we do nothing to them but put the drains, water and roof right. Everything else is added in proportion to the tenants' own care.' While

[1] 1884–5 C.4402, xxx. Royal Commission on the Housing of the Working Classes. Q. 8825.   [2] Ibid., para. 8866.

rent-collecting, she got to know as many of her tenants as possible, 'picking her way over the filth and through the rough crowd; noticing everything and saying nothing'. Sometimes all her patience was of no avail and tenants had to be evicted; when this was so she felt it a personal defeat, but was still quite ruthless about it, as tenants had to learn that she was not bluffing.

Another principle of hers was that tenants must be made to see the evils of overcrowding. A pupil remembered seeing a room in which eighteen people lived. Octavia put a stop to much of this in her own property by preventing sub-letting, and by encouraging tenants to take on a second room to live in; though this was not easy, as many of them had known no other existence than life in one room. No detail was too small for her personal attention—'it is only when the detail is managed as soundly as the whole plan, that a work becomes really good', she said. The 'whole plan' depended for its success on friendship—'the individual friendship which grows up from intimate knowledge'.[1]

3   The development of various services for her tenants was a principle obviously inspired by her early baptism in Christian Socialist doctrines. Rooms were marked off as clubrooms for her tenants, and she soon found a spontaneous demand by her club members for classes in singing and drawing. More important still, she encouraged them to think of themselves as a community whose rules they had made, and so should naturally observe. Many of her tenants suffered from irregular employment, so when she could she found jobs for them on the property itself. To help them harbour and keep stable their finances, she started a savings bank. Above all, she was able to provide for some of the Courts a garden or a playground, a project very dear to her heart, though not accomplished without difficulty. Her first playground, in Freshwater Place, aroused much hostility from the neighbours, who resented the clearing of the waste land they had used for fighting, loafing and rubbish-depositing. These services, along with her funds for training apprentices, for pensioning the infirm, and for other projects were constructively used for the development of the community spirit, and to aid individuals who by timely help might be expected to get on their feet again.

4   A fourth principle was to be as frank as possible with her tenants on money matters. She made it quite clear to them that

---

[1] Moberley Bell, *op. cit.*, p. 85.

she must make the property produce a fixed dividend, but over and above that any surplus was potentially theirs to enjoy in better conditions and increased opportunities in life for their children. And it was through their children that Octavia often made the most progress; not that she herself was naturally at her best with children. She admitted that she had little patience for teaching young children. Her efforts for the little ones nevertheless were the best proof to many tenants of her disinterestedness, which at first had been greeted by hostility and suspicion. This frankness, along with her general supervision and detailed care, gave them a sense of security novel to people accustomed to living from hand-to-mouth, with the result that they increasingly planned their lives and their incomes, instead of living just for the day, while the growth of community spirit enabled them to help each other on many occasions and to do their best in their homes. One of her proudest moments, she used to remark, was when one of the tenants told her 'them drains are a feather in your cap, Miss'![1] The landlords were impressed by the way the rents came in, often from property which previously had yielded the most fluctuating and uncertain returns. In time they learned that money spent on repairs was not wasted, once the tenants had been trained to pay some respect to their own homes.

5 A fifth and central principle was her pursuit of beauty. Her contacts with the Christian Socialists and Ruskin, her own interest and ability in drawing, her early experience of education through the Working Women's Classes and the family school at Nottingham Place, all impressed her with the urgent need to bring beauty and culture into the lives of the London poor. When later she helped and inspired Barnett in the Settlement at Toynbee Hall, it was because they both had this same aim in mind. The ugliness and squalor of the Courts had shocked her when she first saw them at the age of thirteen; they appalled her at thirty, and her whole life was dedicated to doing something to overcome such conditions and to bring some of the beauty of the world to drab and uninteresting lives.

Conclusion

In assessing her importance in the history of social work, as much attention must be paid to her methods of training her

[1] *Ibid.*, p. 123.

assistants as to the completely new field of social work that she in-augurated. Selection was of first-rate importance. She did not want helpers who were too young or too impetuous, nor those with only irregular time to give or who were not prepared to receive training. 'The work', she said, 'is more like a profession, it has so much that is technical in it.'[1] Furthermore, she considered that an efficient housing manager should have a thorough knowledge of accounts, of the rating system, of housing finance, at least on such practical points as the recoupment of capital invested; and a general knowledge of legal matters concerned with housing, and practical acquaintance with housing technicalities such as damp courses, cost of repairs, etc. Some of her workers were full-time, some part-time, but from all she expected the same high standards. From the beginning she gave each a court or street to look after, increasing their responsibilities as they proved themselves. She forced herself not to intervene, but rather to allow the workers complete independence and initiative, as long as they satisfied her of their accurate account-keeping and businesslike manage-ment. Emma Cons, her first independent co-worker, was a case in point; her ways were different from those of Octavia Hill, but the latter realized that the same results were being achieved, and was satisfied. The same tolerance and vision marked her whole out-look. When at the end of the century a group of admiring friends and colleagues presented her with her portrait by Sargent, she particularly stressed the need for new methods as circumstances changed. 'When I am gone', she said, 'I hope my friends will not try to carry out any special system, or to follow blindly in the track which I have trodden. New circumstances require various efforts, and it is the spirit, not the dead form that should be perpetu-ated.' Her insistence on training for intending social workers was an important factor in the rise of social work as a profession, with, she hoped, its own ethics and techniques. Her regime heralded the decline of the well-meaning amateur, for although voluntary workers and part-time workers were welcomed, they had to be trained.

While her methods of training are today of much interest, it was to housing management that she gave her thought and energy. It could have developed as a purely technical matter of rents collected and houses repaired, but to Octavia Hill it became

[1] C.O.S. papers, 1899.

social work, a loving responsibility for the less fortunate, involving friendship and social casework. When she was still able to, she knew all her tenants personally, but when the field extended too widely for personal contact she made sure that her helpers kept in closest touch with all the tenants and their families. For it was the family unit on which she concentrated—the house was nothing to her if it was not a home.

Because of her concern for personal effort and spontaneous help she did not welcome the efforts of the State. She felt that when social work became enmeshed in regulations and detailed legislation the personal touch was bound to disappear. Nevertheless, the housing legislation of her days owed a lot to her example, and her efforts were bound to have widespread repercussions on that and related fields.

The energy of this 'unobtrusive, plainly dressed little lady' was amazing. Housing, social clubs, parties for her tenants, savings clubs, settlement activities, casework for the C.O.S., campaigning for open spaces, cadet movements, teaching, lecturing, writing, giving evidence to and sitting on committees—all these activities and many others were her work. Before she died in 1912 she had already seen many of her dreams realized. Her methods and principles remain today as fundamental as they were then.

CHAPTER 8

CARE OF DEPRIVED CHILDREN

IN no sphere of social work today can the roots be found so directly in the poor law as those of the modern Children's Officer. Nineteenth-century experience is responsible not only for some of the large bleak institutions in which many of the State's children still live, but for the pattern of a Children's Officer's duties—receiving into care, arranging for foster-care, and in a very limited way, adoption. If change there is, it is in the spirit of the work and therefore in the methods and techniques of the service. Though even in this respect the nineteenth century was not the period of grim and repressive treatment of children on a wholesale scale the readers of Dickens and of the Curtis Report might suppose. This is not to argue that the 'deterrent' principles of the poor law did not show themselves in the attitude of many boards of guardians towards the children who came into their care; but from time to time private individuals, or local boards, would venture to experiment, and having done so would inform the world of the results. Thus a new opinion began to grow and by the end of the century it was more widely accepted.

CONDITION OF CHILDREN AROUND 1834

Ever since 1601 it had been the duty of poor law authorities to care for orphan and other children whose parents or guardians were no longer available, but they had no coherent policy. In some places children received out-relief and lived where they could; in others they were cared for in workhouses or in charitable institutions, such as the Blue Coat Schools. The period of the early industrial revolution was one of change and experiment both in the spirit and principles that determined child care, and in the methods used. Education was one example; Joseph Lancaster and Richard Bell

126

were already opening their schools because they believed reading and writing were essential to the moral upbringing of all. Work was another—children had always been useful as workers, whether on the land or in domestic industry, but the new factories, particularly the cotton and woollen mills of the industrial North, provided many openings for juvenile labour. Nor was there any scarcity of children; the large and growing birth-rate of the late eighteenth and early nineteenth centuries provided a seemingly endless stream of recruits for employment in the factories.

Boards of guardians and the creation by the Act of 1834, of 'unions' of parishes with greater resources of rateable value made the erection of houses for the care of paupers, including children, a financial possibility. Had practice followed the advice of the Report of the Royal Commission on the Poor Laws, 1834, separate houses for different classes of paupers would have been established, and children might have been segregated from the rest. But the poor law commissioners from 1834 to 1847 pursued no such policy, and on the grounds of economy and efficiency, declared in favour of the all-purpose workhouse. As Sir Francis B. Head, the civil servant representing the commissioners, said:[1] 'The very sight of a well-built efficient establishment would give confidence to a board of guardians. The appointment of a chaplain would give dignity to the whole arrangement, while the pauper would feel it was utterly impossible to contend against it.' Thus the workhouse became the instrument of the repressive policy which was to characterize the administration of poor law, and each union thereafter had one building bearing no little resemblance, from the plans published in the first annual report, to the prison plans of the period. It was in these that children, orphaned or abandoned, were housed. The conditions of many workhouses were appalling. Sanitation was primitive, though as a result of the enthusiasm of Edwin Chadwick for public health and an outbreak of serious illness in Sevenoaks workhouse in 1842, elementary sanitary regulations were applied in some workhouses as a result of official policy. It is not surprising that commentators in 1852 stated they had 'seen nothing in the prisons and lunatic asylums of Europe to equal conditions in the English workhouse, where children, lunatics, incorrigible, innocent, old, disabled were all mixed together'.[2]

[1] S. Webb, *English Poor Law Policy* (1910), quoted p. 58.
[2] *Ibid.*, p. 88.

I SCHOOLS

Even the most rigid of guardians could hardly blame the children for their plight, and it was among some of the more enlightened that a new policy began to appear. In order that children should have some hours a day at their lessons, guardians by 1844 were encouraged to employ and pay workhouse teachers, but few took advantage of this and those that did often failed to employ capable or qualified ones. An Act in 1862 gave guardians the power to pay for the education of pauper children in the voluntary schools. This was mainly intended as a means of educating children whose parents were on poor relief either in the workhouse or out of it, but it could have been applied to the 'children of the State' as well. It also was little used.

Meanwhile another idea, the building of 'District Schools', was gaining favour. With the laudable intention of taking children out of the ordinary workhouse, many of the larger boards began to build boarding-schools where a thousand or more pauper children could be housed and educated. The scheme was no new one: what was probably the first had been established as far back as 1821 in Central London, and a very well-known one was founded at Quatt, near Bridgnorth in Shropshire in 1836. The latter school was placed in the midst of farm land, and 'while the children do the work of the house, they also tend the animals and land. It started with forty children, but increased to one hundred and seventy, though the older ones looked after the younger, thus creating the family atmosphere and saving expense.'[1] The 'District School' was strongly recommended by Sir Jas. Kay-Shuttleworth, who argued that the children's health improved, the death rate fell, and the children became brighter and more knowledgeable. But the schools were not universally acclaimed and by 1870 there was a reaction against them.

Some mysterious charm [said Miss Florence Hill (sister to Octavia Hill) in 1868] affects the beholder in witnessing many hundreds of children dressed alike, acting in unison, and rendering instance obedience to the word of command—but we are constrained to ask how will individuality of character develop itself from this complete subjection to the will of others, from this routine of duty which leaves open no temptation to wrong and annihilates the choice of right.[1]

[1] F. Hill, *Children of the State* (1894), pp. 72, 74.

This general condemnation of the district schools was supported by grave suspicions about health conditions. At Hanwell, for instance, Mr. Nettleship, the Inspector, reported in 1870 that 80 per cent of the children had been affected by ophthalmia. The problem of the 'in and out' children, that is, of parents removing their children when they became old enough to earn, had also to be faced, and was not remedied until 1889. The large 'barrack' school meanwhile had ceased to be acceptable to many, though they were persisted in by many boards of guardians either through lack of alternative accommodation or the will to find any.

2 ORPHANAGES

(a) Dr. Barnardo

One answer to the problem was being worked out by individuals and voluntary associations, of whom Dr. Barnardo was perhaps best known. Born in Dublin in 1845, Thomas John Barnardo was the ninth child of a prosperous business man of European stock, who had married into an English Quaker family. Thomas John was a puny lad, though he grew up strong enough. His first seventeen years were ordinary school years, with some scoffing at religion, and reading of secularist literature. In 1862, however, he was converted, and thereafter resolved to become a missionary. Within a few months he had gone to London to begin his training for the China Missions. It was quickly decided he should take a medical degree and thus become a medical missionary. It was not long before he became associated with the Ernest Street Ragged School and by 1866 had opened his own in Hope Place. To this broken-down building in the slums Jim Jarvis came one night for shelter and warmth, and from him Dr. Barnardo first learnt of the boys, who without home or protection were sleeping out in London and picking up a living as best they could. It was here too that 'Carrots' came asking for shelter, but as the house was full he was told to come back in a week. Before the week was over he was found dead from exposure. This experience was responsible for the principle, 'No destitute child refused admittance', for which Dr. Barnardo was later to be so justly famous.

Several years elapsed during which he completed his training and experimented in different kinds of youth club work in the East

End, and by 1870 he had started a Home for destitute lads, and thus his life's work began. For some time he had been boarding out Jim Jarvis, and many more lads in like straits, among private families. Now he thought the time had come to recall them from their foster homes and house them under one roof where their training could be carefully supervised. The original Home was not solely for destitute boys—finances would not run to that—so three types of boys were catered for: (1) the wholly destitute who would be 'fed, clothed, housed and taught trades'; (2) lads temporarily out of work, for whom jobs should be sought, and (3) 'good, steady, respectable lads in work'[1] who needed somewhere to live at a modest fee. Believing that idleness brought sin, Dr. Barnardo arranged his daily programme so that every minute was filled. Some schooling was included, as well as training in a skill, and the usual physical training and household duties. By 1873 he had opened 'Mossford Lodge' for girls, which was also to be run on the barrack system, as for the boys. He soon discovered how misconceived his method of rescuing girls was. The answer to his difficulty, we are told, came when he dreamt of Psalm 68, verse 6, 'God setteth the solitary in families.' Thereafter he began his scheme of cottage homes, each supervised by a homely and capable housemother with fifteen or sixteen girls in each cottage. His appeal for this work in *The Christian* brought the desired response, and in 1875 his Village Home with eleven cottages was opened. His own organizing capacity, quick perception, charm and powers of inspiration were his greatest assets and made possible the work he accomplished. In 1905, when he died, he had fathered nearly 60,000 destitute children.

As Dr. Barnardo gained experience, several principles emerged from his work which were peculiar to him, but of interest in the development of social work generally. First, his later Homes were open only to the destitute; for instance in 1888 no fewer than 7,298 applications to enter were made, but only 1,768 were accepted. The rest were not really destitute and were therefore ineligible; though he did help a further 1,200 either materially or by finding a job. Secondly, he believed in small groups, especially for girls, though by 1887 he had begun to classify his boys on age, ability, and circumstances. He became an ardent exponent of the cottage home. Thirdly, he believed that there should be a school on the

[1] J. W. Bready, *Dr. Barnardo* (1935), p. 104.

premises. When his school received government grants and inspectors examined the children's progress, they reported that the attainment of the children was higher than that of similar children coming daily to school from their own homes. This, he considered, was complete justification of his method, and incidentally evidence that children could be taught if their stomachs were full, but not otherwise. Fourthly, his views on boarding-out were somewhat original. He was never opposed to boarding-out, and in fact used this method from the beginning, provided the foster homes were good and the supervision careful. For instance, a doctor or nurse was made responsible for at least four unannounced visits each year to examine the child, as well as the much more frequent visits by a member of the voluntary local committee (a Dr. Barnardo's Committee for raising funds, etc.). What was original was that at twelve or thirteen the child was recalled to the Home, there to be given two or three years vocational training before going out into the world. It was a cardinal principle that no Barnardo child should be launched on the world without a trade. Dr. Barnardo gave evidence on this before the Mundella Committee on the education and maintenance of pauper children in 1896. Finally, he was a strong believer in after-care, and always took pains to see that a child was established in the world, and was under some supervision until he was twenty-one. This was true as much of his migration schemes, as of placements in Britain.

(b) Thomas Bowman Stephenson

As Dr. Barnardo was opening his Home for destitute lads, the Rev. T. B. Stephenson had embarked on his great adventure in child reclamation by setting up the first of what have come to be known as the National Children's Homes. Stephenson was born in 1839, and entered the Methodist ministry twenty-one years later. By 1868 he had been appointed to a very poor circuit in Lambeth where the plight of forlorn and abandoned children filled his heart with compassion. At this period he learnt of the work being done by Emmanuel Wickern and his mother at the Rauhe Haus in Hamburg, and like other Englishmen was stimulated by what he heard, and determined to create a Home in Lambeth for children in need.

Accordingly, in 1869, to a house in Church Street he welcomed a small group of friendless lads. He aimed at keeping the group small, so that the children would have a feeling of belonging, and a sense of identity. Within a couple of years he had opened a further home in Bonner Street, South Hackney, and thereafter other homes were opened in different parts of the United Kingdom and in the Dominions. They were not all boys' homes; some were for girls, and some were mixed, as Stephenson had always been in favour of the mixed home. He believed in prevention and by establishing mission centres strove to influence parents so that children would not be cast out or left friendless. He organized careful house-to-house visiting, and recruited a band of Home Sisters for the work. By 1890 he had opened Mewburn House as a training school for these sisters, where a skilfully devised programme of instruction in housewifery, home nursing and religious knowledge was followed. Like Dr. Barnardo, the Rev. Stephenson was one of the many volunteers of the second half of the century who sought to provide a shelter other than the workhouse for homeless and friendless children.[1]

3   COTTAGE HOMES

Meanwhile experiments were being made by boards of guardians and others in establishing homes where children could live on the 'enlarged family' basis. The origin of the idea undoubtedly lay in the Hamburg Rauhe Haus and the Farm School system of the Continent, described by Mr. Joseph Fletcher in a paper to the London Statistical Society in 1851, in which the more natural environment of the family-size group was stressed. It was claimed that pauper children had as a rule been brought up in misery and filth in an atmosphere of low morality and tended to be of poor mentality. Moreover their health was usually inferior, and most were 'below standard in beauty, form, and health conformation'.[2] Such exceptional material, it was argued, needed exceptional methods of physical and moral treatment which could better be provided in the cottage home than in the large institutions. In the latter, the 'evils' of such children were more likely to spread than in the small group, where strict discipline could be assured without crushing the vivacity and spontaneity of child life. The Victorians,

[1] J. H. Litten, 'I sat where they sat', *National Children's Home Convocation Lecture*, 1954.

[2] 1878 (285), lx. Home and cottage system of training and educating the Children of the Poor. F. J. Mouat, Local Government Board Inspector, Capt. J. D. Bowley. *Report*.

who advocated this idea, added one shrewd argument by pointing to the large capital outlay required for one huge institution, compared with that needed for the cottage homes where house could be added to house as and when the need arose.

The question of mixing the sexes in the cottages had to be considered, since many Continental experiments had been successful in mixing boys and girls as in the natural family. Quoting Mr. Fletcher again, experience in the Swiss farm schools had shown the desirability of both sexes being included, as 'imagination is more excited when sexes are separate, than when in daily and fraternal relations'.[1] Four precautions, however, were thought to be necessary; that both a mother and a father should be appointed to each cottage; that there should be vigilant supervision by them; that children should be under twelve years when admitted, and sent away at seventeen years; and that each sex should have a dormitory of its own. Given these conditions the advantages were great. Not only was the family of say twenty children a more economic size, allowing the labour of the boys and girls to be better distributed and the general oversight and prevention of waste more efficiently achieved, but such a system was alleged to soften the disposition, strengthen the fraternal ties, and unite the children into one family.

During the 'fifties Mary Carpenter had been in the van of this kind of movement, with her Industrial and Reformatory Schools, and the idea was soon adopted by some of the voluntary societies concerned with orphan children. In 1865 when the Home for Little Boys, Farningham, Kent, was founded, each family group of up to thirty children was presided over by both a father and mother. Similarly in 1870, when the Princess Mary's Village Homes, Addlestone, were founded, families of not more than ten girls were put under the care of a carefully selected housemother. It was said that a widow with or without children was preferred, 'as best calculated to win the hearts and understand the ways of children'. Dr. Barnardo's 'Village Home for Orphan and Neglected Girls' in Ilford, founded in 1875, was as we have seen made up of eleven cottages, each containing some twenty girls under a housemother. In all these Homes a school was provided on the premises; it was not until the twentieth century that the general practice was adopted of sending children to the schools of the neighbourhood.

[1] *Ibid.*

These pioneer efforts had not escaped the notice of the boards of guardians, and the whole idea received the blessing of a committee reporting to the President of the Local Government Board in 1878.[1] Between 1874 and 1878 six boards had sought and obtained permission from the Local Government Board to build grouped cottage homes on the family system. They were West Derby, West Ham, Bolton, Swansea, Neath, and Bridgend-and-Cowbridge. Kensington, Chelsea and Birmingham and other boards were subsequently to do the same. However those in rural areas often found it inexpedient to group their cottages, and preferred instead the 'Scattered Homes', where each unit was sited in a different parish. While this development was started from the motive of expediency, it has now been found to provide a more normal life for the 'deprived' child. When a child lives in a house in an ordinary street, he can mix more freely and naturally with other children than if he lives in an institution or in one of a group of cottage homes.

As the examples quoted above suggest, the Continental practice of mixing the sexes did not receive general support in Britain, where separate homes for boys and girls were usually preferred, though little boys under ten were housed with girls of all ages.

4 BOARDING-OUT

Prominent in the mid-century campaign to establish 'fostering' as a method of caring for children were Louisa Twining and Florence Hill. Their arguments ranged round three points. First was the unsuitability of the district schools and the workhouses, where they said not only was health undermined and general education indifferent, but where the development of moral fibre was ruled out. Writing of a visit to a workhouse in 1868, Miss Hill said:[2]

Accompanying an observant friend, we asked how her mind was affected by the establishment, a very large and well ordered one. She answered, the one overriding impression was that of Power. She was awestruck by the unlimited authority over those yielding it up, an authority which saps the very foundation of individual self-government,

[1] 1878 (285), lx. Home and cottage system of training and educating the Children of the Poor. F. J. Mouat, Local Government Board Inspector, Capt. J. D. Bowley. *Report*
[2] F. Hill, *op. cit.*, p. 12.

e.g. it is illegal to pay wages to paupers . . . thus in performing work they are reduced to slavery, and the vices of the slave, lack of self-control, indifference to the value of property, and absolute dependence on others, are painfully apparent.

Or, to quote from *The Times* in 1866, 'the children are brought up in a formal unnatural way, cut off from the lessons of actual life, and when at length they are sent out into the world, they are like caged canaries turned adrift among sparrows'.

Secondly, being boarded-out was a far more natural life for a child than any other. It was agreed that he probably lacked the demure and well-mannered appearance of an orphanage child, but he was said to gain in buoyancy of spirit, confidence of manner and happiness of countenance. And, it was argued, the domestic training he received from the 'cottager' and the love he gained as an individual were experiences so valuable that no child should be denied them. Especially was this so for girls, who by nature were made for domesticity and home-making. How paradoxical it was, to expect girls to become competent wives, mothers and home-makers, if they were denied this vital education in their own youth.

Thirdly, the advocates supported their arguments by citing successful experiments in other countries; in France, boarding-out had been practised for centuries; even as early as 1450 a regulation was made to arrange the salary and emoluments of the agents in Paris who 'bought' the nurses in the country. Some of the children were paid for by the poor law authorities and others by private individuals, but in all cases foster children had to go to a school from six to fourteen years, and 'nurses' were rewarded if their children remained free from accident up to twelve years. Russia also had its boarding-out system, though it was claimed the foster-mother sometimes neglected her own children in favour of the foster child for whom she was paid! Several of the States of Germany had well-established 'fostering' systems under the poor law authorities. Thus in 1854 Hamburg opened an 'Orphan Office' to undertake friendly visits to the children. In Berlin fostering was common and general oversight was exercised by the clergy.

Ireland and Scotland preceded England in the use of the method. In 1828 the Dublin Protestant Society was formed to send children to the country to be boarded with respectable protestant families. Here they went to school, were inspected by the churchwardens, and were reported on regularly. Constant watch was kept on the foster-mother to prevent ill-treatment, and when she attended the annual meeting of the society, she had to produce a certificate from the clergyman that the child attended school and Church regularly! For all this she was paid £4 per annum. In Scotland the Edinburgh poor law authority started sending children to the country in 1852[1] 'where they might have the physical advantage of the country air as well as the moral one of being separated from bad associates and brought into contact with people of good character'. Most large Scottish parishes, such as Glasgow, Aberdeen and Dundee, copied this plan. Boarding-out in Scotland had a strong modern flavour. Every care was taken to choose the right foster-parents, i.e. persons with good character and a steady income apart from the allowance, who would be prepared to take children for love rather than for the remuneration. The accommodation was carefully examined to see that it was healthy and commodious, regular inspection was insisted upon, and inspectors were appointed for the purpose. It was said visits were paid at least eight times a year to see that the children were healthy, well fed, clean, and their education attended to. Moreover, if a child were young enough when boarded out to have no recollection of his former state, he would have 'no idea he was a pauper and would treat such a condition with the same horror and contempt as is entertained by all respectable working people'.[2]

In the meantime some boards of guardians in England were already experimenting with this method of dealing with their young. The first was probably Warminster, which began to practise it in about 1850. Eight years later they were joined by Ringwood, and in 1861 Mrs. Archer inaugurated a scheme in Wiltshire, which was much publicized. According to one poor law inspector's report no fewer than twenty-one Unions had schemes of one sort or another by 1870.[3] But throughout, there had been a good deal of opposition from the central authority to any general use of the method. It was willing to believe the scheme had been successful on the Continent, and in Ireland and even in Scotland, but England was different, it said, 'except perhaps in Cumberland, Westmorland and Durham, where small crofters of sufficient character and education existed, to give pauper children a chance, and to

---

[1] F. Hill, *op. cit.*, p. 150. [2] *Ibid.*, p. 169.
[3] 1872 C.516, xxviii. Local Government Board. *1st Report*, 1871–2.

keep them in order'![1] Even as late as 1869 a Miss Preusser of Westmorland applied to take foster-children from Bethnal Green, but was refused on account of the difficulties of supervision. The problem was solved by Miss Preusser's taking charge of the children without payment.

The turning point came in 1870, when a Boarding-Out Order was issued empowering all boards to place their children with foster-parents, provided the children were healthy, and provided too that foster-parents could be found who would give them wholesome food, warm and clean lodging, and the necessary personal inspection and see that they attended school regularly. All supervision was to be by the relieving officer. The extension of boarding-out meant that the question of whether children were to be fostered 'within' the Union or 'without' it had to be faced. Mrs. Archer claimed that no more than one hundred cottagers in Wiltshire would be prepared to foster children from some of the urban unions. It was argued by certain people that children were more easily and more suitably placed in country areas than in the large towns. As many boards in large towns agreed with this view, a number of children were placed in foster homes at some distance from the responsible board, and voluntary boarding-out committees of local ladies and gentlemen were formed in the rural areas, to find suitable homes and to supervise the children. This, at any rate, was the theory. For though by 1895 about 1,955 committees were in existence, 'some were only nominal, and some covered so large an area as to be useless for proper supervision'.[2]

Two further orders were made by the central authority in 1889 to guide boards of guardians in the framing of their rules for 'fostering'. (The central authority itself had been assisted by model rules drawn up by a few local voluntary societies, such as the Bristol and Clifton Boarding-Out Society.) The rules stated that the foster-parents must not be related to the child, and must not themselves be receiving relief. The father should not be ordinarily employed on night work, and both foster-parents should, if possible, be of the same religion as the child. Other rules concerned the accommodation. Not more than two children were to be boarded in one family, and no home was to be chosen where the total number of

---

[1] W. Chance, 'Children under the Poor Law' (1897), p. 29.
[2] Ibid., p. 30.

children, natural and boarded, would exceed five. Sleeping accommodation was to be carefully inspected; there had to be sex separation in the bedrooms; no child over seven could be allowed to sleep
in the same room as an adult; and care had to be taken not to
board a child where an adult lodger was living. Some rules stated
the exact nature of the child's clothing, but this was not set out in
detail in the general regulations, which were confined to demanding that no uniform should be worn, and that the clothing should
be good, but of an ordinary character so that the child could merge
naturally into his environment. A special clothing allowance of 10s.
to £1 per quarter was paid to the foster parents; the weekly maintenance allowances seldom exceeded 5s. and were often much less,
the argument then being, as it is now, that greater sums would
excite the mercenary, jeopardizing the welfare children.

(a) Supervision

What is perhaps most interesting were the arrangements made
for supervising the children. After the 1870 order making it legal
for all guardians to board-out children, the work was done mainly
by the relieving officer along with his other duties, supplemented
by half-yearly visits by members of the board of guardians, and an
annual report from the Vicar. But this system was not always
entirely satisfactory, as Miss Hill remarked:

Zealous and kind-hearted as officers appointed to this important duty
may be, it must be performed by them rather as a matter of routine.
The time of their visits may be calculated and they cannot go very often.
Moreover a man, however thoughtful for the children's welfare, does
not possess the knowledge of their wants and difficulties, which comes
to a woman almost intuitively. Some supervision by women appears to
us the keystone of the system.[1]

Supervision remained in the hands of the relieving officer until
the end of the century, though after 1889 a member of the local
board, or the boarding-out committee was required to visit every
six weeks, and in most towns the Medical Officer inspected quarterly. Perhaps the most useful and informative work was done by
inspectors from the Local Government Board, as they could inspect children 'without' the parish. (This service was not extended
to locally boarded-out children till much later.) While Mrs. Nassau

[1] F. Hill, *op. cit.*, p. 238.

Senior had been appointed in 1873 to inspect girls in workhouses and schools, the first woman appointed to inspect 'boarded out' children was Miss Mason, and this was not until 1885. It is to her reports in the next twelve years we must turn for insight into the methods and techniques of supervision she employed.

Regarding the choice of the home, Miss Mason thought the personality and character of the foster-parents every bit as important as the accommodation they had to offer. She did not think that children should be placed with anyone who had been convicted, nor with those who drank or had illegitimate children. For however satisfactory the home might be in other respects, children could scarcely be expected to turn out well if brought up to regard such things as normal. Foster-parents should be of the highest moral character, and possess the humanity necessary for the important job of bringing up these children. 'In addition to the necessary enquiries,' she said, 'a little conversation may show their ideas on many essential points.' Young couples with increasing families of their own were not, she thought, the best material, as children boarded with them might so easily become 'nurses' or drudges; while to board out boys with widows or single women was almost always a mistake, since boys so easily got out of control. Careful preliminary investigation was justified because of cases of abuse that had arisen. For instance[1]

a girl of four years old was placed with a small farmer and his wife, whose home was clean and comfortable, and who had the best of reputations, regular church-goers and communicants. They beat and knocked this child about till her screams one day attracted the notice of the neighbours, and she was found a mass of bruises, tied to the bedposts by her thumbs, which had been cut through by her struggles.

Rules were laid down about sleeping arrangements, but Miss Mason quickly found they could be evaded, and she therefore recommended a thorough inspection of all the beds and bedrooms in the house every six months. None could tell if the child really slept where stated without seeing the other rooms and ascertaining who and how many were the inmates of the house. For instance 'a girl of twelve years old was found to have been in the habit of sleeping in her foster-mother's cottage in the same room with three men'.[2]

[1] W. Chance, *op. cit.*, quoted p. 199.
[2] 1892 C.6745, xxxviii. Local Government Board. *21st Report*, 1891–2.

Her main concern, however, was a regular and thorough examination of the child himself to see how he was treated. She was a strong advocate of undressing the child to examine his body, and here she felt lay the strength of women visitors, who could undress a girl or a young boy with impunity. Reliance on hearsay was useless. In the Hockley case two maiden ladies, in respect of whom excellent references had been received from the Vicar and 'all in the village who mattered', took babies for hire, but were found to have received a lump sum of £5 to £18 each, and then to have killed off the children. To ask the child was useless because it undermined his confidence in his foster-parents to be so questioned, and if he were ill-treated, he was often too afraid to say. The only alternative was personal examination in surprise visits.

At least once a quarter [she wrote] it is necessary to remove a shoe or stocking. For it is in the hollows of the ankles that strata of dirt accumulate most visibly, and by taking off one stocking I am generally able to tell the date of the last bath to a week, if it is only weeks since. There is very little visible difference between dirt of some months and a year's standing. The human skin cannot retain strata of more than a certain thickness. The removal of a stocking also often reveals broken chilblains, blisters and sores, nails uncut and broken below the quick, or growing into the foot. The neck, shoulders and upper parts of the arms also show dirt, bites and marks of vermin, skin complaints and blows. Beating is generally begun on the upper parts of the arms. I sometimes find bruises there evidently made by sticks, and where this is the case, I undress the child as much further as necessary. I have thus now and then found a child covered with bruises. An examination underneath also shows whether the underclothing is sufficient, and the linen and stockings clean and in good repair.[1]

Two other principles she adhered to are also of importance in her contribution to modern methods of social work. She was convinced of the importance of treating all foster-parents alike. If they were doing their duty, she argued, they would not resent inspection which could only prove their trustworthiness. But if thorough inspections were carried out in suspected cases only, offence would be given. Every foster-parent would understand that visitors were bound to report to the committee from their own knowledge at first hand. The other point she stressed was the necessity of keeping records of the dates of visits, the particulars noted and of action

[1] 1895 C.7867, 1. Local Government Board. *24th Report*, 1894–5.

taken. Record-keeping was no new device in Miss Mason's day, already the C.O.S. had shown the necessity for it, both to remind a visitor of her own past impressions and actions, and facilitate the passing on of a case from one worker to another. But in poor law work it was possible that Miss Mason's advice was necessary.

One other point in Miss Mason's approach needs to be stressed. It is true that she was not unduly concerned about the child's emotional security, or whether his relationships with the foster parents and the rest of the community were adequate for his full personal development. But such questions arise from the psychological knowledge of today. What did concern her was whether the child was well-fed and humanely treated, and in this indirect way she did try to see that he had the love and care he needed. She was more concerned about this than about scrupulous cleanliness and order in the home; and at a time when hygiene, cleanliness and absence of smell were becoming the idol of the civil service (it had been said of Edwin Chadwick that he gave us all noses) it showed some enlightenment to be able to pick on what we now regard as the essential. She said, 'I do not report the condition of the house at all, unless its condition and smell are likely to be injurious to health, because I regard the treatment of the child not the manner in which the house is kept as the material point of the boarding-out system.' She was not an indiscriminate supporter of boarding-out. She thought it was good only if the foster-home were good, but much worse than the workhouse if it were bad. Wholesale boarding-out was not to be thought of. In fact by the end of the century, fewer than 9,000 children, or less than one-seventh of those in institutions connected with the workhouse, and a twentieth of those on out-relief, were boarded out.

(b) After-Care

Though there is more to be said on the after-care of the children than Miss Mason tried to tell her guardians and boarding-out committees, it is worth examining her contribution, as it corresponds fairly closely with modern practice. She constantly urged both on herself and other government inspectors, and more particularly on the local visitors, how necessary it was to be considered a friend by children and foster-parents alike. Suggestions were then taken in good part, and when the time came for the child to go out into the world the visitor could help to find a suitable situation for him, see that his outfit money was properly laid out, encourage the child to correspond regularly and if possible to join a youth organization such as the G.F.S. in the case of girls.

Efforts had been made in earlier years even by some of the boards themselves to offset the weaknesses of the workhouse system and give the older boys and girls a chance. Norwich was an example of a town with guardians enlightened enough to open for adolescents houses from which they could go out to work in the town and in which they could live under some sort of supervision, yet pay for themselves out of their wages. The feeling that they had money improved their morale, and the fact that they worked in various parts of the town gave them a position which was useful when they came to stand on their own. The first of these 'Preventatories', the inelegant word used by the Norwich guardians for the hostels, was started for boys only in 1845. Another was started for girls five years later, and was run on similar lines, though opportunities for wage-earning in the town were fewer for girls than for boys. The hostel therefore became an industrial school, producing a certain amount of saleable goods, as well as being a dormitory. It is significant that when the central authority discovered what this enterprising board was doing, they declared the scheme illegal. So this example of enlightened after-care came to an end in 1854. After that, initiative seems to have been seized by voluntary effort on behalf of female paupers. The names most closely associated with this in the early 'sixties were the Hon. Mrs. Way, Louisa Twining and Mrs. Nassau Senior, though many others including Mary Carpenter, Margaret Elliott, Frances Power Cobbe, and Octavia Hill should also be remembered.

The phrase 'after-care' suggests a point at which complete care becomes partial care and while today this may be at a definite age, the absence of a compulsory school-leaving age made the point of transition less definable. It is convenient however to include under the heading 'after-care' two types of service for young people, one broadly concerned with residential accommodation and training, the other confined to 'befriending'.

1 *Residence*. One of the earliest homes for these young girls from the workhouse was established by the Hon. Mrs. Way of Workham Manor, Reigate. In February 1859 she opened a small home for girls in Surrey, called Brockham Home, where children aged ten or eleven could go when leaving school, to be trained in domestic

work, and placed in suitable situations. At first the Home was registered under the Industrial Schools' Act to enable it to receive grants from the guardians. The objection to this was that it gave the Home a reformatory flavour, and Mrs. Way sought to obtain another Act to obviate this. In 1862 the Pauper Education Act was passed, making it possible for such voluntary homes to be grant-aided by the guardians. The Home was kept small, not exceeding twenty girls, so that each could have individual attention, and feel that her present development and future progress mattered to someone. But many of the girls lost their first job and the question arose, what was to happen to them? Were they to return to the workhouse or to the Home? If the former, experience had shown the effect was demoralizing. Many girls (Mrs. Way said 80 per cent) sent out into the world had already succumbed and had returned to the workhouse to have their babies. But conditions in the adult female wards, where the young girls were put, were such that a girl depressed by her lack of success in the world would rapidly lose all hope in such an atmosphere. So Brockham Home had to open its doors to friendless girls out of a job and with nowhere else to go but the streets or the workhouse. There had to be an age limit, however, and none were admitted over twenty years of age. In the following year a similar Home was opened by Mrs. Archer in Wiltshire, while Miss Twining, impelled by her knowledge of workhouse conditions and the plight of girls out of a situation, opened another in New Ormond Street, London, in 1862, which continued to house respectable girls until 1878, when it was taken over by the 'Metropolitan Association for Befriending Young Servants'. A further Home was opened in Liverpool in 1866 by Lady Emma Standing and Lady Cecilia Molyneux, and there were many other examples.

There were perhaps two principles of note in this particular form of after-care. Whenever the girls were in residence there was ample work for them to do of a domestic or handicraft nature, and this work had in it an element of training. Thus the deadly monotony of the oakum sheds, which was the chief workhouse employment, was prevented and the un-creative repetitive jobs of the domestic worker were replaced by educational work. The second principle related to the girls' virtue. None but the 'respectable' could be housed. The object to prevent contamination by 'street' girls was laudable enough. Yet Miss Twining recognized that a characteristic of many of those who had grown up as paupers, a total want of gratitude and affection towards individuals, deterred many institutions for fallen women from taking girls so raised, as the possibility of reclaiming them was negligible. For them the only refuge seemed to be the workhouse.

2   *Welfare.* The "Befriending" type of after-care started spontaneously in various centres at the beginning of the 'sixties, influenced no doubt by the speeches and writings of Miss Twining. In 1863 some ladies of Marylebone, headed by Miss Tucker, formed the 'Preventive Mission for Workhouse Girls'. This mission ascertained the names of all who left the workhouse to take a job. They were then visited regularly, and should they be in need were helped in whatever way seemed suitable. But the inspiration for most subsequent effort of this kind came from Bristol. Here Dean Elliott, at the instigation of his daughter, Miss Carpenter, Miss Cobbe and others, started a befriending scheme. The method was first to obtain the goodwill of the mistresses, and then to invite the girls to tea at the Deanery. Many came and the meetings became regular. Others who could not come were visited at their 'place' by the 'Lady Visitor'.

This experiment so much impressed Mrs. Nassau Senior that she recommended its wider adoption when in 1873 she was asked by the Local Government Board to become an assistant inspector to report on the effect of education in pauper schools. Born in 1828, the daughter of Mr. J. Hughes of Newbury, and niece of Judge Hughes, she married in 1848 Nassau John Senior, son of the political economist. She had been a workhouse visitor for many years, and a well-known figure in social work circles. The report she prepared in 1874 was painstaking, and the conclusions new.[1] She found that generally when a workhouse girl was considered ready for service, she was put into any situation that was offered, provided the relieving officer thought there were no serious objections. Here she was visited by the relieving officer until she was aged sixteen years, when the visits ceased. Should she leave the job before sixteen, no more visiting was done, and no effort was made to find her another. Mrs. Senior declared that many of the situations were totally unsuitable, and the supervision largely unsatisfactory. Moreover, she argued, girls needed more protection not less, when they were out of a place. She therefore suggested the general adoption

[1] 1874 C.1071, xxv. Local Government Board. *3rd Report*, 1873-4.

of a visiting scheme on the lines of the Bristol pattern, regular meetings and careful supervision of the girl's situation. She went further than this and urged the necessity of employing properly qualified women to find suitable posts for girls, using the help of the voluntary ladies in follow-up work, and general 'mothering'. This was too new to be accepted then, but, had boards of guardians sought to make such appointments it is difficult to know where they would have found the 'qualified women'. At a time when women had hardly been elected to the boards at all, and when the education of women as well as their professional training was in an undeveloped stage, it is not surprising this suggestion was not implemented. In 1880, however, a society for the 'Return of Women as Poor Law Guardians' was formed, and may have increased the number of women coming forward for election. Other services, such as the Employment Exchanges and Youth Employment Bureaux, have now appeared, so that those recommendations of Mrs. Senior will probably 'lie on the table' for ever.

One result did ensue, and that was the formation of the 'Metropolitan Association for Befriending Young Servants (M.A.B.Y.S.)'. It was concerned solely with the London area and covered all the different poor law union areas, and each of the boards at some time subsidized the association. The whole Metropolitan area was divided, as it was by the Charity Organization Society, into thirty districts, each with ladies who visited the young servants in their area. The girls were not only those from poor law establishments, but included any who needed help. Should they be out of employment, there was a choice of eight Homes for residence and training (including one at Ramsgate for delicate girls and one at Hitchin for mentally defective ones!). When new jobs were found, the active sympathy of the mistress was enlisted, and a visitor as well as the relieving officer and a member of the guardians approved. Further visits were made at least once every six weeks to 'protect the girl and give her simple pleasures such as books, Sunday instruction, etc.'[1] Each visitor made herself responsible for two to eight girls, and would help them, materially or otherwise, in the way she thought best. Regular reports were made, which ultimately found their way to the guardians themselves. M.A.B.Y.S. was a non-denominational body, though when a girl left London she was passed to the Girls' Friendly Society in the Provinces.

[1] E. A. Pratt, *Pioneer Women* (1897), p. 237.

In 1895 attempts were made to gauge the success of the association and the effect of its work on the girls. It had been said in 1862, by Miss Cobbe, that when the subsequent history of eighty girls brought up in a single London workhouse was investigated, every one of them was found to be on the streets. But when in 1895 nearly 4,000 institution girls were visited by the association, 23·2 per cent were stated to be 'excellent', 45·7 per cent 'good', 23·1 per cent 'fair' and only 8 per cent were 'bad'. As the criteria of this assessment are not given, we have no means of knowing exactly what is meant. But one may assume that at least 68·9 per cent had not gone on the streets, since they were designated as 'good' or 'excellent'!

A well controlled apprenticeship system might have been one answer to the problem of the welfare and employment of young people in the care of guardians, especially as the new factories and mills of the north offered skilled and remunerative jobs. Much has been heard of the abuse by the guardians and mill-owners of their opportunities to train young people in so-called 'apprenticeships', yet all employers were not conscienceless, nor all boards of guardians oblivious of what happened to their charges when they went away, as a contemporary writer has indicated. Thus Miss Hill, writing in 1868, quoted the case of an employer in the early nineteenth century in Lancashire who took workhouse children and apprenticed them to his trade. No premium was paid, and no wages, though in the later apprenticeship a small sum was laid aside each week as a nest egg to be the property of each child when he should go out into the world. The children were fed and clothed and taught lessons, and given freedom to play in the fields on a Sunday. While this may sound grim to modern ears, the regime compared favourably with what it would have been in many of the workhouses at the same period. Courtauld's of Braintree tried to develop a similar though modified scheme towards the middle of the century, but were not so successful. It was however Miss Hill's opinion that had more employers persevered with this idea, and had the guardians been more willing to negotiate suitable schemes of apprenticeship, much good would have been done to many of the children.[1]

(c) The private boarding-out of children

Though Parliament was reluctant to give approval to the boarding-out of children by boards of guardians, it was not unknown for

[1] F. Hill, *op. cit.*, p. 38.

parents to board-out their own children. This was particularly the case with illegitimate children, who were often boarded-out while their mothers worked. 'Fostering' of this type sometimes led to the scandals of 'baby-farming', the methods of which had been described in 1867 and 1869 in papers read by Dr. J. B. Curgenven to the 'National Association for the Promotion of Social Science'. Though a committee was set up to investigate the matter and to make representations to the Home Secretary, the government took no action. In 1870, however, in the year when the first boarding-out order for boards of guardians was issued, the sensational trial of Margaret Waters for the murder of a baby that she had accepted for fostering had resulted in her execution. The immediate result was the establishment, largely as a result of the influence of Dr. Curgenven, of an 'Infant Life Protection Society', and to the appointment a year later of a Select Committee on *The Protection of Infant Life*.[1] The evidence given showed that the worst forms of baby-farming were practised on an extensive scale, and that the mortality of the babies was enormous—it was estimated to be between 60 and 90 per cent. Among the recommendations of the committee was the compulsory registration of all persons receiving for hire two or more infants under one year old. This was embodied in the Infant Life Protection Act, 1872.

Under this Act the local authority could refuse registration to any person not of good character, or whose house was unsatisfactory, or who would be unable to maintain the child. If the child died, the coroner must be informed. The Act was strengthened in 1897, after another sensational baby-murder case (Mrs. Dyer was hanged in 1896), and the age of children so covered was raised, while foster parents were forbidden to take out insurances on the lives of such children. Relatives or guardians of the children were however expressly excluded from the Acts. The original purpose of infant life protection legislation was to prevent starvation, cruelty and murder and was thus the protection rather than the welfare of babies. Hence the authorities responsible were the Home Office, and either the borough council (the Metropolitan Board of Works or the Common Council in London) or the local magistrates in petty sessions. In consequence direct supervision was in the hands of the police, and there was no question of inspection by a 'Miss

[1] 1871 (372), vii. Protection of Infant Life. Select Committee. *Report, Minutes of Evidence*, etc.

Mason' from the Local Government Board. Under the 1897 Act local supervision was passed to the boards of guardians, whose relieving officers undertook the work, but central administration still remained in the hands of the Home Office. The care of these children was said to be regarded by the relieving officers as a less important part of their work than the care of the other children whom they also supervised, for whom the guardians were solely responsible.[1] The evidence before the Select Committee in 1871 indicated that some privately fostered children were well treated and happy, but this was not always so and many were vulnerable if their own parents took little interest in them.

5 ADOPTION

While the main work of the present Children's Officer in adoption cases is based on twentieth-century legislation and practice, two events of the latter part of the nineteenth century are worth recording. One was in 1889, when boards of guardians were given the power to assume parental rights, permanently or temporarily, if a child were deserted or the parents in prison because of an offence against the child. This power still exists, though a local authority passing such a resolution must give the parents the right to object within a month. It meant in the nineteenth century that a person other than the natural parent might become the child's guardian even in the parent's lifetime. The other, in 1891, was the Custody of Children Act, usually called the 'Barnardo Act'. This arose over the public tumult about the 'Roddy' and 'Gossage' cases. In both cases the parents had asked Dr. Barnardo to take the children into care, and subsequently had wished to withdraw them, owing, it was said, to the influence of Cardinal Manning. Litigation ensued, and Dr. Barnardo was forced to give way. The new Act reversed this position to some extent, by providing that no parent, having given up the custody of his child, could take him back at will. Moreover the court was now given the power, having regard to the character of the parents, and the fact that they had 'abandoned, deserted or flagrantly neglected' the child, to refuse an order of *habeas corpus*. In either case the wishes of the child were to be consulted, if he was of an age to understand.

[1] G. F. McCleary, *The Maternity and Child Welfare Movement* (1935).

6 NATIONAL SOCIETY FOR THE PREVENTION OF CRUELTY TO CHILDREN

Though the work of the N.S.P.C.C. runs parallel to that of a modern Children's Officer, any study of nineteenth-century social work among children deprived of a normal home would be incomplete without reference to the work of this great society. It is a sad reflection on both the state of the law and the public conscience that though Britain had a society for the prevention of cruelty to animals, it was not until 1883 that anyone had enough courage to form a similar society for the protection of children. This cannot have been due to public ignorance, for through the century social workers had uncovered instance after instance of child suffering, and government reports had drawn attention to its existence in factories and public institutions. But while legislation had ameliorated the lot of children outside their homes, so sacred and so private was home life itself that nothing, it was thought, should interfere with it. Even Lord Shaftesbury, when appealed to on the matter, while admitting the cruelties practised on children by some parents warned that 'they are of so private, internal and domestic a character as to be beyond the reach of legislation'.[1]

In spite of public reluctance to penetrate into family life, events were moving in the direction of some sort of social protection for the young and of giving legal rights to a child against his parents. The first of these events occurred in America. The Association for the 'Prevention of Cruelty to Animals' in New York had, on the instigation of several people, taken up the case of Mary Ellen, a foster child, who was so beaten and ill-treated by her 'parents' that when they were all brought to court 'strong men who looked on that battered little body wept like children, and wondered how they had been blind to it all for so many years'.[2] The publicity given to this case resulted in the formation of a 'Society for the Prevention of Cruelty to Children' in New York.

Another event was the correspondence in the 'Liverpool Mercury' begun in 1881, by the Rev. George Staite, Vicar of Ashton-Hayes, Cheshire. These letters described cases of gross cruelty to children, and called for some remedy. Meanwhile another Liverpool man, Mr. N. F. A. Agnew, was in America, and although

[1] Rev. A. Morton, *Early Days* (N.S.P.C.C., 1954).   [2] *Ibid.*

unaware of the newspaper campaign, discovered the existence of the New York society, and determined to introduce something of the same nature in England. Consequently, on his return he called a meeting in Liverpool of interested people, including the Rev. Staite, and in 1883 the first 'Society for the Prevention of Cruelty to Children' in England was founded. In the following year the Baroness Burdett-Coutts and her collaborator Miss Hesba Stretton, having studied the Liverpool experiment, instituted a similar society in London. Other towns quickly followed suit, and by 1889 no fewer than thirty-three towns had committees. The time was obviously ripe for a national society, which came in 1889 and with which the name of Benjamin Waugh is so closely connected. For some reason Liverpool remained aloof until the mid-twentieth century, and the Scottish society when it came was also separate. But by 1895, so generally accepted had the English national society become that it obtained a Royal Charter, with the additional powers and status that this implied.

The contribution of the National Society to the welfare of children was broadly twofold. It sought to promote legislation for the protection of children; and it developed a staff to prevent cruelty and take action against those guilty of it.

The most famous Act was that of 1889, generally called 'the Children's Charter', for which Mr. A. J. Mundella, its sponsor, was supplied by the society with over forty cases illustrating the need for every clause. The Act made it an offence for any person in charge of a child to ill-treat, abandon, neglect or expose him; and gave the court powers to remove a badly treated child from his home to a place of safety, while making an order if necessary on the guilty parents to contribute to his upkeep. Further sections in the Act prohibited begging by children, and controlled their employment, especially in street hawking, or in any form of entertainment. In 1894, again as a result of experience gained by the N.S.P.C.C., an amending Act was passed, which among other changes, made it obligatory for boards of guardians to accept children brought to them under the Acts, provided they had room for them. Meanwhile the police were empowered to remove a child from his home, even without a court order, should they suspect cruelty of any kind, a power which was extended to officers of the society by 1904.

The other, and less spectacular part of the society's work was the actual prevention of cruelty, and the help and supervision given to those families where cruelty had occurred. For this work paid officers were recruited, though it is clear that the local committees took more than an administrative interest in the day-to-day work. The methods of the officers were partly admonitory, and partly concerned with welfare. Having received information, usually from neighbours, which was always treated as completely confidential, they proceeded to investigate. If on inquiry cruelty were evident, the officers did not necessarily bring the matter before the Justices at once, but by warning and exhortation, sought to frighten or persuade the parents to moderate their behaviour. If this was of no avail the case was brought to court. Thus while hundreds of offenders were tried in Court, thousands more were induced to mend their ways by other means. The possibility that their function of investigation and warning might overlap that of the police was obvious, but a clear distinction was made in the last decade of the century by the society and by official enquirers. Thus Mr. Asquith, the Home Secretary of the day speaking in the House of Commons in 1892, stated—'The main function of the police in this country is to maintain order and to punish crime. The object of the society is . . . not to detect and not to punish, but to prevent crime.'[1] Moreover, he went on to say, the society had advantages over the police, who in this matter had difficulty in obtaining authentic information, 'while to a body of humane and philanthropic men and women looked upon by the people as their friend, information would be more readily and freely forthcoming'. Another impartial witness to this point of view was Lord Herschell, a former Lord Chancellor, who was invited to investigate the society's affairs in 1897.[2] He considered the possibility of the police doing the society's work, and decided that the activities were beyond the scope of the police. In this he was supported by the Assistant Commissioner of the Metropolitan Police and others.

The admonitory method used by the N.S.P.C.C. officials was by no means their only one. For in order to prevent cruelty, or to build up a family after a court sentence, some positive case-work was necessary. There is no doubt that by kindness and common sense these officers did some excellent work in this respect. Nor was this work on the plane of material relief, as the N.S.P.C.C. never became a relief society, and its officers were seldom paid enough to

[1] Rev. A. Morton, *Early Days* (N.S.P.C.C., 1954).   [2] *Ibid.*

enable them to afford much out of their own pockets. Sometimes it was necessary to house children if parents had turned them out, or the magistrates had ordered their removal. As long as boards of guardians could refuse admission to their institutions the society met the need by opening shelters, but when this was rectified in 1894 the shelters were gradually closed. As a means of relief to hard-pressed families, and of succour to ill-treated and neglected children these shelters must have been an invaluable standby for the officers in their work. In spite of their wide experience and unique opportunities to study families who were social misfits, the N.S.P.C.C. have few records to indicate that they saw the wider implications of their material or reflected on their methods. This may have been because the officers received no case-work training (though the C.O.S. by this time was eloquently proclaiming the need for it, and other societies like the Salvationists were beginning to train their missioners) or because the weight of their case-work made it impossible.

Two things emerge from this review. First, the developments were due to a combination of statutory and voluntary effort. Thus it was Norwich Board of Guardians which instituted the 'preventatories', but it was Mrs. Way and others who established permanent hostels. Secondly, a series of steps, from the earliest and obvious one of providing food, clothing and shelter, to experimenting with cottage homes and boarding-out with foster parents, and finally developing after-care in the form of hostels, and the selection of suitable jobs, led up to many of the duties of the modern Children's Officer. After-care was not adequately developed during the century, and adoption came later. Yet the scope, and even the techniques and aims of our modern Children's Officers can be discerned in the experience of those years.

CHAPTER 9

THE PENAL SERVICES

THE outstanding contributions in the nineteenth century to social work among law-breakers were the prison work of Elizabeth Fry, After-Care (particularly by the Discharged Prisoners' Aid Societies), the Reformatory and Industrial School movement associated with Mary Carpenter and Probation. There was also a vast amount of unco-ordinated work done with and for ex-criminals by case-work societies, by Ragged Schools and other agencies, which was incidental to their main activity.

I ELIZABETH FRY

Though Elizabeth Fry's fame is mainly that of a social reformer, her contribution to the development of social work should not be overlooked. Mrs. Fry was born in 1780, the fourth of twelve children of John and Catherine Gurney of Earlham, Suffolk. She was a Member of the Society of Friends, and about 1799 became a 'Plain Quaker', thereafter adopting the dress and manners peculiar to this strict sect. In 1800 she married another Quaker, Joseph Fry, and bore him eleven children. During the years that followed she presided over his house, whether it was at Mildred's Court in London, or at Plashet, his family house in the country bequeathed to him at the death of his father, or, when there came a reverse of fortune, back in London at Upton Lane. She died in 1845 having suffered considerable ill-health throughout her life, especially at the birth of her numerous children.

Her social work began at her house at Earlham, before she was married. The Gurneys were a lively family, influenced by the teachings of John Wesley, and the reverberations of the French Revolution. Stirred in social conscience and humanitarian feeling,

Elizabeth turned still closer to her faith, and aspired at one time to 'travel in the Ministry' and visit Friends elsewhere to strengthen them and herself by their mutual prayers. Meanwhile she was not inactive in everyday matters, for she brought what help and comfort she could to the labourers and their families in the village, and for the children she started a kind of school that was partly youth club as well. This activity she repeated when years later in 1809 she settled in Plashet with her own children. Her benevolence was undiscriminating, for she believed that it was the duty of all who had money to do their best for the benefit of their immediate neighbourhood, and for any other of their fellow creatures who aroused their interest. While her almsgiving at that time may have lacked method, the school she inaugurated did not. A competent school-mistress was engaged, trained in the Lancastrian method, and seventy children were enrolled. They quickly learnt to read the Bible and to write. For though her motive was religious she was not troubled by the inhibitions of Hannah More. She liked nursing, and as she could not hope to nurse all the sick cottagers in the village, she would send the doctor along, and advise those undertaking the nursing care. This interest led her in 1840 to visit Kaiserwerth, six miles from Düsseldorf, where among other pioneer work, Pastor Fliedner had started a hospital to train volunteer nurses—a training school Florence Nightingale was to visit some years later. Stimulated no doubt by what she had seen there, Mrs. Fry came home and started one of the first Nurses' Training Homes in London in 1840. Like Mrs. Nightingale, Elizabeth did not for a moment consider nursing as a fit profession for her daughters, and the training given to 'Fry Nurses' or 'Nursing Sisters' was of the most elementary type, and fitted for the kind of girl who was then considered suitable.

But it is for her work in prisons with prisoners that she is chiefly remembered. In the winter of 1812-13 there came to London an American Quaker of extraordinary power and personality and, like most Quakers, Stephen Grellet soon found himself accepting the hospitality of the Frys. Now Grellet had travelled through Europe in the midst of the battlefields, had visited many prisons on his way, and on reaching England he was not long in finding his way to Newgate Gaol, where the misery and depravity that met his eyes was such that none of his previous experiences could equal. The women, especially, aroused his pity and concern, as he told Mrs. Fry when he returned from the gaol.

> On going up I was astonished beyond description at the mass of woe and misery I beheld. I found many very sick, lying on the bare floor or on some old straw, having very scanty covering over them, though it was quite cold. There were several children born in the prison among them, almost naked. . . . They occupied two long rooms, where they slept in three tiers, some on the floor, and two tiers of hammocks over one another. When I first entered, the foulness of the air was almost insupportable, and everything that is base and depraved was so strongly depicted on the faces of the women, who stood crowded before me with looks of effrontery, boldness and wantonness of expression that for a while my soul was greatly dismayed.[1]

The response of Elizabeth to this was simple and direct, as would be expected of the lady whose benevolence was a byword in her Suffolk village. She collected what flannel and clothes she could and with them repaired to the prison next day. This was in January 1813. Three times she went on her errand of mercy, and then for four years ceased to go. It had been enough, however, to leave a deep and lasting impression on her, and when, in 1816, the 'Society for the Reformation of Prison Discipline' was formed, she and two of her brothers-in-law, Samuel Hoare and Fowell Buxton, were concerned in it.

It was in January 1817 that she began her consistent work with the prisoners in Newgate. Against the advice of the gaolers who never went singly to the women's yards, she entered the gaol alone. Janet Whitney describes her actions.

> At once she was surrounded by the mob. Her first action was to pick up a child. 'Friends,' she said, 'many of you are mothers. I too am a mother. I am distressed for your children. Is there not something we can do for these innocent little ones? Do you want them to grow up to become real prisoners themselves? Are they to learn to be thieves and worse?' It was in this wise that she reached them.[2]

Her first step was to establish a school for the children and for the juvenile prisoners. From the prisoners themselves a teacher was forthcoming (Mary Conner) and the principle of 'Self Help', so much a part of Chalmers' doctrine, was introduced. With the

[1] B. Seebohm, *Memoirs of the life of Stephen Grellet* (1860), p. 224.
[2] J. Whitney, *Elizabeth Fry* (1937), p. 152.

reluctant consent of the prison authorities a room was set aside and with help from friends, school equipment was obtained.

The school for children was quickly followed by another for women. They clamoured for it partly because they wanted education, believing, as Hannah More had found the women of her villages did (see Chapter 13), that education was the key to something better, but mostly because they were so bored in prison. For the problem of finding work to keep prisoners busy was bigger than the authorities could tackle, and in Elizabeth Fry's experience the result of enforced idleness was a direct incentive to vicious behaviour. The 'School' for the women was a much tougher proposition than that for the children, so she called into being the 'Ladies Association for the Improvement of the Female Prisoners in Newgate', composed of ten women, who pledged themselves to go daily to Newgate, and to provide materials for reading and writing and handwork. Furthermore a paid matron was appointed by them to supervise the work. Access to prisoners was much easier then than now, but even so, permission to use the rooms in this way was only achieved after considerable opposition.

Elizabeth Fry's work in the prison was group work of a really novel kind which has no counterpart in modern social work. It aimed at providing education in the narrower sense, and some constructive employment in a monotonous life; more than that it tried to give these prisoners, failures in society, experience of responsibility in living together harmoniously and of growing in self-respect to fit them to become decent citizens. Thus with the help of Elizabeth Fry and her friends, the prisoners formulated rules for their school, and saw to it that they were obeyed. The women were divided for work purposes into small groups of about twelve, each with a monitor chosen by the women. She was, in practice, usually one who could read, and seemed capable of taking responsibility. If she were unsuitable, her place was taken by another. Each morning and evening the prisoners would assemble for a short Bible reading by one of the visitors, work would be distributed and collected, and material checked. A yard-keeper was also elected who would inform a prisoner of any friends who had called to see her, and would accompany her to the grating and see that she spent time only with her friends. In this way it was hoped to prevent the women begging at the prison gates or from chance acquaintances, a habit that had led to the drinking and other vices which so depraved prison life.

The problem of what to do with the articles made by the women soon began to cause concern. To Mrs. Fry the answer was that they should be sold and the profits go to the prisoners, or be saved against the day of their discharge or transportation. This policy was soon criticized by those who thought that such goods would be sold at a lower price, and undercut the products of free labour. Nothing daunted, she replied that it was better to employ our criminals than to let them rot, and that the small output of prisons could not seriously affect the market price of goods made by free labour; whereupon she proceeded to arrange the marketing of her wares. Indeed in the first year, the women were knitting 60-100 pairs of socks per month, and had made 20,000 articles of wearing apparel.[1] As some of the profits were at once available to the prisoners a small shop was opened in the prison where food and a few useful articles were sold—doubtless to the detriment of the prison 'tap-room'.

The methods she adopted in prison she extended to the transportation ships. The departure of women in a 'transport' was the signal for great unrest among the prisoners. The night before the women were due to be carried in open carts through the streets of London to the docks, there were wild scenes of fighting, drinking and debauchery. The warders went in fear of their lives, and frequently had to put the women in irons to get them away at all. Even so it was a hazardous business, as the women, spitting, biting and scratching, strenuously opposed them. Elizabeth tried to modify conditions by obtaining permission to accompany the women in closed conveyances. Before they set off she stayed late to be with them, reading to them and comforting them. Her voice and manner must have been her strength. For not only did the prisoners listen intently but others, interested in her work, came to hear her. She did not welcome this publicity, but felt it was the price she must pay to interest others in a cause that troubled her so much. After preparation of this kind, the women went quietly and composedly to the 'transport' ships, there to remain sometimes for six weeks, till they were ready to sail. Mrs. Fry visited them daily, and for the rest of her life, if she were in London,

[1] 1818 (275,392), viii. State of Prisons within the City of London, etc. Select Committee. *Report.*

never failed to visit the ships if women were aboard. It is said that a total of 106 ships and 12,000 convicts were thus visited.

Nor were her visits merely friendly pastoral calls, as she quickly organized a routine for the women. Each was given a number to help her to safeguard her small possessions and her place at meals. The women were divided into groups of about a dozen, as in prison, each with an elected monitor, for sewing, reading and other purposes. The children were provided with a school and one of the convicts made mistress of it, while a library was organized and each woman was allowed to borrow a book as a reward for good conduct. The books were of travel, biography, history, serious poetry and religious works; plays, novels or other 'improper books' being carefully excluded! Meanwhile her Ladies' committee collected among themselves, and provided each convict with an imaginative collection of articles to take with her into her new life.

Towards the end of her life Elizabeth Fry promoted a society for the after-care of discharged women prisoners, the purpose of which was to find suitable posts for them, or to help them to emigrate.

2 DISCHARGED PRISONERS' AID SOCIETIES

One result of the work of John Howard, the prison reformer of the eighteenth century, and of Elizabeth Fry in the nineteenth century was the growing interest in the after-care of released prisoners. Aid societies had begun to appear at the end of the eighteenth century, though philanthropically disposed people had founded charities for aiding discharged prisoners much earlier than that. Howard had campaigned nationally and even internationally for reform in all prisons, but the societies and the charities were essentially local in character, and autonomous in operation. In consequence little is known of them or their personnel until 1862 when Parliament recognized their existence. Those who worked in this field did not leave much behind them about their aims, their methods, their successes or failures which might have been a pointer to later workers.[1] Despite the fact that the aid societies have persisted to the present time, after-care of prisoners has not developed as a branch of social work with its own techniques and training, and the modern tendency in certain cases is

[1] The Prison Commissioners began to appoint prison social workers in 1955-6.

to use local probation officers to 'aid and advise' prisoners discharged from long-stay prisons on their return home, rather than to inaugurate new aid societies to fill the gaps.[1]

In spite of the uneven development of the societies during the earlier part of the century, some interesting work of after-care was done mainly in the neighbourhood of the local or county gaol. In Manchester about the middle of the century a Mr. Wright was active in finding employment for ex-prisoners, while in many parishes the clergy were doing their best to rehabilitate those who had erred.[2] Outstanding was Sarah Martin of Yarmouth, about whose work for the prisoners of that city much has been written. Born in 1791, the child of a Caister tradesman, Sarah Martin was brought up by her grandmother, who apprenticed her to dress-making, from which she made her living for the rest of her life. At nineteen years old she joined a body of Nonconformists in Yarmouth, and resolved to discover ways of serving others. Having heard of Elizabeth Fry's work, she determined to follow her example, and after repeated efforts at last was allowed to enter Yarmouth gaol. For the rest of her life (she died at the age of sixty-one in 1852) she gave all her spare time to this and became well-known and much respected both for her work inside the gaol, and for the ex-prisoners outside it. She kept a meticulous record of her after-care in her 'Liberated Prisoners Book', and tried by every means to find lodgings and work for those discharged from prison. 'In every way she laboured that the wrong-doers would go forth, better members of society than when they entered the prison doors; and to prevent deterioration after their release by continuing the inducements to conduct themselves well.'[3]

Important though these efforts were, they were sporadic in character, and no general system of after-care was established. As early as 1847, Lt.-Col. Jebb, C.B., Director of Convict Prisons, had urged the need to provide in some way for the care of criminal children on their discharge from prison, and by 1853 was declaring that the need was equally urgent for adults. 'It is vain,' he said, 'to expect they will be able to avoid a repetition of their offences unless they can obtain some means of subsistence on their

---

[1] As a result of the Maxwell Committee Report on Discharged Prisoners' Aid Societies (1952-3 Cmd. 8879) a few new aid societies have been inaugurated.

[2] 1852-3 (1572), i. Discipline and management of the convict prisons. Lt.-Col. Jebb. *Reports*, p. 35.

[3] Religious Tracts Society, *Sarah Martin*, p. 61.

discharge.'[1] But in spite of these warnings, little was done except in a few local areas; and what was done was unco-ordinated and the activities of neighbouring societies were unrelated. As far back as 1792 Parliament had recognized the principle of assisting a prisoner to go back to his home on discharge, but no money was voted and the Act was little more than a dead letter. In 1823, however, Peel's Gaol Act had given power to the Justices to levy a county rate to provide up to £1 per head for deserving prisoners, which was to be spent on necessary clothing.[2] Further, the Justices were empowered to divert any charitable bequests connected with the prison to the provision for poor prisoners of food and clothing, implements of labour, and the means to return home. So, given willingness on the part of the local Justices, there need not have been any shortage of funds, especially for 'deserving' cases. It is doubtful, however, whether much use was made of these powers.

Meanwhile, discharged prisoners' aid societies had been growing up, sometimes independently of the justices, sometimes in collaboration with them, when in 1862 an Act was passed giving some form to the rather chaotic position of grant-aid to discharged prisoners. This was a turning point as it brought to an end the distinction between justices' aid and society's aid. For justices were now empowered to give a certificate of recognition to the society or societies connected with the prison in which they were interested, and to pay to those so certified a sum not exceeding £2 per prisoner, with which they could help him return home to honest employment. It cannot be said that this Act brought any change to the work being done among ex-prisoners, as aid was confined to small grants of money or gifts of clothing, but it did stimulate the societies to try to put their house in order. In the next year, 1863, a conference was called by the 'Reformatory and Refuge Union' to discuss the new status of the aid societies under the 1862 Act. This led to the formation of a central committee, and later to a relief committee under the chairmanship of Lord Shaftesbury, whose object was to establish more aid societies. By 1872, after a second general conference, not only had a central organization in London been set up, but it had been designated to act for all societies in places where no society operated. Thereafter regular conferences were called, relations with the Prison Com-

[1] Lt.-Col. Jebb, *op. cit.*, p. 35.
[2] L. W. Fox, *English Prison and Borstal System* (1952), p. 258.

missioners (after 1877) put on a firm footing, and in theory at any rate, the old isolation of the societies was at an end. Even so, by 1878, when the Prison Commissioners took over the control of prisons from the justices, inheriting at the same time their right to give grant aid, only twenty-nine societies were in existence.[1]

At this period the story of the societies revolves round their relations with the Prison Commissioners and the system of grants-in-aid. When the Commissioners took over from the justices they discovered how economical they had been. For instead of the £2 per prisoner permitted under the 1862 Act, the average amount spent was only sevenpence, and in the light of this, the Commissioners decided to withdraw the grants altogether, and substitute the payment of gratuities to the prisoners as reward for good conduct. At this, the societies took action, and after a further conference, approached the Government for a renewal of grant of the very modest sum of a shilling for every prisoner released. The request met with a sympathetic response, and the determination in future to relate the grant for each society to the voluntary subscriptions it received and the number of prisoners dealt with. Thus the active societies could expect encouragement, while those not receiving help were inactive anyway. How stagnant many of them were is shown by the fact that though the grant was assessed at £4,000 in 1879, by 1886 it had fallen to £1,726, and by 1888 to £1,500. It was evident indeed, that the situation needed review and in the following year, 1889, it was agreed that the societies should have the right to administer any prison charities peculiar to their prison, and that the grant in future would equal the sum of such charitable income, plus the average grant of the previous three years. This broke the link between voluntary subscriptions and grant aid. After the Gladstone Committee on *Prisons* in 1895 the grant was partially replaced by equalizing it to the sum of the voluntary subscriptions and the charitable endowment.

While the government was feeling its way to the most effective method of giving monetary assistance, some of the societies were pursuing their work of helping discharged prisoners. Fortunately some evidence of how this work was done was collected in 1895 by the Rev. G. P. Merrick, M.A., M.B., in response to a recommendation of the Gladstone Committee on *Prisons*.[2] The report

---

[1] 1897 C.8299, xl. 'Operations of Discharged Prisoners' Aid Societies.' G. P. Merrick. *Report.* [2] *Ibid.*

makes depressing reading; if the twentieth century opened with hopes of reform, the nineteenth century ended in the knowledge that the policy of after-care, which had been publicly recognized for fifty years as essential to the ex-prisoner, was as far from achievement as it had ever been, except in the case of a small number of societies.

The number of aid societies found to be in existence was fifty-six, as some prisons had more than one society; and of these, forty employed an agent, either voluntary or paid. In so far as any social work was done, the agent was the man responsible, and it is to his methods and approach, that our analysis must be directed. In theory he was required to interview the prisoner before his release, communicate with friends regarding his accommodation, and his former employer about his old job. He was to meet him at the gate on his release, and provide him with board and lodging if he had nowhere to go, or purchase a railway ticket, and perhaps some tools and clothing, if the prisoner had a home and a job to go to, at a distance from the prison. The agent was in any case to find him employment, and report all the facts to the committee. It is clear from this that the work of an agent with imagination and also with a progressive committee behind him, though largely composed of giving material aid, could be to create a helpful relationship and a steadying influence on the newly released man. In probably fifteen of the societies case-work of this kind was achieved, for the evidence shows that the zeal, organization and imagination of the agents did succeed in finding employment for the ex-prisoners, and one can assume that there was a constructive effort to make a reality of after-care. But in the rest of the societies, the finding of jobs was said to be 'almost impossible', and doubtless little else but the giving of small grants of money was ever considered.

No case-work is possible without adequate knowledge of the client, and careful preparation for the helping process. The way information was obtained was, therefore, relevant to the quality of the work. Here again the report shewed marked differences in practice. Some agents visited prisoners in their cells and talked to them before their discharge, but many did not, feeling that as the warder was generally present, the man was unlikely to speak the truth, and that 'he is more reliable when he has his liberty than when he has not'. Other agents did not even trouble to talk to the man about his circumstances at all, but contented themselves with obtaining their information from the prison records.

Societies seem to have differed about the type of prisoner they were disposed to help. Some were prepared to do what they could for the short-sentence man; others refused to have anything to do with him. Some helped only prisoners newly released, while others were willing to consider applications from those who had been at liberty for some time, but were in danger of falling again if no help were forthcoming. Many limited their help to first offenders only. The Liverpool Society claimed that experience shewed the hardened criminal to be only encouraged in his ways by frequent doles. The first offender, they said, was the most hopeful object for their limited resources. All societies found the woman ex-prisoner difficult and costly to maintain. For in spite of a recom-mendation by the director of convict prisons as far back as 1854 that hostels for women without homes should be provided, by the end of the century they were still insufficient and inappropriate.

'Labour Homes', or hostels where discharged prisoners could stay for a period and do some remunerative work, such as stick-chopping, were used extensively by some societies to tide a man over the time between his release and the making of other arrangements, or to test a man's willingness to work. Other societies made no use of them, but were only too eager to rig a man or boy out for work at sea and to pay his fare to the port. This, Mr. Merrick thought, was often short-sighted, since many of the ex-prisoners instead of going to sea became entangled in the flotsam and jetsam of the port and quickly drifted back to prison.

3   THE WORK OF MARY CARPENTER—REFORMATORY AND INDUSTRIAL SCHOOLS

In 1756 the 'Marine Society' had started a school for the children of convicts and by 1788 a few philanthropic individuals formed a society 'to educate and reform destitute and depraved children'. This was the origin of the so-called 'Philanthropic Society', which initiated a number of institutions, the first being established at Hackney, but later (1848) removed to Redhill Farm at Reigate. There was some confusion in the purpose and methods of these schools, which were concerned at the same time and in the same institution with both prevention and cure. The schools admitted sons of convicted felons, presumably as a preventive measure, and boys guilty of criminal practices for penal and curative purposes. The methods were experimental; at first the boys were made to submit to sedentary occupation, but later were given the opportunity to do active manual work on farms and in other trades. The youngsters were expected to respond to a 'rough life', and at the same time to a 'strong religious influence and the irresistible law of kindness'.[1]

As the various institutions of the early part of the century were founded either by voluntary or State effort or by both, it is not difficult to understand their somewhat chaotic state by the middle of the century, when Mary Carpenter first published a plan of what she thought these institutions should be. There were probably four distinct ways in which a youth in trouble could at that time be dealt with:—

1   *Prison*

In spite of the work of John Howard, Elizabeth Fry and the others, a large number of children found their way into the gaols of the country. In 1844, for instance, over 11,000 children and adolescents between ten and twenty years old were in prison, or 1 in 304 of the whole population in that age group.[2] Nor did the numbers decrease with the passing of new legislation empowering magistrates to send juveniles to reformatories. For whereas in 1847 1,274 children under twelve years old were in prison, by 1856 there were 1,990 of the same age span there. Certainly some prisons had schools for the education of the young, and Parkhurst was established as a Juvenile Prison in 1837 with the school as an integral part of it. But as the schools were run by fear, the boys frequently wearing irons when in school, and the school masters were usually themselves convicted felons, it was seldom that they achieved any education or reformation. Otherwise, as prisoners were not classified, the young mixed freely with the hardened and depraved, and prisons became a forcing ground for the criminal. Moreover, when once the young had been in prison 'they do not fear it any more. To them the disgrace of prison is never so potent as to the adult.'[3]

[1] M. Hill. *Prize Essay on Juvenile Delinquency* (1853).

[2] 1847 (447,534), vii. Criminal Law (Juvenile Offenders and Transportation). Select Committee. HL. *1st and 2nd Reports*, etc.

[3] M. Carpenter, *Reformatory Schools for the Children of the perishing and dangerous classes* (1851), Cap. VI.

2 *Reformatories*

These were schools started by voluntary effort (in London, Warwickshire, Gloucester, and elsewhere) for the reception and education of youngsters already convicted, or those in criminal surroundings. Before the 1854 Youthful Offenders Act, the legal power to keep young people in them against their will was doubtful in the extreme, but it is evident that some magistrates did send children, as an alternative to prison, and some school managers did detain them in the schools, bringing them back if they absconded and forcibly keeping them there.

3 *Industrial Schools*

These schools were started to teach a trade, and to instil a habit of work among classes of children where discipline, moral and industrial training were lacking, and were not primarily for convicted children. Delinquents did find their way into the schools however, sometimes being sent by magistrates on a 'free pardon', conditional upon their attendance. For example, one of the first to be opened was by Sheriff Watson in Aberdeen in 1841 for 'the education and feeding of the children of the lower orders and their industrial training'.[1] By 1849 the Magistrates of Aberdeen were directing 'the police to apprehend all children found begging in the town, and carry them off to school. They soon had seventy-five in process of cleansing, scrubbing, dressing and feeding. After that they had no begging children'.[2] In 1854, under a local Act the Middlesex justices inaugurated a school at Feltham, though this differed from the others in being exclusively for convicted cases. The distinction between industrial and reformatory schools was thus not very clear, and it was the earnest hope of Mary Carpenter that the position would be clarified. Acts of 1857, 1861, and 1866 did something to help, but during the whole of the nineteenth century the confusion remained.

4 *Feeding Schools*

'Feeding Schools' were a variant of the industrial schools, being set up in local centres for day attendance. Some general education and training in a trade were given, and the children were fed

---

[1] E. A. Pratt, *Pioneer Women* (1897), p. 194.
[2] M. Hill, *op. cit.*, Cap. VI.

during the day, but they were allowed to go home to sleep. These schools were originally intended for the non-convicted, but justices were alive to their value and sometimes released a youngster on condition of regular attendance. This could not be enforced until after the Act of 1857 (Industrial Schools Act), but it had been in common use long before that, and some parents had even been obliged to make contributions.

This was the state of affairs in 1851 when Mary Carpenter published her book *Reformatory Schools for the children of the Perishing and Dangerous Classes and for Juvenile Offenders*, which had such a profound influence on both public opinion and legislative reform. She was not content merely to set out a plan for dealing with delinquents, she followed it up by founding schools and actually supervising one herself for some twenty years or more. Born in 1807 in Bristol, her interest was first drawn to social evil when in the year 1833 along with Dr. Joseph Tuckerman, the Boston philanthropist, she saw a little ragged boy running down the street. Said Dr. Tuckerman 'that boy should be followed to his home and seen after'.[1] This led her to found the 'Bristol Working and Visiting Society' in 1835, of which she remained secretary for twenty years. Later she organized a 'Ministry to the Poor' in Bristol, and in 1846 a Ragged School. In this she was faced with the riotous behaviour of untamed and poverty-stricken children, yet she succeeded in holding their interest by her ability and enthusiasm. It was as a result of her experience here that she began to concentrate on the welfare of the toughest of the youngsters, who were usually young offenders as well. It was commonly thought that some 60 per cent of adult criminals had learnt their first lessons in crime before they were fifteen years old; and while there was little the courts could do either in prevention or reclamation, there was no shortage of dens in which crime was taught. Mary Carpenter thought this intolerable, and by studying how other countries were dealing with the same refractory problem, she gradually developed for herself the solution with which her name is associated.

In 1825 New York State and Philadelphia had established 'houses of refuge' for the reception of delinquent children and those out of control or in moral danger. From these 'Houses' children were apprenticed to understanding masters who would

[1] J. E. Carpenter, *Life and Work of Mary Carpenter* (1881), p. 149.

care for them and teach them a trade. If they misbehaved during their apprenticeship they would be returned to the 'House' for a further period. Thus was the idea of 'Release on Licence' developed in America. In Europe experiments of various kinds were being made. Pestalozzi's work in Switzerland was worth the closest study, as were the farm schools of Belgium and other European countries, including Russia. But it was the reformatory colony at Mettray in France, and the Rauhe Haus in Hamburg in Germany which gave her the greatest stimulus and hope.

The Mettray Colony derived from a French statute of 1832, whereby any child under sixteen could, though guilty of an offence, be acquitted if he acted 'sans discernement', when he could be returned to the care of his parents, or sent to a House of Correction. Owing to the efforts and generosity of M. M. Demetz and de Brétignères de Courteilles, an alternative to the House of Correction was founded in Mettray in the year 1839. This farm school set out to procure for young delinquents religious instruction, moral education, and the acquisition of a trade, especially in agriculture, and also provided for their benevolent guardianship 'as long as they have need of it'. Thus after-care was an integral part of the whole scheme. By 1850 the Mettray experiment had so impressed the French authorities that private associations were encouraged, with state help, to form these 'colonies penitentiares' all over the country. At first they concentrated on farm schools, but freedom to experiment later produced colonies with industrial workshops of all types.

In Germany, though the first reformatory school was started in Stuttgart in 1820, the best known was the 'Rauhe Haus' founded near Hamburg in 1833. The principles of this school were similar to those being advocated in Britain over a century later: that voluntary effort should be fertilized by state grants to aid the foundation of such schools; that the schools should be run as a family—and should be kept small, or subdivided into family groups; and that, under due precautions, boys and girls should be associated together 'thus placing the children in their natural relations to each other'.

In 1851, after the publication of her book, Mary Carpenter called a conference in Birmingham to discuss the whole question of the institutional care of young offenders. The interest aroused was so great, that in the following year the Kingswood Reformatory

School at Bristol was founded, in premises originally erected by John Wesley, providing accommodation for over a hundred children. Such a venture was not without its growing pains; for instance, as the school had no legal sanctions behind it, there was difficulty in dealing with runaways. Parties of children, led by some more daring spirit, often a girl, would make their way into Bristol and get into mischief. They would be locked up in gaol, where Mary Carpenter would visit them and obtain their release if she could, and take them back to the school. At first the school was mixed on Rauhe Haus principles, but by 1854 she decided to start a girls' reformatory at Red Lodge House, and for the rest of her life she maintained close supervision over this establishment.

Meanwhile she continued her writing and in 1853 published *Juvenile Delinquents, their Condition and Treatment*. She also corresponded regularly with others, such as Mr. Barwick Baker of Hardwicke Court, Gloucestershire, who were similarly employed in the supervision of these schools. By 1856 a 'British National Reformatory Union' had been inaugurated, and here she read papers, as well as at the 'Social Science Association' founded in the ensuing year. She also played a leading part in promoting legislation, and submitted evidence to various Royal Commissions on reformatory and industrial schools and juvenile delinquency. By 1854 the Youthful Offenders Act gave power to the Home Secretary to grant certificates and financial assistance to reformatories, in return for which they were to be inspected and reported on annually by the inspector of prisons. Courts were empowered to send juveniles to them on summary conviction for a period of years, and parents could be obliged to make contributions. But it was not until 1899 that the fourteen days of preliminary imprisonment which Mary Carpenter hated so much, were abolished.[1]

Principles and Methods advocated by Mary Carpenter

It remains now to analyse the principles and methods of social work in these institutions, which Mary Carpenter advocated, and which she practised during her long years of service at Kings-

[1] An interesting personal description of Mary Carpenter is given by Louisa Twining. 'Her appearance was somewhat singular,' she wrote, 'with plain old-fashioned dress and small grey curls on her forehead. Her eye was remarkable for expression and power, and her voice low and gentle.' L. Twining, *Recollection of Life and Work* (1893), p. 134.

wood and Red Lodge. She started on the assumption that there was not one cause of juvenile crime but many, and that poverty was not a prime cause of delinquency. Furthermore, the children who appeared before the courts were mainly limited to one class, namely 'Moral Orphans', or children whose parents could not or did not exercise authority over them. The best place for a child was with his parents, she averred, provided parents exercised proper parental authority over him. Where they did not, or where their own conduct might harden or corrupt him, then society must act in their place, so that when the child was restored to ordinary life, he would adequately fill his station in it. To achieve this it was the duty of society to provide a refuge for the child that would approximate as closely to a home as possible.

1 Treatment then, must be founded on the love of the child, and so awaken in him the trust, affection and sense of security, which the normal child could expect to develop in his own family. She followed here the precept of the Rauhe Haus, and visualized the unit of the reformatory to be as close as possible in size to that of a family, where discipline and training could be given, and where individual needs could be individually dealt with. Each of these family units was to be self-contained, and all the members of it were to have a relationship one to another of mutual dependence and responsibility.

She recognized early the need for a capable and skilled staff, and though this was expensive, she felt that in the long run the more effective system was the cheapest. Work of this kind was difficult, more so even than that of a physician, for

his healing art is to be exerted on the body, his agents are physical means, his hopes of success are founded on certain laws which he can comprehend. But to restore health to the mind diseased is a task to be accomplished by very different agencies. No beating of the pulse can reveal to him the condition of the patient; he must often discover it by symptoms unnoticed by any but the most experienced observer, and must learn even from the cessation of songs the discordant state of the inner nature.[1]

2 She realized the need for co-operation on the part of the child. He must be willing to reform, and convinced that progress was possible. Without his active participation, the energy necessary for

[1] M. Carpenter, *Juvenile Delinquents, their Conditions and Treatment* (1853), p. 301.

change would not be forthcoming. This was true, she said, not only of his industrial training, but in his moral development as well.

3 Work was to be a means to an end, not an end in itself. There should be no forced work, as that had no educative quality. It would be better for a child to be idle, even refused access to work, so that when he was tired of his idleness work could be made available as a favour. On the other hand, the basis of the curriculum should be work, particularly of the kind that excited a lively interest, calling forth all a boy's powers, and making him see that what he did was useful, and that what he did well was best. The actual choice of work was difficult. Mary Carpenter thought farm work the most universally satisfying, but as few found their way into it afterwards, urban skills suitable to age and sex should be taught, always provided they developed the necessary stimulus to growth in the youngster.

4 Recreation was just as important as work. Children needed sport, and opportunities to indulge in it. In this she reacted violently from the thought of her day, which believed in repressing recreation. Moreover, the masters in the school had more opportunity of discovering the true nature of the boy in his periods of recreation than at any other time.

5 Corporal punishment was reduced to a minimum, and to her the story of Anselm contained a pointed lesson. Anselm visited a monastery, where the Abbot consulted him about the perversity and incorrigibility of the boys there. He was continually beating them but they grew worse, and when they left they were dull and brutish. Then said Anselm

this must surely be a poor return on all your expenditure of time and money. Yet surely if you gave the young trees in your garden no freedom they would become crooked and useless. So it is with boys, as they do not observe any love or kindness in your dealings with them, they think that you have no other motives in your discipline than envy and hatred, and so it turns out most unhappily that they grow up full of hatred and suspicion. He who is but young needs gentle treatment. Cheerfulness, kindness and love are the means whereby such are to be won to God.[1]

Over-indulgence was just as bad as constant severity, and discipline should be consistent, while punishment such that it

[1] M. Carpenter, *Juvenile Delinquents, their Conditions and Treatment* (1853), p. 316.

could be easily understood as the direct result of wrong-doing. Pilfering was a habit difficult to overcome, and here she thought that boys should earn, or be given possessions of their own to prize and guard, arousing in them feelings of respect for property, and helping them to realize that what belonged to others was as prized as what they themselves possessed.

6 Her methods were largely educational, but as no training was conceivable to her unless founded on Christianity, Christian and moral instruction were to accompany the teaching of a trade. The delinquent would thus be equipped in every way to occupy his station in life on his release. There was no question in her mind of educating him 'out of his station', and the able child had no more chance of promotion to a higher status than the dullard.

How long it would take to accomplish the reformation of the young criminal was a matter for experience. The Rauhe Haus thought an average of four to five years was needed, while the American reform schools thought one to two years would suffice, but Mary Carpenter would not stipulate a fixed time. Each case should be dealt with on its merits, release being dependent on the progress made, and decided by the school managers under a government inspector.

Later in her life (1864) she appointed a 'Children's Agent' to visit boys and girls, discharged from the Bristol schools, if they had obtained situations in Bristol. For those who were homeless he found lodgings, for those out of work he sought employment. He was in fact the forerunner of our modern 'after-care' officer, though his duties, being localized, became wider in scope. He not only looked after the ex-reformatory youths, but investigated the condition of special neighbourhoods, bringing to light cruelty and neglect in much the same way as N.S.P.C.C. officers do now. That she appointed this official so late in her life does not mean that Mary Carpenter was neglectful till then of what happened to the boys and girls on leaving the schools. She and her co-managers took an intense interest in finding them suitable jobs, and seeing that they did not fall into bad company. Emigration, she thought, was the most helpful means of establishing boys in a 'respectable position'.

The problem of what to do with delinquent girls was as much a difficulty to Mary Carpenter as to us today. She realized that though fewer girls were brought before the courts than boys, they were more hardened and difficult to manage. The reason, she thought, was that girls were not often brought before a court until all lenient methods had failed, and seldom came at all unless their home life were utterly degraded. Such girls should be prepared for domestic service, not for emigration or factory work, should be brought under restraint and control, be reformed by steady discipline, and educated by understanding teachers in a kindly home-like atmosphere. She fully realized the need for skilled supervision, and insisted that the women appointed to carry out this training and education must know as much as possible of each girl's character and antecedents. She felt it to be highly important that a 'lady', capable of understanding the intentions of the managers, should live in or near the school, to exercise a general superintendence, and to regulate the daily working of the school.

4 PROBATION

Of these four aspects of the penal services, that of 'probation' work is the most clearly seen as 'social case work', because today its members require a special training, its sphere of operation is clearly defined, and it has a professional organization of its own. But clear though its present pattern is, there has been much speculation, and some special pleading about its origin. It has been pointed out[1] that the idea of probation involves two conceptions: 'binding over', an old idea, and 'supervision', the new element which when added to 'binding over' produces 'probation'. 'Binding over' to be of good behaviour for a specified period was inherent in English common law, and therefore probation took root more easily in countries familiar with common law, such as America and the Dominions, and it is not surprising that both Britain and America claim to have been the first to introduce it. It is said, for instance, that a rudimentary form of probation was practised by the courts of Massachusetts in the seventeenth century, and that a cobbler at Boston in 1841 stood bail for a drunkard and volunteered to look after him, thus inaugurating there the system of binding over with supervision. It is also said that in England in the early 1820's, some of the magistrates in the county of Warwick were experimenting with young first offenders

[1] 1935–6 Cmd. 5122, viii. Social Services in Courts of Summary Jurisdiction. Departmental Committee. *Report*, p. 35.

by sentencing them to imprisonment for one day, and releasing them on condition that they returned to the care of their parents or masters for more careful supervision. This process is said to have been carried one stage further by Mr. Matthew Davenport Hill, the well-known Recorder of Birmingham, who in 1841 instituted a register of men volunteering for this work. These friends, relatives, or masters were allowed to take the children from the court in return for a guarantee of care. The sponsors, in their turn, were to be visited at frequent but undetermined periods by officers of the police to see that their charges were well cared for and of good behaviour.[1]

The return of the young delinquents to the care of their parents or masters, could be regarded as an extension of the medieval guild system of supervision expected of masters over apprentices, or the common law guardianship duties of parents over children.[2] To liken this to the modern probation method, by which a stranger to the young offender undertakes to guide and befriend him, while leaving him under the legal care and guardianship of his own parents, is to strain history too far. Perhaps closer to the modern probation officer was the children's agent mentioned above, appointed by Mary Carpenter in Bristol, to visit boys and girls discharged from the industrial and reformatory schools. But he had no access to the courts, and could not therefore be cited as the forerunner of the probation officer.

But there did come into existence an organization which was some years later to be the cradle of probation work in this country. In 1861, the 'National Temperance League' presented each member of the clergy of the Church of England with a pamphlet on temperance called *Haste to the Rescue*. Written by Mrs. Wightman, wife of the Vicar of St. Alkmund's, Shrewsbury, it set out to show how the labours of the Church were being neutralized by the prevailing drunkenness. So impressed was the Dean of Carlisle by this pamphlet, that he convened a meeting of abstaining clergy in London to discuss the matter, with the result that in 1862 the Church of England Total Abstinence Society was founded. Ten years later the name was changed to Church of England Temperance Society, so that those who were not total abstainers, but who

---

[1] 1847 (534), vii. Criminal Law. (Juvenile Offenders and Transportation) Select Committee. HL. *2nd Report, Minutes of Evidence*.
[2] E. Lipson, *Social and Economic History* (1931), Vol. III.

believed in temperance, could be included. It was to the office of this society in 1876 that a letter was sent by a Hertford journeyman printer, Frederick Rainer, deploring the quick degeneration of individuals, who got into trouble through drink or any other cause. 'Offence after offence, sentence after sentence seemed his inevitable lot. Could anything be done', he asked, 'to prevent this downward fall?'[1] With his letter he enclosed a five shillings postal order, in the hope that some rescue work in the courts could be started. The letter made an immediate appeal to the committee, and some remembered the words of Charles Dickens in the 'Chimes', words which have been so often quoted by them since: 'Gentlemen,' said Toby Veck, 'dealing with men like me, begin at the right end. Give us in mercy better homes when we're a-lying in our cradles; give us better food when we're a-working for our lives; give us kinder laws when we're a-going wrong; and don't set jail, jail, jail, afore us wherever we turn.' Accordingly it was resolved that a 'Special Agent' should be appointed to the Southwark, Lambeth and Mansion House Courts to deal with individual drunkards, 'with a view to their restoration and reclamation'.[2] In August 1876 Mr. G. Nelson was appointed, and in the following year he was joined by Mr. W. Batchelor. The numbers grew until by 1889 nearly every police court in London had its missionary. Nor were the Provinces unmindful of the work to be done in their Courts. In Handsworth near Birmingham a missioner was appointed in 1877, and in other Dioceses similar workers began to appear. The numbers grew, until by 1885 there were nine missioners; by 1890, thirty-six; by 1895, seventy-seven; and by 1900 there were a hundred missioners, as well as nine missionary women employed by the Women's Union.

Meanwhile a parallel movement in Massachusetts was developing as a result of the voluntary efforts of social workers there. For several years some State courts had suspended judgment and kept the power of recall, though they had no adequate control over the conduct of the offender in the interim. But in 1878 Massachusetts passed the first Probation Law, and a full-time paid probation officer was appointed to the Boston courts to provide supervision for defendants, released for a definite period, on an undertaking of good behaviour. It was not for another twenty years that this

---

[1] Church of England Temperance Society—*Sixty Years Old*, p. 8.
[2] H. H. Ayscough, *When Mercy Seasons Justice* (C.E.T.S., 1922), p. 13.

example was followed by Chicago, and thereafter by the whole State of Illinois.

In England the tentative Summary Jurisdiction Act was passed in 1879, Section 16 providing that magistrates could discharge offenders conditionally, with or without sureties if the offence were trifling, and including a condition of good behaviour. Failure to comply with the conditions meant that they could be called upon to appear for sentence. Adults guilty of indictable offences were expressly excluded. A Bill to establish a system of supervision on bail failed to reach the Statute Book in 1881, and though provisions for supervision on American lines were embodied in the First Offenders' Bill introduced into Parliament in 1887, they were deleted before the Bill became law as the *Probation of First Offenders Act, 1887*. Whereas the 1879 Act referred to the trifling nature of the offence, that of 1887 extended conditional discharge to first offenders convicted of more serious offences, provided the 'youth, character and antecedents of the offender' were taken into account. This was the first time probation made its appearance in English law, and its provisions were extended to the higher courts. From 1879, therefore, though the law did not expressly provide for supervision, magistrates had the power in certain circumstances to hand the offender over to a supervisor—the police court missioner or other suitable person—if any were available. Even before 1879, according to Mr. Curtis-Bennett, the Metropolitan magistrate, the London courts had begun to use the system by a 'Missioner's bail.'[1] Supervisors, however, could not be provided by the courts until the Probation of Offenders Act 1907.

Probation therefore depended on the voluntary provision of officers by charitable agencies. Of these, by far the largest was the Church of England Temperance Society, with their police court missioners, though there were other societies in the field. In Liverpool for instance, four societies sent missioners to the courts: the Church of England Temperance Society, the Wesleyan Mission, the Catholic Aid Society and the Liverpool Ladies' Temperance Association. All were recognized, and their missioners made probation officers after the 1907 Act.[2]

At first most of these missioners were men, but in 1884 the

[1] 1910 Cmd. 5002, xlv. Probation of Offenders Act, 1907. Departmental Committee. *Report, Minutes of Evidence*, para. 1–6.
[2] *Ibid.*, para. 1435.

Liverpool societies reported to the C.E.T.S. the need for a woman worker to help Mr. James Mercer, the prison gate and police court missionary. Drunkenness among women had increased so much, that some direct attempt to tackle the problem seemed to be called for, and it was thought that a woman could best be reached by one of her own sex. Accordingly the first appointment of a woman appears to have been made in Liverpool. The C.E.T.S. was, however, acutely aware of the need for women workers, and the Women's Union, a body associated with the C.E.T.S., made this one of its main concerns, but it was greatly hampered by lack of funds and pleas are to be found in all the annual reports of the period for more money for women missioners. For 'poor women' they said 'frequently apply to them for sympathy and encouragement in resisting their temptation'.[1] Nor would it have been very costly greatly to increase the female staff, if we may judge by the large advertisement in the C.E.T.S. Report of 1895 stating '£50 per annum will provide a mission woman'! The first woman was appointed in London in 1886, and by 1897 there were nine.

No worker operated in a court without the consent of the magistrates, whose general goodwill, as well as that of the police and court officials was made very clear. Mr. Curtis-Bennett in 1910 spoke highly of the work, and evidently prepared a daily routine to keep in close contact with it. 'I see the missionary,' he said, 'every day when I am eating my lunch',[2] and as he had presided over a court since 1886 he had doubtless had many opportunities to get to know his missionary. The police also were co-operative, and according to Mr. Nelson, it was common for them to bring girls from the streets to him, for his advice or help.

Purpose of the Work

In assessing the contribution of the police court missionaries to the development of probation in this country, one must be clear about their purpose. At the beginning they were intended as an answer to the plea so effectively made by Frederick Rainer, that someone should be at hand in the courts to promote temperance; and to try by personal influence, with material help if necessary,

---

[1] Church of England Missionary Society, *Annual Report for 1889*.

[2] 1910 Cmd. 5002, xlv. Probation of Offenders Act, 1907. Departmental Committee. *Report, Minutes of Evidence*, para. 9.

176

to persuade those who had found their way into the dock through drink to lead a sober and steady life in the future. It was soon clear, however, that the function was to be wider than this, for though drink was a potent factor in crime, it was not the only one, and many needed help who had not suffered from insobriety at all. As the Rev. Hasloch Potter (who was a member in 1876, and became C.E.T.S. Secretary in 1878) revealed, there was some doubt whether the work should be confined to prisoners convicted of drunkenness, or extended to those convicted for other offences.[1] In the end those with larger vision prevailed, and Magistrates were encouraged to hand over to the missionaries an ever-widening variety of cases, from drunkenness, prostitution and attempted suicide, to larceny and housebreaking. In spite of this, however, the society was primarily concerned with temperance. The annual reports show, that in addition to their court work and prison gate attendance, missioners had to address meetings in factories, on building sites, and among cabmen, and to use their evenings to assist in the general temperance work of the diocese. Some measure of their success was indicated by the number of 'pledges' signed, though a more sophisticated generation would not place too much reliance on this criterion.

Scope of Probation Work

The change in emphasis opened up a field of police court social work unthought of until these men appeared, and much of the pattern of the modern probation officer's work can be seen in the developments of the last quarter of the nineteenth century. Convicted defendants were handed over for care and supervision, as they are today. If they were fewer in number than they are now and were first offenders, this limitation was imposed by the state of the law. It became the habit, particularly among the London magistrates, to defer selected convicted cases for a 'home surroundings' report, to be made by the missionary. This was done in case extenuating circumstances might affect the sentence, or to see if the employer would give one more chance; to find a home where a new start could be made; to see if a reconciliation could be effected; to enquire if the home could be kept together while the husband was in gaol; or whether a few shillings spent on stock-in-trade would help a man to get an honest livelihood and

[1] J. H. Potter, *Inasmuch* (1927), pp. 8–9.

make a fresh start. Though the purpose of the report was not primarily to help the magistrate to understand why the man committed the crime, the fact that missioners were asked to provide some kind of a picture of the home, and make suggestions about the defendant's future, showed the value that was beginning to be placed on this important information.

When the Summary Jurisdiction (Married Women) Act of 1895 made it legal for maintenance and separation cases to be heard by magistrates in the lower courts, new functions increased the dependence of the Bench on the police court missionaries. In the delicate work of conciliation in matrimonial disputes, it was they who were most suited to deal with the intricate and lengthy work involved; and if in spite of all their efforts, the case came to open court, the issue might be clearer in the disputants' minds for having been discussed with the missioner. A further branch of modern probation work is after-care, which then took the form mainly of follow-up work on drunkenness cases. The missioner would keep in touch with families in his district, where there seemed danger of back-sliding, or refer a family to the Vicar if it moved away. By 1894 after-care of this nature was an integral part of the Church temperance work, and 'Rescue Bands' of voluntary workers were formed in many parishes.

Two other developments, which are now less important but seemed invaluable then, were the provision of institutional accommodation and the Labour Yards. The institutions were mainly shelters for the drunkards, where time, habit and training were expected to effect a reform. Most dioceses had one or more of these Homes, and doubtless they were of some help to the missioners in dealing with their cases, but as there was no power to direct anyone into a Home, only those willing to co-operate went into them, and for the vast majority they were quite useless. The labour yards were different. Many convicted men, whether sentenced to imprisonment or not, became unemployed. Frequently they had no trade, and having been convicted, no 'character' either. The C.E.T.S. therefore founded 'Labour Homes or Yards', in Peterborough in 1888, in London in 1890, and later in other parts of the Provinces. These yards, where wood sawing and chopping were the main occupations, had a double purpose. They provided a livelihood to tide the man over the crucial period when he might lose hope and resort to further crime; and they provided the manager with an opportunity to assess the man's capacity to work and to earn a reference. At the same time openings in the labour market were diligently looked for. These labour yards, to which hostels were occasionally attached, were much relied upon by the missioners, as the many enthusiastic references to them in the Annual Reports indicate.

In view of Mary Carpenter's work, it is surprising that the one aspect of modern probation work which had not really developed before the turn of the century was that concerned with juveniles as a class. This may have been due to the preoccupation with temperance, though drunkenness was not confined to adults,[1] or to the conservatism of the law, which did not establish the Juvenile Court until 1908. The young were not necessarily ignored. Obviously the missioner would have much scope in the reformation and training of children and adolescents who appeared in the courts, but there is surprisingly little reference to them in the reports. In 1890, for instance, the London missionaries reported that they had decided to devote as much time as possible to juvenile work, as there had been a singular increase in the number of lads appearing before the courts. Three years later, a special labour yard for boys between fourteen and eighteen years of age was opened at Bethnal Green. In the same year juvenile work for temperance was entrusted in London to a 'Juvenile Board'. But as compared with the overriding importance of the young to the modern probation officer, the police court missionary of the nineteenth century spent only a modicum of effort on them.

Methods of Police Court Missioners

The methods used by the Police Court Missioners were essentially case work, in the sense that they were 'individual to individual'. They were probably influenced by the teaching of the C.O.S., which was well-known before Mr. Nelson was appointed, though there is little evidence of the missioners having been trained by the C.O.S. unless they came through the training channels of the Church Army (cf. Chap. 11). The only training, if any, they had

---

[1] For instance, H. H. Ayscough, in his book *When Mercy Seasons Justice*, states that in 1877 in Liverpool alone 1,846 boys and girls of eighteen years and under were arrested for being 'drunk and incapable'. Of this number no fewer than 115 were under ten years old.

was by the Church Army, or the Church College for Lay Workers.[1] This meant, of course, that all the men and women entered the work with strong Christian beliefs, and the work was pursued as God's work. The personality of any applicant for a post as missioner was carefully considered in this light by the selecting committee. He had to be sympathetic, be able to discriminate in his judgment of human nature and character, and must 'with a patience that is unwearied and a vigilance that never sleeps, devote himself to what he has in hand'.[2]

Work of this kind demanded that the missioner should get to know his individual cases thoroughly; one of the first principles of case work, minute investigation of all the relevant facts, was inherent in it. His object was reclamation and the restoration of self-respect. To achieve this he sought to help his client to become independent, either through the labour yard, by finding him a job, or by material help, if a small expenditure would help a man to his feet again. As Mr. R. O. B. Lane, Q.C., said at the Annual Meeting in 1892:

> People who have fallen into crime are at a low ebb, gloomy, dark and weak. The police court missionary meets them as they step out of the dock, takes them to his home, follows them into their own homes; he provides assistance for them, brings to bear on them all that amount of sympathy without which it would be impossible to carry on this work; binds up the broken reed, teaches them to look with the eye of hope for the future; and when he has found them a new life to start in, and a safe work to do, he does not leave them there, he still keeps in touch with them, to watch, to counsel, and to see there is no relapse.[3]

Conclusion

While there was general concern about criminals, how best to treat them, and to whom they should look for help and guidance, there was no co-ordinated effort that could be said to have led to a 'Court and Prison Social Worker'. This chapter has been concerned with the work of two outstanding individuals, and two philanthropic movements whose influence has been felt down to the present day. Elizabeth Fry's pioneer work aimed at fundamentals; she recognized that in helping women prisoners she was

---

[1] Private letter to the authors from Rev. McAuliffe, one time Principal of the Church College for Lay Workers.
[2] London Police Court Mission, *Annual Report for 1894*. [3] *Ibid.*

helping mothers and potential mothers and she appealed to the maternal in them. Her methods were not new, but she realized that method would not succeed without the guidance and friendship of the worker. It has been said that Mary Carpenter's work was the turning point between individual philanthropy and reform through organization, between the individual work such as that of the Misses More and Elizabeth Fry, and the organization of a society with officials, committees, appeals for funds and the full panoply of organized work so typical of the later nineteenth century.[1] Reflecting on the work of Chalmers, and the many societies already in existence for the prevention of mendicity, it is a little difficult to accept this assessment of Mary Carpenter's contribution. What she did do was to enunciate and test a body of principles upon which institutional care for the 'perishing and dangerous classes' ('perishing' through lack of knowledge, 'dangerous' because lacking in moral discipline) and juvenile delinquents should be developed.

There is no doubt that the Discharged Prisoners' Aid Societies were started and continued from the highest humanitarian motives, and did succeed in giving help, usually financial, when help must have been sorely needed. But that they were doing after-care in the sense of helping the ex-prisoner to get on his feet again, and of supporting him in his moments of weakness is very doubtful. It is probable they did not really believe in after-care of this type; most of the societies, while stressing to Mr. Merrick the difficulties and objections to their work, alleged that the men themselves were opposed to any follow-up, dubbing it 'snooping', and they were not prepared to pursue a relationship in the face of such manifest opposition from those whom they designed to help.

The great temperance movement of the last century was the sole example of a service for the criminal which has had an uninterrupted progress towards a clearly defined branch of social work. The words of Mr. Lane 'to watch, to counsel' were prophetic of the function of the probation officer of the future. For 'to guide and befriend' is precisely what the probation officer sets out to do. It is difficult to tell from the statistics of the period what the case load of the temperance missioners was and therefore how deep their work could be, though in 1894, with some thirteen male officers and perhaps five women nearly 13,000 visits to and about

[1] E. A. Pratt, *op cit.*, p. 212.

offenders were paid, while nearly 1,200 special cases were handed to their care by the magistrates. It is significant, however, that the money expended on material aid in the same year was barely £780. For the missions never wanted to be, and never became, relief agencies. The work itself, as one would expect, was full of set-backs. Mr. Batchelor, the second missioner in London, reported (1884) that when he went 'into the cells, they curse me and use fearful language', or again, 'I have to confess my great disappointment in much of the work of those I work among. Regarding the women I get into Homes, many leave before they have been there long.' Even Mr. Nelson, who seems to have had a more cheerful temperament than his colleague, had to complain in one report (1885) of some of his pledge-signers: 'I am sorry to say many of my cases fell away during the hot weather last summer.' Yet though these early police court workers experienced difficulties familiar to all social workers, they were eminently successful, because they gained the confidence of the courts, and through them of the public, and they marked out a pattern for court social work similar to that of today. If there has been a change in the depth and scope of the work, it has arisen out of the wider knowledge we now possess of human needs and motivation, and the greater efforts we make to select probation officers and train them in the skills associated with 'case-work'.

CHAPTER 10

THE HANDICAPPED

'HANDICAP', whether of the senses, hearing, sight, or of the mind, or whether by physical deformity through birth or accident, excited considerable interest during the nineteenth century, and has furnished the twentieth with a plethora of voluntary organizations to cope intermittently, and often selectively, with those who are less well-equipped in these respects than the normal person. But little in the form of a closely defined branch of social work has been bequeathed to us, though the Charity Organization Society and other case work agencies of a century ago recognized the stricken' as a particularly suitable and deserving object of their care. Much of the concern which led to the creation of special ervices for the handicapped centred round their need for education when they were young, and for spiritual care at all times. In consequence, it is often for its schools and missions that the work for the handicapped has to be studied.

I   THE BLIND

Blindness, above all other defects, has captured the public imagination and evoked its pity, but up to the nineteenth century the blind were considered as utterly helpless, doomed by Providence to be always dependent on others, and absolutely unfitted to take part in affairs around them. So, though everyone was sorry for them, it was assumed that those who could not be supported by their friends must secure a pension from whatever source was available, or retire into a Home, or become beggars on the street The Poor Law of 1834 tacitly recognized this, by exempting the blind from their rigorous regulations relating to out-relief, and from the ordinary means test. In the 'thirties, a number of residential asylums for the blind were started, such as that of the

Henshaw Blind Asylum, Manchester, founded in 1839, for the impotent and aged blind.[1] Mendicancy remained, however, a favourite method of earning a living, and in some cases even the education they had received was used to arouse sympathy in passers-by, for often the blind would sit at street corners reading Scriptures printed in raised characters. Even as late as 1889 a Royal Commission reported that too many of the blind had too little to do, and became mendicants, or relied on charity.[2]

But a new attitude was developing and among those who propagated the new ideas was Miss Elizabeth Gilbert. Born in 1826, the third child of A. T. Gilbert, Principal of Brasenose College, Oxford, afterwards Bishop of Chichester, she became blind at the age of three, after a severe attack of scarlet fever. Her parents were determined she should have as good a chance as her ten brothers and sisters, and saw to it that she did and learned as much as they. Her mind was cultivated by learning and experience, so that though the last ten to fifteen years of her life before she died at the age of fifty-nine, were spent as an invalid with spinal trouble, she had many personal and spiritual resources. Her most active years seem to have been between 1850 and 1875.[3] In 1851 she wrote (on her Foucault frame, which she always used for writing) to Mr. W. H. Levy, a young blind teacher at the St. John's Wood school, about a system of printing he was using in his work, and so began a partnership that was to have far-reaching results for the blind. Levy, an intelligent man of poor origin, was able to supply her with information about the needs of the blind poor, and together they devised a scheme of providing work for the blind and selling the finished goods, and of social welfare and home visiting, which was to develop into a nation-wide system.

Principles

Miss Gilbert and her associates started with the premise that the blind were not doomed to be parasites on society. Given the necessary opportunity, the handicap of blindness could in some measure be overcome and the blind could become useful, self-respecting, self-supporting citizens. In order that this might be

---

[1] 1889 C.5781-1, xix. Blind, Deaf and Dumb, etc., of the United Kingdom. Royal Commission. *Report*, etc., Vol. II, App. 2.
[2] 1889 C.5781, xix. *Ibid.*, *Report*, para. 87.
[3] F. Martin, *Eliz. Gilbert and her work for the blind* (1887), Cap. I.

possible, society must first treat them not as sick and impotent, but as potential citizens and workers able under certain conditions to hold their own in the company of the sighted. It was therefore advocated, as a first principle, that children and the newly blind (if educable) should be educated in the use of the various reading and writing media, and should not be segregated from sighted people any more than necessary. Secondly, they wanted to develop trade schools, so that the blind would have a means of livelihood. Thirdly, they argued that all possible means of employment should be made available whether in the home, in industry, or in sheltered workshops. And fourthly, on the grounds that social ties are more necessary to the blind than others, they tried to foster the family, to promote home-visiting, and to provide the financial or other support this principle involved. In this they were spurred on by the example of the 'Dresden Institute for the Blind', where experience had shown it was possible to offer the blind an adequate variety of training, whilst enabling them to keep contact with the intricacies of everyday life. Dresden had also developed a scheme of grant-aid, particularly in tools and raw materials, for those leaving the institution and setting up for themselves, and had bought raw materials in quantity to be sold at cost price to the blind worker. In return, the worker was encouraged to sell his goods privately. If he were not successful, the Institute undertook to sell them for him. To assist the scheme, following perhaps the precedent of the Elberfeld experiment, voluntary guardians, living near the blind, were recruited to advise and befriend them.[1] Though this country has never developed such a thorough-going system of care, it was an example eagerly watched and studied here during the nineteenth century.

Methods of rehabilitating the Blind

1   *Education.* As would be expected, the earliest institutions, dating back to the eighteenth century, were concerned with the education of children. M. Hauy had founded the first institution for the blind in Paris as early as 1784, Liverpool following suit in 1791, Edinburgh started one in 1793, and the London School for Indigent Blind came in 1799. These pioneer efforts were followed by others both in London and the Provinces until, by 1870 and

[1] 1889 C.5781, xix. Blind, etc., of the United Kingdom. Royal Commission. *Report*, para. 119.

the passing of the Education Act, a fair number of schools had been founded by voluntary effort for the education and training of blind children. Moreover, by an Act of 1862 Boards of Guardians were empowered to maintain, clothe, and educate the blind children of the poor in special schools, provided their total cost did not exceed what the child would have cost in the workhouse.[1] Though this Act was not used to any great extent, it did show some public concern for their education. When the School Boards came into being in 1870, it became their duty to provide classes or schools for all children, but even as late as 1889, a Royal Commission[2] reported that far too much of the education of the blind children had been left to charity. The chief controversy concerned the problem of how far blind children could be taught in the ordinary schools with the sighted, and how far they should be segregated in special schools. There was a large and influential body of opinion (notably the C.O.S. in London) in favour of teaching these children in ordinary schools with sighted children, but providing special classes where Braille and the 'blind techniques' could be taught. In support of their contention they cited the Scottish experience where, as in Glasgow, blind children had been successfully taught in the ordinary schools for a number of years.[3] In spite of this, the tendency was to create special schools for the blind and this soon raised questions of whether there should be special training of teachers, the appointment of an inspectorate, and whether the education of the blind should be compulsory up to the age of sixteen years. The C.O.S. answered these questions in an emphatic affirmative.

2 *Training.* Closely allied to but not inseparable from the schools for children who were blind, were the training establishments for youths and older people. The Liverpool school (1791) which obtained a private Act of Parliament in 1829, offered children schooling up to sixteen years, and thereafter taught them a trade, and many later schools and institutions followed a similar pattern. In spite of the Dresden example there was still real difficulty in finding a sufficient variety of trades to fit the varying needs of the blind, and though some were apprenticed in 'sighted' workshops, they do not seem to have been as suited to this method as the

---

[1] 1886 C.4747, xxv. Education of the Blind. *School Inspectors' Reports.*
[2] 1889 C.5781, xix. *Op. cit.*
[3] C.O.S. *Report on Training of the Blind* (1876).

deaf. A profession (or art) thought particularly suitable for the blind was music, and the Royal Normal College, Norwood, was concerned exclusively with their musical education, usually with a view to their making a living afterwards as teachers or musicians.

3 *Employment*. Though so many schools and institutions (61 by 1889) set out to provide training in a skill, some of them interested themselves no further than this, and their pupils had to sink or swim unaided in the industrial market. Throughout the later nineteenth century constant reference can be found to this lamentable state of affairs; and it was here that Miss Gilbert and her friends made what was probably their greatest contribution. For in 1854, on capital largely subscribed by her, the first depôt for the blind was opened in a cellar in Holborn, with Mr. Levy as the general manager. At first, seven blind men were employed in their own homes, working on goods supplied by the depôt; later, women were also found employment. The principle of home-work was what Miss Gilbert really believed in, though later she had to modify this, and allow the store to become a workshop where the blind could work on the premises. Care in selecting workers was, she felt, an integral part of the scheme, as it might be so easily abused by the unworthy; and as it was never self-supporting, she felt it her duty to subscribers to see that their money was well spent. Soon she was faced with the question of finding teachers for the new workers who came to learn brush-making, knitting, basketry and the other trades for which the workshop catered. The teachers had to be paid, and subscriptions were needed to meet the cost. But she was always adamant that they should be blind, on the grounds that they alone knew the needs of the blind. Later opinion differed from that of Miss Gilbert and advocated the use of sighted managers.[1]

The problem of finding employment for the sightless was much larger than this, however, and certainly much larger than that of educating blind children, for most adults who were blind had lost their sight after childhood—one authority suggested thirty-five years as about the average age at which people went blind in the later nineteenth century[2]—Miss Gilbert stated (in 1874 to a C.O.S. Special Committee) that of the 30,000 blind in the United

[1] C.O.S. *Conference on the Blind in York* (1883).
[2] W. J. Ray, *Work among the Blind.*

Kingdom, nine out of ten were over twenty-one years of age. Not all of them were capable of supporting themselves, but of those who were, only about 10 per cent were being dealt with by voluntary societies. Apart from the poor law officers, who could give out-relief and provide training if they thought it desirable, the societies were the sole means of obtaining help and finding employment. The workshops and depôts were only one answer to the problem, and though they were copied in all parts of the country, they could not hope to deal with so complex a situation. Even a later generation, with its variety of social and industrial services for the handicapped, has not been wholly successful in this. In the nineteenth century the principles were laid down, that the blind should be made as independent as possible, and should work with the sighted when it could be arranged. Although the difficulties of getting the right supervision, and of buying and selling in the best market were recognized, it was thought that the workshops should be run on commercial lines, and be self-supporting.

4 *Home Visiting*. While training and employment were the only effective ways of achieving self-respect and independence, the fact that many were aged and had gone blind late in life, or were in poor health and unable to work, made social work in the home of peculiar importance. The need had been recognized as early as 1834, when the 'Indigent Blind Visiting Society' was founded in London. Similar to their work was that of the 'Home Teaching Society' founded in 1855, both kinds of society acting as models for others that were established during the rest of the century in different parts of the country. (There were fifty-three home teaching societies in the British Isles by 1876, and forty-five visiting missions to the blind by 1889).[1] These home teaching and visiting societies were the origin of what is becoming a new branch of social work for the blind.

One of the difficulties was the existence of charities for the dispensation of doles and pensions. In their early years, the visiting societies were active in dole-giving, as it was they who knew where the deserving were to be found, and it was to them that the blind would often make application. The foundation of the C.O.S. in 1869 however, and its vigorous propaganda against indiscriminate money-giving, influenced many blind societies and traces of their

[1] 1889 C.5781–1, xix. Blind, etc., of the United Kingdom. Royal Commission. *Report*, etc., Vol. II, Apps. 2 and 12.

dilemma can be seen in their annual reports. In its 1886 report the 'Home Teaching Society' commented on the fact that some £30,000 annually was distributed in doles and pensions, but 'the Committee are persuaded that there are many disadvantages attendant on the giving of pensions to the young and able-bodied blind. Often a small dole or pension entirely destroys the efforts which the blind might otherwise be induced to make towards self-help'. It is this dilemma—on the one hand of a philanthropic and pitying public giving largely to charitable funds for the blind, and on the other of the societies feeling the need to use the money creatively and constructively—which has never been satisfactorily resolved. But it is clear that the societies in the nineteenth century were very much alive to it; and one proposal to deal with it was to set up a central system of record and information, in order to discourage the giving of small doles to travelling blind who went from agency to agency. There is no evidence, however, that this was ever successfully implemented on a national scale, though the 'Teachers' Society for the Blind' developed the scheme throughout London.

Of the moral effect of sending teachers or visitors to the homes of the blind they were in no doubt. The fact of going blind usually meant despair, while the visitor brought hope, and the knowledge that here was someone with an understanding of their difficulty such as they could not expect to receive from most of their sighted friends. From the learning of Braille or Moon or other techniques of communication they were able to renew their contacts with the world. Or again those sunk in lethargy were stimulated to make an effort for themselves, and thus achieve the sense of purpose that would make life worthwhile.

The development of recreational and other facilities in the home, or if necessary at the mission itself, became an important part of the work, and was one of the major factors in combating the demoralization that can so easily beset the blind, whose own resources have had no chance to grow. In this, the library movement was a vital link. Many of the teaching societies had their own libraries of books in embossed type. The 'Society for Printing and Distributing Books', for instance, had by 1863 produced about a thousand books, which were sold to the blind at a quarter of their cost. It was regretted by some that so large a proportion of the books were purely religious and so few of general information and amusement.[1] But this disparity was redressed as the century advanced.

There was still a strong body of opinion following Miss Gilbert's lead in favour of the idea that home visitors should themselves be blind, even though it meant employing sighted guides to lead them round. There was a difference, it was said, between the workshop manager, who had to carry on a business in a sighted world, and the visitor whose function was to understand and be understood by the blind person in his own home. It was the visitor, himself blind, who was most welcome in the home; and of course this fact created employment for a few of the blind, and had therefore a double advantage.

The religious and spiritual activities of the visiting societies and missions were naturally of great importance, though there was no reason why the blind should not attend church in the ordinary way, if they were able-bodied, or receive spiritual comfort from the pastor. There was no need therefore to develop, as the deaf were doing, special religious services for the blind. Yet many societies, as for instance the 'Association for Promoting the General Welfare of the Blind', founded by Miss Gilbert in 1856, had as one of their chief objects the promotion of the religious welfare of the sightless.

2 THE DEAF

Unlike the blind, the deaf have been slow to evoke general public sympathy. This is largely due to the nature of their defect. For it has to be understood that the real calamity of deafness is their separation from normal human beings through the absence of language and power of communication. Seldom has it been possible, and almost never in the nineteenth century, for the deaf to explain to the world what deafness really means in loneliness, in lack of understanding from the world around them, and in the feelings of suspicion of their fellow men that come from being shut-in upon themselves. Since the ordinary channels of communication are barred, normal people tend to become impatient of the deaf, and fail all too often to understand their difficulties. Furthermore there has been a tendency in this country and in others to rank the deaf and dumb with the insane and the imbecile. How many have been shut away in lunatic asylums we have

[1] *Social Science Review* (1863).

no means of knowing, but right through the nineteenth century the practice persisted, as the 1886 reports of school inspectors in Manchester, etc., showed.[1]

In spite of this public lack of understanding, there were many who developed the work that had been growing since the sixteenth century. In 1526 Cardano, a Professor of the University of Padua, stated that education was possible for deaf mutes, and that because a child had no hearing, it did not mean that he was wanting in intellect or power to learn. A few years later Ponce, a monk in Spain, declared that he would teach the deaf to speak, so that they could say their prayers. It is said that he had a mercenary motive too, as under the law no dumb person was allowed to inherit and the heirs to some Spanish estates being deaf, there was danger to the succession in some cases. Could he therefore induce the heir to speak, even if only a few words, the law would be satisfied, and the future of the estate assured. His success was limited, but there is little doubt that under his guidance his pupils did utter words.[2] In the succeeding centuries several men in different parts of Europe experimented with the education of the deaf, and gradually built up a body of knowledge concerning them. Up to the nineteenth century two men stand out and much of the history of work with the deaf is concerned with the differences that separated them.

Charles Michel de l'Epée began his work as a teacher in Versailles in 1712, and unlike most of his predecessors, who had worked for the wealthy, his primary concern was with the poor. His great contribution was his codification of the 'Sign' language, for he believed that there are two natural methods of communication, speech and signs. If the method of speech is denied through inability to hear and thus to imitate, the deaf must develop the 'sign' method, which depends on sight. To him 'signing' was the best and indeed the only method of teaching the deaf. By 1782 he had entered into correspondence with the second great figure of the eighteenth century, Samuel Heinicke, the German teacher, who contended that if the deaf were to live in ordinary society, they must somehow acquire speech. The way to achieve this, he argued, was to live and learn in the oral atmosphere. Signs were likely to interfere with this, and were a danger to the promotion

---

[1] 1886 C.4747, xxv. Education of the Blind. *School Inspectors' Report.*
[2] K. W. Hodgson, *The Deaf and their Problems* (1953), p. 85.

of speech. Therefore he became the progenitor and active promotor of what has come to be known as the 'Oral method'.[1] Thus by the end of the eighteenth century there were two distinct schools of thought about the true method of deaf teaching, the 'oral' (mainly German in origin) and the 'manual' (mainly of followers of de l'Epée and his pupil Sicard).

A third man is of interest to the British. Thomas Braidwood was born in Edinburgh in 1715, where in due course he opened a school. To this in 1760 was sent a deaf boy, Charles Sherriff, with a request that he should be taught mathematics and whatever else he could learn. From this Braidwood's interest in the deaf grew, and further deaf children came to his Edinburgh school. Later his fame had spread so far that he decided to move south, and in 1783 opened a school for the deaf in London. To this the wealthy sent their deaf children, not only to keep them out of sight for a time, but hoping to make them into social beings of whom they would not be ashamed when they returned. Braidwood was not without his extravagant claims, though he steadfastly refused to divulge his methods, which throughout his life he kept secret. Through the growing interest in Braidwood's work, a 'Society for the Indigent Deaf', founded in London in 1792, opened in Bermondsey a boarding school for the deaf children of the poor, for the society believed that only residential education was likely to effect any real transformation. At the head of it was placed a pupil and relative of Braidwood, Joseph Watson, who published a book on '*The Instruction of the Deaf and Dumb*' in 1806. Now that Braidwood was dead, he was able to break the bonds of secrecy and proclaim with Heinicke the necessity of speech, and how he taught the deaf to acquire language. Though further schools for the poor came into being in different parts of the country, often with a member of the Braidwood or Watson family at the head, the whole-hearted support for the 'oral' system was not always maintained, and 'manual' and 'sign' teaching were introduced from time to time, as for instance at Birmingham. The result was that in 1889 when there were thirty schools, five taught on the 'sign' and 'manual' system alone, seven on the 'oral', while the rest used a combined method.[2]

[1] K. W. Hodgson, *The Deaf and their Problems* (1953), pp. 130 *et seq.*
[2] 1889 C.5781–1, xix. Blind, etc., of the United Kingdom. Royal Commission. *Report*, etc., Vol. II, App. 24.

This controversy on method has reverberated down the years to the present day and shows no signs of abatement. To the outsider, the truth would not seem to lie in the indiscriminate practice of either method. For some children, the purely 'oral' method is apparently both acceptable and successful, while for others the 'sign' and 'manual' methods are much better, and for yet others a combination of methods would appear to achieve the objective. The situation was perhaps best summarized by the well-known discussion before the Philosophical Society of Washington in October 1833.[1] Dr. Alexander Bell argued that the only defect of the person who was deaf and dumb was lack of hearing, that 'sign' language was not any more natural to him than to anyone else, and that he could and should be taught by the 'oral' method, as no other method would give him the grasp of the English tongue, or the ability to read and communicate. To this Mr. E. M. Gallaudet[2] replied that far from those who were deaf and dumb having only one defect, lack of hearing, they might have many. They suffered as other children did from lack of intelligence, of perception, of imitative faculty and the rest. He quoted the Abbé de l'Epée's view that signs were as natural as speech, and the statement by Moritz Hill of Wessenfels, Prussia, that of one hundred hypacusic children taught by the 'oral' method only eleven could converse readily with strangers on ordinary subjects. From this he concluded that while the 'oral' method should not be absent, understanding of language could be given by the 'sign' method, while far more knowledge of the world could be imparted if precious time were not devoted to the effort, often vain, of trying to make the deaf child talk.

Meanwhile, following the example of the 'London Society for the Indigent Deaf', special schools were founded in different parts of the country, and to these boards of guardians could send their deaf children at a charge no greater than the cost in one of their own institutions, so giving them a chance to gain from the specialized

[1] *Ibid.* App. 31. Quoting from Vol. VI of the *Bulletin of the Philosophical Society of Washington.*

[2] Mr. E. M. Gallaudet was the youngest son of Mr. Thos. H. Gallaudet, who had been sent to England to train as a teacher of the deaf in 1815. He had been cold-shouldered by the secrecy of the Braidwoods, and went to France to become a pupil of the Abbé Sicard who had learnt the 'manual' methods from the Abbé de l'Epée. Thus Gallaudet returned to America with a thorough knowledge of these methods; though he and his sons remained interested in the 'oral' ones.

teaching. Unfortunately this power was little used, and many of their deaf children were probably transferred to lunatic asylums, or allowed to remain in their institutions to be the butt of their contemporaries. The creation of the school boards in 1870 provided the turning point, for when schooling for all children became compulsory, the existence of deaf mutes became a pressing problem, especially to some of the larger authorities. In 1891 Lord Lothian obtained an Act, applicable in Scotland, for the compulsory education of these children in institutions away from their area if necessary. Pauper children were, however, specifically excluded. By 1893 a similar Act for England and Wales made school boards responsible for the compulsory education of deaf children between seven and sixteen years, whereas the Act making twelve years the school leaving age for normal children was not passed until 1899. And while the size of a class for a normal child was about sixty, the Royal Commission on *The Blind, Deaf and Dumb*, 1899, had declared that the size of the class in deaf schools should not exceed ten. Thus considerable enlightenment was shown in the education of these handicapped children. School boards frequently evaded their responsibility, however, and parents were not always co-operative, sometimes being reluctant to admit the defect in their children, preferring that they should earn their living if possible.

The development of schools and of special classes in board schools resulted in the emergence of a specialized branch of teaching, with its own training and examinations. By 1885, when the 'College of Teachers of the Deaf and Dumb' was formed, there were three examining bodies, including the 'Fitzroy Square College,' and the 'Ealing College.' This was an important development, for though they were divided by the 'method' controversy, they were at one in their interest in the deaf children. And this interest was not confined to the school room, but extended to the homes from which the children came, that is, to the after-care of their pupils, and to the general questions relating to the cause and effect of deafness. Two professional associations of teachers of the deaf were formed in 1894 and 1895.

The Adult Deaf

Parallel to the schemes developing for the education of deaf children, were others for the welfare of those adult deaf who were not in poor law institutions or asylums. These schemes, some of which were associated with the effort to found and maintain schools, were concerned with trade instruction, employment and the after-care of children on leaving school, homes and pensions for the aged and indigent, and religious missions to the deaf.

1 *Trade Instruction.* Many of the schools, such as those in Doncaster and Hull, felt that industrial training was an important part of their curriculum. As the century advanced, others followed their lead. Still others declared that so long as the deaf were taught to lip-read and to mix with hearing people there was no need for the school to teach a trade, which was far better taught on the job itself under the ordinary apprentice system. In any case, deaf children differed as much as others in their capacities, and the range of trade classes which could be established in schools was limited.

2 *Employment.* Some societies, like the 'Newcastle Institute for the Deaf and Dumb' founded in 1838, not only educated the young, but became almost an employment agency. The Newcastle Institute was particularly successful, as the shipyards of the Tyne and the heavy engineering works of the North East of England provided a ready market for cheap labour, especially as in many of these noisy industries lack of hearing was not a great hardship. In other areas the difficulty was more acute, and practically all the missions and societies founded to help the adult deaf were brought up against the major problem of finding employment. The chief obstacle was the reluctance of employers, who feared that the deaf would be more liable to accident. This objection gained point on the passing of the Workmen's Compensation Act in 1897, which put upon employers the onus of compensating workers who sustained accident at work. So serious was the situation in Oldham that a number of deaf workmen banded themselves together to present a petition to Parliament, praying that the employers of the deaf might be excluded from the operation of the Workmen's Compensation Act.[1] They failed in this, and employers have continued to be chary of employing the deaf. Thus associations, and all who worked for the deaf, had to continue the campaign, to persuade employers that not only are the deaf usually as capable in their work as their hearing comrades, but that they are on the whole no more liable to accident.

[1] K. W. Hodgson, *op. cit.*, p. 253.

3 *Poverty*. It may be readily understood that many of the deaf were in acute poverty during the nineteenth century, and the peculiarity of their position was recognized by the regulations made under the Poor law (Amendment) Act of 1834 which exempted the deaf as well as the blind from the rigorous 'workhouse test' and allowed them to receive out-relief on the basis of the needs of the applicant. In addition a 'Charitable and Provident Society for granting pensions to the Aged Poor and Infirm Deaf and Dumb' was founded in 1836 and operated mainly in London. This was a grant-giving body which led an exiguous existence until 1890, when it was re-formed into the British Deaf and Dumb Association. Others in different parts of the country set out to provide material aid, or homes where the aged and poor deaf could live, such as the 'British Asylum for Deaf and Dumb Females' founded in Clapton in 1851.

4 *Religious Missions to the Deaf.* The attention of those concerned with spiritual welfare was quickly directed to those who by their handicap were unable to take part in ordinary church services. Glasgow and Edinburgh were the earliest cities where organized help was given. By 1840 the former pupils of the Old Kent Road asylum school, for the teaching of the indigent deaf, were meeting together for prayer and worship every Sunday and thus a church for the deaf had come into being in London, with Sam Smith as its first missioner. The movement spread rapidly, especially in the North, and by 1889 there were nineteen centres in England and Wales, and four in Scotland.[1] Their first aim was to bring spiritual aid to the deaf, and to hold religious services. Most were Church of England, but a few were Nonconformist. Some met in private houses, others in school premises, and by 1873 there was a specially built church opened by Queen Victoria in Oxford Street, London.

The missioners soon discovered what the teachers had also learnt, that their work was wider than the purpose that had originally brought them in contact with the deaf. They were led to establish a service for the deaf which covered many other aspects of their lives. Their main concern had always been with the adult deaf, though their advice was often sought by parents, particularly hearing ones who found they had a deaf child, and needed consolation in their plight and information on how best to

---

[1] 1889 C.5781–1, xix. Blind, etc., of the United Kingdom. Royal Commission. *Report*, etc., Vol. II, App. 24.

help the child. Otherwise, as the Royal Commission of 1889 stated, the work was mainly 'visiting, relief, conducting educational classes, religious instruction, spiritual welfare, assisting to find work, giving pecuniary help, and support in old age and infirmity.'[1] This developed into a service which can almost be classed as a specialized branch of social work.

Of the need for education and religious instruction little need be said, nor of the profound comfort the religious services were to people made lonely by their handicap. But what was not mentioned by the Royal Commission was the need for interpretation. The missioners were people with speech and usually with hearing who had learnt to communicate with the deaf through the sign language, and could act as interpreters and become 'the buffer between the deaf and the hearing world'.[2] In any of the myriad mishaps of life, the missioner was at hand. For instance he interpreted in the courts of law; he was in constant demand to interpret the deaf person's difficulties or grievances to the employer, and the employer's true attitude and point of view back to the worker. In their personal relationships the deaf have always been vulnerable to social difficulties, so that here the missioners have tried to disentangle many a confused relationship, and in doing so have performed the function of a social case-worker.

It is clear that many efforts were made to develop an educational service so that the deaf could mix as freely as possible with the hearing; that agencies and individuals were concerned that the deaf should earn their living in ordinary society and on the same terms as normal beings; that the poor should be relieved, the aged and sick cared for, and that no deaf person should remain misunderstood or unheard through lack of interpretation. But it is only in the twentieth century that a concern for the whole life of the deaf has emerged as a specialized branch of social work for the handicapped.

3 THE MENTALLY DEFECTIVE, INSANE AND EPILEPTIC

Mentally defective, insane and epileptic persons suffer from very different disabilities, but during a great part of the nineteenth century neither work on their behalf nor the law relating to them

[1] 1889 C.5781, xix, *op. cit.*
[2] A. F. C. Bourdillon, *Voluntary Social Services* (1944), Cap. V.

always made these sharp distinctions. Social case work with such sufferers while they were living in their own homes did not develop rapidly, and the care envisaged was mainly of an institutional character. An exception was the provision for paupers living at home with their friends, but receiving out-relief under the 1834 Poor Law Act in the same way as other handicapped persons. These were visited from time to time by the Medical Officers to the boards of guardians, and reports on their physical and mental improvement, or otherwise, were made.[1] As the Medical Officers were not paid for this service, the boards could not demand reports, which were sometimes not written at all, and were often only perfunctory.

The institutions were either educational or for safety, the latter being mainly the lunatic asylums, maintained by local rates, where little if any social work was done. A government report in 1860 discusses the opportunities and improvements in some of them[2] and there is no doubt that by the middle of the century a strong urge to 'cure' insanity had appeared. It was suggested that a large percentage of the insane could be cured if a patient had asylum treatment in the early stages. However, though experiments of this nature were being made, asylums continued to be mainly places of safe keeping, and in any case the social implications of insanity and defect were not considered.

The provision of education for children and young people either mentally defective or epileptic did show some response to the social needs of this particular type of handicap. The boards of guardians had the power under the 1862 Act to maintain in special schools feeble minded children (not idiots or imbeciles) of parents unable to pay. By 1891 the power was extended to include maintenance in voluntary homes and by 1899 school boards had taken over responsibility for this and for the education of epileptics. Meanwhile the charitably minded had not been idle, and by the end of the century there were six schools for the education of defectives, though the fees charged were sometimes fairly high, and six special homes for girls, financed partly by the boards of guardians who used them, and partly from voluntary subscriptions. Here instruction was given in manual occupations and in

---

[1] 1860 (2675), xxxvii. Poor Law Board. *12th Annual Report*, 1859–60.
[2] 1860 (495), xxii. Care and Treatment of Lunatics. Select Committee. *Report*, etc., App. 1.

some reading and writing.[1] Further, there were ten institutes for the care of idiots and imbeciles. In these, as in the Earlswood Common Home founded in 1853, manual trades like handicrafts and light farm work were taught to men, and laundry and household work to women. Instruction was 'mingled with games in a judicious way', so that games like shop-keeping would teach the value of money, weight of articles, etc.[2] It was generally agreed that for such institutions to be effective they should be organized in small groups. Miss Cooper, of the 'National Association for Promoting the Welfare of the Feeble Minded', suggested to the Departmental Committee in 1898 that units of fewer than twenty were the desirable size. The same plea was echoed by Mr. Nicholls, Chairman of the 'National Society for the employment of Epileptics' (founded 1894). In suggesting that epileptics who were badly afflicted should go into a colony, he advocated that they should live in small units, work at the trade they liked best, play games and lead as normal a life as possible.[3]

As in all other work among the handicapped, opinion was moving in the direction of keeping the mentally defective and deranged in ordinary society. What was not happening, however, was a parallel movement to develop home visiting and social welfare work. And though many case work societies must have been dealing with this type of handicapped person, all too many found their way into the workhouses, where as the 1889 Report pathetically described them, 'they just sit in a row all day'.[4]

4 CRIPPLES

Information about work among the orthopaedically deformed and handicapped is remarkably scanty, considering the incidence of 'crippling' in the population. Government reports and other literature have stressed the way accidents, particularly in factories and mines, led to deformity, and we now know that insufficiency in the diet and various diseases were responsible for rickets and other malformations. Yet, little seems to have been done by the

[1] 1898 C.8747, xxvi. *Defective and Epileptic Children*, pp. 145–59.
[2] *Social Science Review*, 1862, p. 107.
[3] 1898 C.8747, xxvi. Defective and Epileptic Children. Departmental Committee. *Minutes of Evidence*, qq. 3293 *et seq.*
[4] 1889 C.5781, xix. Blind, Deaf and Dumb, etc., of the United Kingdom. Royal Commission. *Report*, etc.

philanthropically-minded for those who through their inheritance or their environment were unable to lead a normal life, and were often condemned to remain dependent on others. Some became beggars, and the workhouses must have contained a large number, but of the thousands of cripples who were in the ordinary population there is very little information. There was no government report of any kind which considered the needs, either general or particular, of this kind of handicap. Even the schooling of children, which one would have expected to attract official attention, appears to have been ignored and while school boards all over the country were struggling to provide instruction for the blind and deaf, it was not until 1901 that the London school board opened its first day-school for cripples.

In spite of this curious silence there can be no doubt that the paralyzed and lame not only roused pity, but became the objects of much good work by the visiting societies, the C.O.S., the religious bodies and the charitably minded. But there was no propaganda about their need for independence, or the ways it could be achieved, and few facilities were available to look after their spiritual needs or their physical and mental development. The state of medical knowledge may have been partly responsible, for in spite of the pioneer work of Dupuytrew and Delpech on the Continent, and of W. J. Little, H. O. Thomas and Sir Robert Jones in Britain, our scientific knowledge of the causes and treatment of orthopaedic handicap was then only in its early stages. Some work among the crippled did develop, however, though it was usually entirely local in scope, and took broadly four forms: (1) medical, (2) residential, (3) educational and (4) charitable (in the sense of providing for the recreational and material needs of cripples living at home).

1   The first orthopaedic clinic was started in Geneva in 1780, and later centres were opened in Montpellier (*circa* 1820), Bavaria (1832), New York (1863). But in England the real pioneer work was done by William John Little, himself a cripple, who qualified as a doctor and began to specialize in deformities of the foot. His book published in 1839 on this subject was to have a profound effect on all medical thinking and practice, as did his later works on other orthopaedic matters. Largely due to his influence what came to be called the Royal National Orthopaedic Hospital was founded in London in 1838-40. Though it was not the first of

such hospitals (Birmingham claims to have founded one in 1817), it had much influence, and many general hospitals, including St. Bartholomew's, developed orthopaedic departments inspired by Little's work. Subsequently other specialist hospitals were founded in London and the Provinces (particularly in Liverpool where Hugh Owen Thomas, inventor of the Thomas splint, opened an orthopaedic clinic in 1870, and Sir Robert Jones was put in charge of the newly formed Heswall branch of the Royal Liverpool Children's Hospital in 1899). Thus by the end of the century some of the medical aspects of deformity were well understood, and a beginning had been made in a few centres to develop the use of manipulation and of special exercises like swimming, and to advocate rest and splinting for certain conditions. The greatest developments on the medical side have however occurred in the twentieth century, and it is perhaps significant that 1900 saw the foundation of the Baschurch centre for cripples (later the Oswestry Orthopaedic Hospital) by Dame Agnes Hunt.

2   While hospitals of this kind may in a sense be considered a residential aspect of work among cripples, the various holiday homes and refuges had a wider purpose than the cure and study of a physical condition. They were concerned with social and material difficulties as much as with medical ones, and though many were originally founded to relieve distress among poor and neglected children, they were often forced to devote special facilities to cripples because the need was so manifest. Among these were Winchmore Hill Cripples' Home and Industrial School for Girls (1851), the Wright's Lane Home for Cripple Boys (1865), and the Boys' and Girls' Refuges and Homes founded in Manchester in 1870. The Manchester Refuges[1] came to develop their cripples' section because so many cripple children were discovered in the squalid slums of Manchester and Salford by the visitors of the society. Existing Homes were unsuitable, and many children had to be refused admittance because their physical disabilities were so severe. Accordingly in 1890 the 'Bethesda Home for Crippled and Incurable Children', Cheetham Hill, was opened. It had thirty-five beds, and it housed patients who might respond to medical treatment and thus be cured sufficiently to return

---

[1] Information about the early history of the Manchester Refuges has been kindly supplied to the authors by Mr. R. E. Hughes, the Secretary of the Society.

home, or those who might be able to lead a fairly satisfying life under constant treatment, or incurables who were taken in for their terminal illness. The staffing of the Home was necessarily by skilled and trained nurses because of the immediate condition of the children, but the Home was not intended for medical purposes alone. It concerned itself with the wider aspects of a child's development including character-training through Christian teaching and influence, and ordinary schooling. Evidence is scanty about the early schooling in the Bethesda Home, though case-papers suggest that the founders realized the need of bringing the school to the children, and supplied teachers from voluntary sources until the local authority took over in the twentieth century. Education was not confined to the ordinary school subjects, as children were given some training in a skill if they were suitable. Thus girls were taught needlework, and were often able to earn their living in this way, when they left the Refuge. Boys were taught trades of various kinds, particularly tailoring, where the needle was found to demand less physical effort than the tools of carpentry and other skills. When the child left the Home effort was made to find him a job, and to keep in touch with him, though no articulate scheme of after-care was developed; nor was there any system of 'home industry.' In London the most active society concerning itself with the residential care of cripples was the Ragged Schools' Union, later (1894) to be re-named the Shaftesbury Society. To this in 1869 the authoress 'A.L.O.E.' gave her cottage in Sutton where cripple children could go for a holiday. Later other holiday homes were opened, some after 1890 being specially designed for the purpose. It was but a short step from this to the establishment of convalescent and treatment homes, and by the 'nineties many children were beginning to be cured. For instance at the Southend Home an utterly helpless girl had been admitted, and the Home's honorary surgeon, Dr. Clough Waters, determined to operate on her; presently she was able to walk on crutches, and before long without any aid at all. Or again, another little girl was sent to the Margate Home in a 'cage jacket'. Within a few weeks she too was able to run about. On one occasion Queen Victoria visited the People's Palace in London, and among the children was a little boy lying on three chairs He too was sent to one of the holiday homes, and within a year was attending school like any other normal child. All this, it was said, was due to 'nourishing food, fresh air, sea baths, exercise and the joyous atmosphere of the Homes'.[1] This work, though of great value, was in no way comparable to that of the Manchester Refuges, and was intended for short-stay recuperation, rather than the rehabilitation of the whole body and character of the crippled child. Other examples of residential care for the physically handicapped are relatively rare and it is clear that this type of social provision had not been much developed until the twentieth century.

3 We have seen how experiments in adapting education to the needs of the child were being made in the Manchester Refuge, and it is known that the first hospital school in the country was established in 1892 by the Royal National Orthopaedic Hospital in London, yet no effort to provide special schools for crippled children living in the ordinary population came until the late 'nineties when Mrs. Humphrey Ward began her campaign in London. Due largely to her efforts, a voluntary school was opened in 1898 which received rate aid from the London School Board in the following year (under the Education Act of 1899 which gave such power to school boards). At the school meals were provided as well as teaching and a small charge to the parents was made. The effort to provide special schools for cripples did not go unchallenged, as many, particularly the Medical Officers of Health,[2] thought the best arrangement would be to educate the physically and mentally handicapped together. Apart from London there is no record of special educational facilities for the crippled child living in his own home until after 1900, when many experiments began to be made elsewhere.

4 Even about miscellaneous charitable efforts for the orthopaedically handicapped very little evidence is available. The one exception is the work done by the Ragged Schools' Union in London. In the early days this took the form of 'treats', particularly the annual 'day in the country' for city children, and especially crippled ones. Treats were to remain important and when Arthur Pearson began to interest himself after 1892, the 'Fresh Air Fund' became a useful means of financing what must have been a red-letter day in the dull and monotonous lives of these children. By 1895, in answer to some moving articles in the Daily

[1] J. Stuart, *Mr. John Kirk, the Children's Friend* (1907), p. 77.
[2] Mrs. G. M. Trevelyan, 'Mrs. Humphrey Ward,' *The Cripple*, 1928–30.

Telegraph, it was decided to hold a Christmas banquet for crippled children in the Guildhall, London. For this the co-operation of Alderman William Treloar (later Lord Mayor Treloar, the founder of the famous orthopaedic hospital at Alton, Hampshire) was sought; and what had started as a modest venture became an annual treat, in which thousands of crippled children in London either came to the banquet, or were sent hampers of Christmas fare. Another aspect of the 'treat' idea was the formation in 1895 of the 'Christmas Guest Guild', in which about five hundred crippled children were invited by the well-to-do to spend Christmas with them.

By the early 'nineties, the R.S.U. had opened a 'Cripples' Department' at its headquarters, with full-time paid staff, and with a variety of different items in its programme. One of the interesting and valuable contributions of this department was its register of crippled children in London, and in 1895 some six to seven thousand names had been entered, the list being lengthened every year as more people heard about what was being done. It was useful as a basis for another activity of the department, the visiting of crippled children in their homes by voluntary workers. Between 1894 and 1897 upwards of a thousand men and women offered to do this work, the whole of London being divided territorially amongst them. Their task was primarily to bring religious teaching to those who would otherwise lack it; but visiting quickly uncovered other needs, such as the distressing loneliness of house-bound cripples, lack of surgical aids, and in many cases of proper clothing. To combat loneliness, the 'White Dove League' in North London was founded by a band of workers who agreed to devote all their spare time to the help of cripples. The 'Crutch and Kindness League' developed a system of pen friends, and obtained volunteers from all over the world as well as from the home country. Where surgical boots or spinal carriages or similar aids were not available elsewhere, the cripples department set out to supply them. The families of the cripples were expected to contribute if they could, and in any case the 'aids' were on loan if possible, a receipt being signed by the parent or guardian to produce the articles on demand; this was in order to prevent their pawn or sale. Clothes were also carefully collected and distributed by the department, whole rooms at headquarters being taken up with storage. No application for clothing was considered without the counter-signature of an agent of the R.S.U., or a subscriber, who guaranteed personal knowledge of the child's circumstances and need. Already in 1892 the 'Guild of Good Samaritans' had been formed to organize working parties to make garments for crippled children. And in 1895 the 'League of Hearts and Hands' was started among the children of the well-to-do, who each guaranteed to make at least two garments a year for crippled children.

While this work, some of it admittedly sentimental and ephemeral in nature, took up much of the time of the full-time organizers, they did not neglect another aspect of the work, the need for companionship among the cripples themselves. In different parts of London clubs for cripples, 'Cripples Parlours'; and other means of bringing them together were explored. Many of them had weekly meetings where all kinds of pastimes were introduced. Particularly valuable were the choirs, some of which became quite well-known. Handicrafts such as rug-making, fretwork and lace-making were also popular. Should children show special aptitude they were sometimes apprenticed; employers in such trades as printing, saddlery, bookbinding and cobbling were often willing to accept them. Indeed, the finding of employment for these children quickly came to take an important place in the programme of the Shaftesbury Society, though apart from the cases where apprenticeship was possible, the opportunities were often limited to the traditional 'ragged school' trades of boot-blacks, boy messengers, house-boys, and rag collecting.

CONCLUSION

Few aspects of the lives of the handicapped are divorced from their disability; their need is to accept it both intellectually and emotionally, and to overcome it as far as possible. What began in the middle of the nineteenth century was a revolution in attitude from one of hopelessness to one in which the aim should be to integrate the handicapped into society, and make people aware of their responsibility to accept those with some defect, as far as possible, as equals and colleagues. Continuous propaganda about the potentialities of the handicapped was just as much part of the function of the social worker, as the face-to-face relationship which taught them Braille, or how to speak, or helped them to find jobs or tried to disentangle some of the social and emotional difficulties.

Because each class of handicapped person had to be fought for separately there grew up distinct services for each, and distinct groups of workers with their own training, skill and function. In spite of this separation, as a review of their work suggests, the workers for the handicapped are trying fundamentally to do the same thing. Their skill, and the scope of their work being so similar, suggests that a common training might be to their advantage. Specialized knowledge concerning the kind of defect and its psychological implications for the sufferer would seem to be necessary according to the branch of work chosen and might be superimposed upon the basic training. But the isolation of the last century, understandable though it was, was ceasing to be valuable even before 1900.

CHAPTER 11

MORAL WELFARE

THOUGH the earliest known home for 'the fallen' was begun in the eighteenth century, the branch of social work we call 'moral welfare' owes its existence to the field work and propaganda of a few idealists, and to the impact on the public mind of the scandals they laid bare. For the struggles to repeal the Contagious Diseases Acts, and to raise the low age of consent, with which 'white slavery' was intimately concerned, have meant that in probably no other field have social work and social reform been so closely intertwined. The pressure of events and the test of experience suggested that if immorality were to decline the attack should come from two quarters, field rescue work and residential training, and that both sexes required 'rescue'.

I CONTAGIOUS DISEASES ACTS

The *Contagious Diseases Acts* of 1866–9 were essentially public health measures and typical of the powerful hygienic drive then apparent in this country. They stated that if a woman living within fifteen miles of a garrison town should be designated by the police as a prostitute, she must sign a form agreeing to be medically examined by the police surgeon once a fortnight. Should she be found to be infected, she was obliged to go to the Lock, or any other hospital (often the prison one), for treatment, until she was cured. If she did not sign this 'voluntary submission', she was to appear before a magistrate to prove she was not a prostitute.

The person most closely associated with the campaign against these measures was Mrs. Josephine Butler. Born in 1828 in Rilston, Northumberland, the daughter of Mr. John Grey, she married in 1852 Mr. George Butler, who having entered Holy Orders after his marriage, subsequently settled in Oxford. They moved to Cheltenham when Mr. Butler became Vice-Principal of Chelten-

207

ham College in 1857, and nine years later to Liverpool when he became Principal of Liverpool College. It was in Liverpool that Josephine's work for 'moral purity' began. Many years earlier, in late adolescence, like Florence Nightingale, she had suffered long periods of acute depression, a state which temporarily returned to her on the tragic death of her daughter Evangeline. 'I became possessed with an irresistible desire to go forth and find some pain keener than my own,' she wrote, 'as my heart ached night and day. I had no clear idea beyond that, no plan for helping others . . . My sole wish was to say to afflicted people, "I understand: I too have suffered." '[1] It was under this impetus she began, in the oakum sheds of Liverpool workhouse, her campaign for moral purity and for the abolition of the degrading Contagious Diseases law. She wrote articles and pamphlets, and addressed meetings of protest in which her eloquence was deepened by her sincerity and feeling. Sometimes she was received sympathetically, at others with ignominy and even with actual violence. Her chief arguments against the Acts were the degradation imposed on women and the complete neglect of the responsibility by men for moral and physical standards. She advocated the abolition of the double sex standard, and the substitution of a degree of moral purity in both sexes that would raise men and women above the moral and physical dangers which abounded. Though she was joined by a notable band of supporters, including the great journalist, W. T. Stead, it took many years of unremitting effort, before the Acts were repealed in 1886. She then turned her attention to other sides of her campaign, including work for moral purity in many European countries.

2 WHITE SLAVERY

Meanwhile the existence of juvenile prostitution at an incredibly tender age, even as early as ten, and sometimes at three years old,[2] had been made plain to various workers, particularly those of the Salvation Army. This, along with a traffic in young girls, decided Bramwell Booth in the year 1885 to try to collect real evidence to present to Parliament and the public about the evils arising out of the low age of consent and the so-called 'white slave traffic' that

[1] G. W. and L. A. Johnson, *Autobiographical Memoir of Josephine Butler* (1909).
[2] M. Unsworth, *Maiden Tribute* (1949).

accompanied it. He had been made aware of the situation through his wife whose work in the 'Salvation Army Refuge' had opened her eyes to such things. As it happened, in the year 1884 there had appeared at the door of the refuge a girl of about seventeen, wearing a red silk dress. She had come up from the country to London, she said, and there had met a very nice lady, who had introduced her to a friend. They had gone with the lady, and the girl found herself virtually imprisoned. Attempts were made to seduce her, but finally she escaped to the Salvation Army, whose address she had found on the back of a hymn book she had brought with her. The story was hard to believe, but there was the girl, in a dress so very unlike any a mistress would give to a servant, that they felt it worth-while following up her tale. They called at the address the girl gave them, and though at first blank looks met them, the people in the house finally agreed they knew the girl, and in fact did return her box. It was not long before the Booths got in touch with Josephine Butler, who in 1881 had already presented a petition to the Secretary of State to make 'such changes in English law as shall make it impossible for any young girl or child in our country to be deprived of her liberty by fraud or force, and to be kept in a foreign city in bondage for the basest purposes'.[1] She was therefore very willing to co-operate with the Salvation Army in their task of unearthing evidence that would make the government take action.

The story of how this was done was daring and dramatic, and must have lived in the memories of those who read the poignant accounts in their daily papers. To help them Booth and his friends enlisted the services of two persons of very different origin, but of one mind on moral purity. They were Mr. W. T. Stead and Miss Rebecca Jarrett. Stead is remembered by a younger generation as the great journalist who was drowned on the *Titanic*, and by an older one for his graphic writings on many subjects, including the purity campaign, when editor of the *Pall Mall Gazette*. Rebecca Jarrett was born in Pimlico, the thirteenth child of dissolute parents. When she was about twelve, her mother began taking her to Cremorne Gardens (Chelsea) for immoral purposes. A tall good-looking girl, it was not long before she had all the money she wanted. The men paid her mother, and Rebecca accepted the situation. When she was fifteen one of her

[1] M. Unsworth, *Maiden Tribute* (Salvationist Pub., 1949), p. 16.

brothers returned from sea, and discovering what she was, locked her out of the home. Whereupon she went to a procureur she already knew, who readily gave her accommodation; and by the time she was sixteen she was managing the whole brothel. Thus it went on till she was thirty-six, when her health began to break. She went away for a change and happening to attend a Salvation Army meeting, was influenced by some of the Sisters, and taken back by them to London to be nursed back to health. Later she joined the Butlers, who by this time had moved to Winchester, and helped Josephine to set up a small rescue home. It was from here she was called to help in the plan for collecting evidence on 'White Slavery'.

The plan was that Rebecca, whose past experience left her nothing to learn in these matters, should arrange to buy a young girl and pass her on to Stead, who was to impersonate an elderly debauchee, and take her to a brothel on the Continent. Thus in a street near her old haunts in 1885, where she had seen poor children running about, she paid the sum of £2 over to a woman for a pretty child of thirteen, named Eliza Armstrong. 'The mother did not ask me what for,' recalled Rebecca, 'nor where I was going to take her, nor even when she would see her again. Before I could say another word, after I had given her the money, she was in the public house, drinking.'[1] The child was taken to a well-known brothel, where Stead had engaged a room, and where he stayed alone talking to her for an hour or two. Then Rebecca and another woman officer of the Salvation Army called for Eliza, and took her to a doctor, who examined her and certified her unharmed. She was put on the boat train and accompanied to Paris. Thus the case was proved up to the hilt. For although Eliza received no whit of harm it was shown to be possible for a pro-curess to buy a child for money, bring her to a house of ill-fame, leave her with a man she had never seen before, and send her off to the Continent where nothing more need be heard of her. Stead wrote a moving article about it, and so incensed was public opinion, that a Bill raising the age of consent to sixteen was intro-duced into Parliament and quickly became law. There is a some-what sour postscript to this campaign. For hardly had the echoes of the victory died down, when Stead and Rebecca Jarrett were sentenced to three months' and six months' imprisonment for

[1] M. Unsworth, *Maiden Tribute*, pp. 29–30.

procuring a child for immoral purposes (under an Act of 1861, that had been to all intents and purposes a dead letter up to that time).

3 WHITE CROSS LEAGUE

The other aspect of social reform, less dramatic, but just as important as the protection of young girls, was the crusade for the protection of young men. Ellice Hopkins was most closely associated with this, though she was helped by innumerable men and women who also realized the need. Born in Cambridge in 1836, the youngest child of William Hopkins, mathematician and tutor at St. Peter's College, Ellice was a delicate child and suffered much ill-health throughout her life. When she felt stronger she helped in a Sunday School, and later began to visit a 'Working Men's Club' in Cambridge, where her powers of oratory attracted attention. She was a prolific writer and a profoundly religious woman. From 1866 she began visiting Brighton for her health, and there came in touch with several people interested in social work (such as Mrs. Vicars who conducted rescue work for 'fallen women' and Miss Sarah Robinson, founder of the 'Portsmouth Soldiers' Home'). But it was Dr. James Hinton, a world-famous aurist, whom she met in about 1872, who opened her eyes to the demoralization of many women and the need for moral purity in men to prevent this degradation. As a result she toured the country preaching the need for moral purity, and helping to found hostels and clubs to protect girls, and associations for the rescue of the 'fallen'. Though this was important, she is best known for her work among men, and as a founder with Bishop Lightfoot, Bishop of Durham, of the 'White Cross Society' in 1883. Four years earlier, in 1879, partly through her influence, the Church of England had begun discussing the whole problem, and in the course of time formed the 'Church of England Purity Society' to undertake education and preventive work among young men in the parishes. Meanwhile in February 1883, Ellice Hopkins had arranged to address a miners' meeting in Bishop Auckland, Co. Durham, as part of her personal campaign for moral purity. So telling was her discourse, so compelling her style, that some one hundred and fifty miners came forward and signed the five rules she had expounded, thus becoming the founder members of the society. The rules were: (1) To treat all women with respect, and endeavour to protect them from wrong and degradation. (2) To endeavour to put down all indecent language and coarse jests. (3) To maintain the law of purity as equally binding upon men and women. (4) To endeavour to spread these principles and to try to help younger men. (5) To use every possible means to fulfil the command, 'Keep thyself pure.' At first the 'White Cross Society' was confined to the Durham Diocese, but later it became inter-denominational, and extended over the whole country, and to countries abroad. For a time it co-operated with the 'Purity Society', an arrangement that became so close that in 1891 they assumed the joint title of 'White Cross League', and the connexion with the Church of England was strengthened. Though it was never a major social movement, it certainly exercised considerable influence, and guaranteed that preventive and rescue work among men would be an important aspect of the Church of England Moral Welfare Council, by which it was absorbed in 1939.

The survey of these three aspects of social reform provides a vivid background, against which the unending work of 'rescue' and 'training' may be set. For it has to be admitted that moral welfare workers in those days were mainly concerned with the rehabilitation of the 'immoral' and less with 'prevention' than their modern counterparts would be. Prevention, they doubtless felt, was the concern of all, whilst trying to 'raise the fallen' was work they alone were trained to do.

4 RESCUE

It is convenient to examine the methods these workers used in trying to persuade the most degraded or the sorely tempted to leave the life of 'sin'. Josephine Butler was possibly the first to envisage the method of dealing with them. In 1866, on being permitted to visit the huge workhouse in Liverpool, she made her way to the bare unfurnished cellars set aside for the less tractable women. These were the 'oakum sheds'. 'I sat on the floor and picked oakum among the women,' she wrote. 'They laughed at me, but while they laughed we became friends.'[1] Thereafter she read to them, and prayed with them. They were not easy to deal with, many being there for their habits of fighting and brawling, though they had 'good stuff in them'. Others were, humanly

[1] G. W. and L. A. Johnson, *op. cit.*, p. 59.

speaking, useless—'not quite all there, poor limp fibreless human weeds'. These were the most difficult to deal with, as there was so little to build upon. In her own home she had a dry cellar and some attics, and to those she took as many friendless girls as she could, provided they wanted to go, and were ready to co-operate in making a fresh start. Here she fed, nursed and befriended them. From here she helped them to get work, or to return to their parents, or to set up homes of their own. When, years later, she was to be reviled and accused of treating the girls cruelly, she replied

‘ "Into our house I have received, with my husband's joyful consent, one after another of these my fallen sisters. We have given them in the hour of trouble, sickness and death the best that our house could afford. . . . I have nursed poor outcasts filled with disease, and have loved them as if they had been my own sisters. Many have died in my arms." ’ [1]

At the time this work was developing in Liverpool, William Booth had withdrawn from the 'Methodist New Connexion', of which he was a member and preacher, and established a Christian Mission in Whitechapel. Here, from 1865 onwards, he combined evangelism with rudimentary relief work. By 1878 the name had been changed to the 'Salvation Army'. From the beginning of the mission Catherine Booth, his wife, had been concerned with the problem of the double sex standard, as well as with 'the attitude of those who, in their very efforts to raise the fallen, treated them rather with suspicion and pity than with confidence and love'.[2] Together they had tried to provide a shelter for the girls, but at first the project failed. Nevertheless they persevered, for as the work of the Salvation Army was always in the poorer parts of big towns, the sin and misery associated with prostitution was inevitably their concern, and they realized, that if the women officers of the Army were to do constructive work in this sphere, they must have some preparation for it. Accordingly in 1880 Catherine Booth opened a training home for the women workers where they were instructed in: (a) 'Matters of the heart', i.e. on the basic truths found in the Scriptures. Each cadet was given private counselling where she had an opportunity to search her

[1] M. G. Fawcett and E. M. Turner, *Josephine Butler* (Association of Moral and Social Hygiene, 1928).
[2] M. Unsworth, *op. cit.*, p. 3.

heart and confess her faults. (*b*) 'Matters of the head', including elementary education. (*c*) 'Matters of the Army', which embraced the methods and principles of the Army, and included practical field work, like open air meetings and marches, house-to-house visitation, hunting-up of drunkards, and rescue work among the 'fallen'.[1]

They found, as did Josephine Butler, that immorality and intemperance went hand in hand. Much temperance work, such as that of the Church of England Temperance Society, was 'rescue' work. In 1884, however, the Salvation Army in Glasgow revived a method popular in earlier years, the 'Midnight Patrol', where women workers mingled with the crowds on the busy streets late at night, and made a direct appeal to women, particularly the newcomers and the young. By 1887 the method was widely used in London and other big cities. With them at times went the brass band, and while the bandsmen paraded down the middle of the road, the women workers were diligently mingling with the crowds on the pavement. Besides persuasion, they invited whoever would come to the 'Midnight Meetings' with suppers mixed with evangelical discourses, and calls to the penitence form. Hardly a night passed without two hundred or more taking advantage of the invitation. Some remained to seek comfort after the rest had gone. The overriding objective, in William Booth's own words, was 'to sweep the gutters and seek the lowest', and to offer material comfort and spiritual hope. While this method was scorned by the C.O.S., there is no doubt some were saved by it, and turned to a more moral way of living.

Equally important was the work of Wilson Carlile and his sister through the branch of the Church of England, known as the 'Church Army'. Carlile, who had been a successful business man up to the Franco-Prussian war when his trade in French silks came to an end, fell under the influence of the Evangelists, Moody and Sankey, and decided to devote the rest of his life to the furtherance of religion. He took Orders, without any formal training, and thereafter pursued a vigorous crusade, mainly in the open air, all over the country. It was a hard life and a strenuous one, but though he had been a delicate child he lived till he was ninety-five years old and was active until his death in 1942. Like William Booth, he believed in taking religion to the gutters, and in so

[1] W. Booth, *Life of William Booth*, Vol. III, p. 88.

doing encountered the same problems of poverty, misery and depravity. To meet the challenge, he organized a band of lay missioners, both men and women, and developed a training for them which included, as well as Bible knowledge, the more practical techniques of how to gather a crowd, how to visit, how to render first aid, and some general information on social questions. His first training-home for men was opened in 1883 at St. Aldgates, Oxford, and for women in 1889, in a house in the Edgware Road, London. The special interest of the women's training lay in the lectures on social work given by representatives of the Charity Organization Society, and the period spent in hospital learning the rudiments of nursing. Like the Salvationists the women missioners adopted the policy of the direct approach, and by selling Church Army gazettes in the public houses they made contact with the women they hoped to help, and by parading the streets at night they took advantage of any opportunities there might be to rescue the fallen, or prevent the weak from succumbing. By 1891 a labour home for women had been started, where domestic subjects such as laundry and needlework were taught, in an effort to create a feeling of self-respect, and to provide some training for women who might want to 'take a place'.

In various parts of the country, and usually associated with a 'Home' or 'Penitentiary' there had been formed 'Preventive and Rescue Associations', which maintained a few 'outdoor workers' to work for moral purity and to rescue the 'fallen'. Some evidence about their methods has fortunately been left to us in two books published in the last quarter of the century giving hints on rescue work by the Rev. Arthur Brinckman and the Rev. Arthur Maddison.[1] The duties of the outdoor workers were, they said, to patrol the streets, particularly at night, in order to get to know the girls by sight and the places where they lodged; to speak to a girl if it seemed desirable and the girl were alone, telling her that the worker was ready to be a friend if wanted; and to follow up these cases and others heard of in the course of the conversation. Each worker was supplied with pamphlets and small books, such as *If I had only heeded* or *The Message of the Snowdrops*, to hand to such girls as might be persuaded to read them. The workers were also expected to visit workhouses and infirmaries and to co-operate

[1] Arthur Brinckman, *Notes on Rescue Work* (1885); and Arthur Maddison, *Hints on Rescue Work.*

with prison visitors, police court missioners and any others working with 'girls in danger'.

It is possible that their main work was of an exploratory nature rather than sustained case work in the girls' own homes. For though the 'Hints on Rescue' suggested that in those cases where a girl would return to her friends, or was sincerely attached to a man and wanted to marry him, the workers should help her, the main details of the books were concerned with how to persuade a girl to leave her evil surroundings, and having done so how best to rehabilitate her when she had entered a Home. Thus while detailed advice was given on how to approach women in the streets, what to do and what to guard against if visiting them in a brothel, or in lodgings; how useless it was to speak to a woman if she was drunk, or with others, or in a crowded street; and how valueless most of the 'midnight suppers' had proved to be; no hints were given about helping a girl to adjust herself to her family, or about giving her strength and support when she was struggling to keep a job that was monotonous and hard, while the glitter and easy money of the streets were tempting her. On the contrary, it is clear from both works that they did not believe reform could come except by a long period of re-education in a Home, and that it was the duty of the rescue worker to try to persuade a girl to submit to this process while in no way glamorizing or misrepresenting to her what it involved. They did not underestimate the difficulty of the 'Outdoor Worker's' duties, or the need for a careful selection of the right women to perform them.

Meanwhile in about 1890 the Diocese of London was beginning to feel that there was need for more organized co-operation in the fight against immorality, and this resulted in the appointment of an organizing secretary to develop 'rescue' work. The lead was closely followed by similar action in the neighbouring dioceses of Rochester and Winchester, and by 1913 there were enough organizing secretaries for Mrs. Davidson to invite them to a conference at Lambeth Palace. This she repeated from time to time during World War I, until by 1917 an Archbishop's Advisory Board was established which in 1939 became the Church of England Moral Welfare Council. Thus the Church of England moral welfare workers, who are the backbone of this branch of social work today, did not make their appearance in the field as a separately organized body until the twentieth century.

5 HOMES

Individual rescue work was seldom sufficient, and most workers, sooner rather than later, found it necessary to provide residential accommodation for either temporary or long-stay cases. We have seen how Mrs. Josephine Butler in 1866 used her own home as a temporary shelter for those in need, how Miss Carlile used the labour home as an adjunct to the work of the Church Army sisters, and how Mrs. Catherine Booth in 1868 tried in vain to set up a refuge for girls. Similarly years later, in 1881, Mrs. Cottrill, a leading member of the Salvation Army, determined to take home one of these friendless women. 'The girl was amazed to be allowed into a respectable home,'[1] and was so grateful for the chance she was being given, that Mrs. Cottrill thought that if one girl were sick of the life there might be others, and set about to invite girls to come to her for help. This led to the establishment of the Hanbury Street refuge three years later. Meanwhile Glasgow and other towns were establishing similar short-stay homes under Salvation Army auspices.

Though shelters and temporary refuges were making their appearance in the latter part of the century, the long-stay home was much older. The first 'Foundling Hospital' was founded in 1739 by Thomas Coram, but this was for abandoned children only. The first 'Magdalen Hospital' for unmarried mothers came in about 1758. A pamphlet setting out the need for a *'Place of Reception for Penitent Prostitutes'* was published by Robert Dingley in 1758. His plan was to establish an institution to be called 'the Magdalen Charity House', to which those who petitioned might enter, and become apprenticed to the matron for seven years. Patients were to have their names changed, wear dark uniforms, sleep in separate beds in wards of not more than twelve.

Each shall take her turn in watching throughout the night and traversing the ward at least once every hour. . . . The objects in general shall be clothed and fed meanly, though with cleanly and healthful provision. Each is to work according to her ability, and have half the Benefit accruing from her Labour and ingenuity, part whereof to be deposited in the Committee's hands for her benefit when dismissed on proper behaviour; which sum may also be increased by the bounty of

---

[1] M. Unsworth, *op. cit.*, p. 6.

the House as favourable opportunities offer of establishing them in the world.[1]

Though crude and repressive in modern eyes the scheme was in some ways enlightened, for it stressed the need for long training in habits and methods of employment and for some community living. It also considered how the girl should establish herself in the world after her apprenticeship.

Further homes of this nature were opened in the years that followed, though they were mainly on a sectarian basis. The Jews worked amongst their own people, as the Roman Catholics did amongst theirs. The best known perhaps were those of the Church of England Sisterhoods, such as the 'Community of St. Mary the Virgin', Wantage, which started to work among the 'fallen' in 1848. Ten years later the 'Community of St. Peter's' at Horbury and of 'St. Peter the Apostle' at Laleham started similar work, followed in 1870 by that of 'St. John the Baptist' at Clewer, Windsor. 'The Community of the Holy Name' had been founded in Vauxhall in 1865, and set up a Home in 1879. The objects of these Sisterhoods, though mainly concerned with the spiritual life of their members, came sooner or later to include the reclamation of 'women who by sins of impurity have defiled those bodies which should be the temples of the Holy Ghost' (from the rules of the Wantage Community). These Homes which were for 'Penitents' who honestly sought to lead a better life, later became known as 'Penitentiaries'. Here by love, prayer and religious example the Sisters hoped to transform the characters of the girls, while by work and training, particularly in laundry and domestic work there was preparation for earning an honest living in the world. The methods used in these penitentiaries were not noticeably beyond their time; like most Homes in the nineteenth century, they refused to accept a mother with her illegitimate child, but they moved with the times, and by the twentieth century were accepting both mother and child.

In 1851 a 'Church Penitentiary Association' had been formed to co-ordinate such work of this type as was being done under Church of England auspices. Two years later the Society for the 'Rescue of Young Women and Children,' later to be renamed the

---

[1] R. Dingley, 'Proposals for establishing a public place of reception for Penitent Prostitutes' (1758).

'Society of Hope', came into existence to found further homes (many of which still continue); but it was Josephine Butler's Home in Liverpool that combined both rescue work and long-stay training in the fight against prostitution. With the help of some Liverpool merchants early in 1867 she was able to take a large house, and set up an industrial home for the 'healthy and active, the barefooted sand-girls and other friendless waifs and strays'.[1] It was managed by a matron, and the girls learnt laundry duties and worked in a small envelope factory. Similarly the Salvation Army, in the Hanbury Street Refuge in 1884, and in other Homes founded later, tried by personal influence and industrial training to provide these girls with an alternative way of life. Mrs. Bramwell Booth (née Miss Florence Soper), daughter-in-law to General William, realized that many rescue Homes had failed because they were selective. Many refused admittance to any girl over twenty-five. Rebecca Jarrett had said there was no home in existence that would take a mother and her baby. Mrs. Booth determined to remedy this and declared that she would open the doors to all. She deplored the bolts and bars, the bare dismal rooms, the high walls, and the endless laundry work of many of the Homes, and the fact that if the girls failed to progress or made a slip, they were never given a second chance. She could not imagine herself becoming any better for a long stay in such surroundings. She agreed with Ellice Hopkins, who had said that 'in not making life as bright as we can for the girls we are punishing their penitence as well as their sin'.[2] She determined therefore at the first Home that there would be no rules at all. What the girls needed, she felt, was a real home—not merely a refuge for a short time—and support in their first efforts to earn their living, and to return to respectable society. She therefore planned the Homes as places of movement, life and activity, believing there should be light, colour and noise. She realized that these girls were used to glitter and excitement and could not be expected to adjust themselves to an atmosphere of gloom. So excitement of a harmless sort was introduced as much as possible. Having set the surroundings, it was usually necessary for the girls to be trained, sometimes in laundry work, but also in book-binding, knitting by machine or

[1] G. W. and L. A. Johnston, *op. cit.*, p. 62.
[2] J. M. Cole and F. C. Bacon. *Christian Guidance of the Social Instincts* (1928), p. 7.

general domestic work. Though the opportunities were limited, there was more chance of fitting the job to the girl than in many such Homes. When the girl was ready to leave, there came the task of finding a suitable job, and seeing that she was fitted out with clothes. The clothes were often made by the girls themselves before they left, the cost being repaid out of their wages when they began to earn. After-care was an important part of the process which the Army, now a national organization, could undertake through its local officers.

These views on the best way to conduct a Home were not universally shared, as can be seen by studying the 'Hints' of Arthur Brinckman and Arthur Maddison.[1] Both urged the need for small Homes, and for the careful classification of girls in them, so that the more experienced and depraved would not contaminate and undermine the more 'innocent.' The use of the night shelter or temporary refuge they condemned completely as giving neither time for reformation nor safeguards against further degradation. Danger lay, they thought, in mixing the 'penitent' who might be transferred to a long-stay Home, with the really degraded, who used the shelter as a resting place when tired or ill, often leaving it for the old life after a few days. The object of the long-stay Homes should be to make a girl realize the value of the character she had lost, and to long for its recovery. Having obtained her co-operation, her physical well-being had to be regained. Many girls were simply worn out on entering the Home, and often needed weeks or months of good food and rest to regain their health. Secondly, they needed to be taught how to work, how to manage a cottage in every detail, to repair clothes, and lay out their money to the best advantage; and perhaps also to learn a trade. Teaching in most homes was limited to laundry work, and where financial resources were slender there was sometimes a temptation to use the girls solely in laundry work because it made profits and thus financed the Home. This Brinckman and Maddison thought regrettable. Thirdly, the religious and moral training was of paramount importance, but religion was to be presented in a practical way, not in an emotional one, since anything that roused emotion or excitement was to be avoided as creating more problems than it solved.

Though in many ways the attitude of the Rev. Brinckman and

[1] A. Brinckman and A. Maddison, *op. cit.*

the Rev. Maddison in their respective 'Hints' was enlightened and progressive, in others it was repressive and punitive. Some of the 'Rules for Inmates' they quoted with approval were more suggestive of a prison than a Home. Talking was to be restricted, walking outside the Home was to be only under escort, letters could be written home once a month, and had to be censored. Visits from relatives were to be permitted once a month. The girls were to be seldom left to themselves in case they exchanged confidences, and where there were dormitories, every bed was to be so arranged that it could be easily seen through the window of the night sister's room. On the other hand, they thought separate rooms were to be preferred to dormitories, and should be arranged where new Homes were constructed. After-care by the Home was not, however, an unmixed blessing. For though in some cases a girl was helped and encouraged by letters from the matron, in others and often the most hopeful ones, the girls wished to sever all connection with their past and to conceal from the new employers or friends that they had ever been in a Home.

CONCLUSION

These pioneers created a branch of social work concerned with moral welfare. The need to reform 'fallen women' and to care for the illegitimate child had been recognized by humanitarians many years before, but though their work had been pursued from religious motives, the condemnation that went with it was apt to extend not only to the sin but to the sinner, even to the next generation. Josephine Butler and her friends in the 'Armies' and out of them, while still spurred on by the belief that it was God's work, brought a new attitude of love and hope for 'the fallen'. Having mapped out a field of social work these pioneers set out to strengthen their work by their training schemes, especially for women workers. The training was naturally religious in content, especially for the Salvation and Church Army workers, since evangelism was the important weapon in their armoury, but it included instruction in social case work, especially in the practical field. Thus rescue workers became specialists in their sphere.[1] The people associated with moral welfare work were mainly women,

[1] By 1920 a Training House for moral welfare workers was founded in Liverpool in memory of Josephine Butler.

yet Josephine Butler recognized the need for both men and women workers, and the contribution each could make. She said, 'The feminine form of philanthropy is the independent individual ministering, the home influence. The masculine is the large comprehensive measure, the organization, the system planned by men and sanctioned by Parliament. Separately they both fail. But if these two influences combine there is the greatest hope of success.'[1]

[1] G. W. and L. A. Johnson, *op. cit.*

CHAPTER 12

GROUP WORK—I

SETTLEMENTS

THE first Settlement in England was founded in 1884, and was another and different response from that of the 'case-workers' to the pitiable plight of the poverty stricken in our large cities. There were 'settlers' before settlements. Many clergymen lived and worked among their neighbours in the poorer parishes, and many religious missions, often financed by educational establishments, especially the Oxford and Cambridge colleges, were attached to city churches, in which both clergy and laymen worked for the evangelizing of the poor. But they were not 'Settlements' in the sense in which the word came to be used later, or in the sense thought of by Edward Denison whose ideas were to be so influential in the establishment of the first settlement more than a decade after his death. The story of this young man is baffling. Born in 1840 and in poor health during his last few years (he died of tuberculosis at the age of thirty) one wonders how he made such an impression on men like Canon Barnett, men so much older and more experienced than himself. It is no answer to say that as the son of the Bishop of Salisbury and as a scholar of Eton and Christ Church, Oxford, he was guaranteed a hearing. Other men of good birth and education interested themselves in welfare work, but achieved much less. Family connections may possibly have helped his election to the vacant parliamentary seat for Newark at the age of twenty-eight, but for the explanation of his great influence in social work development we must look elsewhere.

Much may be learned from his collected letters edited by Baldwyn Leighton in the year after his death. He came to London from Oxford in 1864 to live in miserable lodgings in the Mile End Road for two purposes: to learn the real facts of life in the East End, and to be at hand should exceptional distress arise. Though he went originally as an almoner of the 'Society for the Relief of Distress', he soon realized that material help alone was insufficient.[1] 'The evil condition of the poor', he said, 'is largely due to the total absence of residents of a better class—to the dead level of labour which prevails over that wide region.' The solution, he thought, lay not in more almsgiving, 'more sops to an already uninspired and sometimes demoralized population, but in more education, more justice for the downtrodden, and more leadership'. His suggestion of the need of leadership and friendship directly foreshadowed the work of the settlements. He went even further, for in 1868, just two years before his death, at Ruskin's invitation he addressed a small gathering including Green, Vicar of Stepney, Lambert, Vicar of Kensington and Canon Scott-Holland, on the need for educated men capable of leadership to reside in a poor area. Though the meeting was abortive, the notions there expressed grew and flowered later in the fertile mind of Canon Barnett.

Samuel Augustus Barnett (1844–1913) was born in Bristol, the elder of two sons of an iron founder. He spent a sickly youth with intermittent schooling. He went, however, to Wadham College, Oxford, and obtained a Class II degree in History and Law, and after a few years of tutoring, teaching and travelling he was ordained priest in 1868. In 1873 he was called to the living of St. Jude's in Whitechapel. Here he gained an understanding of the meaning of poverty, so that while he began his work among the poor holding stern tenets about relief, before he died he became an advocate of free breakfasts for all school children, gratuitous medical relief and universal pensions.[2] Barnett kept in close touch with social movements in London—such as the C.O.S.—and elsewhere, as well as with academic circles in Oxford and Cambridge. From time to time University men joined him at Whitechapel to learn from him, and through him the point of view of the people who lived there. The presence of these young men was a potent influence in Barnett's life, and underlined once again for him the lessons Denison had taught fifteen years before. Barnett in his turn frequently visited his University, where he thrashed out his economic and social ideas.

Among his friends was Arnold Toynbee, who had become a

[1] B. Leighton, *Collected Letters of Ed. Denison* (1871).
[2] H. Barnett, *Life of Canon Barnett* (1918), p. viii.

tutor at Balliol College, Oxford, in 1878. A brilliant scholar, and one who had a profound effect on the teaching of industrial history, Toynbee was passionately concerned with the lot of ordinary men, and tried to understand their way of life, for instance by living in a half-furnished lodging and joining a trade union and friendly society. He held classes to enable them to share the delights of the learning which meant so much to him, and discussed with them (sometimes, it is said, 'in an atmosphere of bad whiskey, bad tobacco and bad drains')[1] things material and spiritual—the laws of nature and of God. He talked with his contemporaries about the needs of the poor, and the relationship that he thought ought to exist between the 'haves' and 'have-nots'. Thomas Nunn, later to be a settlement resident and staunch supporter of Canon Barnett, told how impressed he was by almost the last words he heard Toynbee speak: 'Workmen, we have neglected you. Instead of justice we have offered you charity, and instead of sympathy we have offered you hard and unreal advice. But I think we are changing. If you would only believe it and trust us, there are many of us who would spend our lives in your service.'[2] Toynbee died in 1883, at the age of thirty-one, but his power lived after him in the thoughts and achievements of his friend to whom he had given such inspiration.

It was in this setting that Barnett's ideas began to be formulated. In the year of Toynbee's death he was asked to give two lectures, one at Oxford and the other at Cambridge. In May, as the guest of the Palmerston Club, he read a paper at Oriel on *Our great Towns and Social Reform*, detailing some of the ways in which Oxford men could help to secure such reform. In November at St. John's College, Cambridge, he read a further paper on *Settlements of University Men in great Towns*, in which he formulated his thesis more precisely. The proposal met with immediate response both in Oxford and Cambridge and was, as C. G. Lang of Balliol wrote, 'one of the most practical outlets for that interest in social amelioration which is unusually strong at present'.[3]

That the people of the Universities had been shocked by the revelation of the condition of the poor was evidenced by the profound effect of such pamphlets as Preston's *The Bitter Cry of Outcast London*, and G. R. Sim's newspaper articles in 1883 on *How the*

[1] F. J. Bruno, *Trends in Social Work* (1948), p. 114.
[2] Anon., *Thos. Hancock Nunn*.   [3] Anon., *Oxford House*, p. 8.

Poor Live. Their feelings about the contrast between the wealth of inheritance and opportunity stored up in Oxford, and the poverty of East London, made them long for some means to redress the balance. Barnett's plan provided this. Within a few months, in February 1884, a Committee was set up in Oxford to found and maintain a 'University Settlement in East London' and to offer Canon Barnett the wardenship. Cambridge quickly followed with their support. A further committee was formed in London to acquire premises, and pursue the practical details attendant upon such a venture. Meanwhile the untimely death of Arnold Toynbee led his friends to start a memorial fund, which was used to establish the proposed settlement in Commercial Street under the name of Toynbee Hall.

Canon Barnett's Principles and Methods

Barnett believed that man must be given every opportunity to effect his own salvation, and that material aid indiscriminately given would but lower his power to fend for himself. He was not concerned with a man's suffering, if his soul could thereby be saved. Yet he believed, with the Socialists, that environment had an effect on character, and agreed with Octavia Hill (whose influence over him was profound) that better housing and a development of garden cities would effect a revolution in men's habits. Above all he thought educated men, particularly University men, living and sharing with the people would have a direct influence by providing not only the example of higher standards, but the leadership that would inspire their neighbours to seek these standards. 'The best for the lowest', meaning that all the best cultural and spiritual influences should be available to the slum-dweller, seemed to him an appropriate slogan. Unfortunately in Barnett's experience (his philosophy was largely empirical) rich and poor were alienated classes, even as they had been when Disraeli was writing. The new suburbs of big towns were inhabited either by the rich or the poor, seldom both. This isolation created different customs, speech, pleasures and above all different ethical standards. What was worse, it prevented either class knowing anything of the other. 'The rich think of the poor as people to send missions to, to amuse, keep out of pubs, and guard from dangerous opinions. The poor think of the rich as idle and self-indulgent', remarked Mrs. Barnett.

The settlement was Barnett's answer to this mutual suspicion and ignorance. His plan was to take a house in some big industrial city, so that educated men could live in close proximity to the underprivileged. There was to be no question of these men living the life of the poverty-stricken; indeed, part of the settlement programme came to include invitations to dine with the residents, as true neighbours would. But while in general settlements did not call for the literal assumption of all the conditions of poverty, the settlers' daily contact with it, and their poignant feelings of sympathy for the difficulties of their neighbours gave them a closer experience than had been generally felt before. Some settlers went even further. For at one time it was the practice for each resident in one settlement to refuse remuneration that gave him a gross income higher than any of his fellows. Barnett's plan was originally confined to men. He felt that social work in the past had been so much the sphere of women or men of mature if not advanced years, that unless he carved out a niche for younger men they might retire from their new role. He was anxious therefore to keep settlements primarily as places for men; what struck Mrs. Barnett as being novel, was not so much that 'men lived among the poor, but that young and brilliant men had chosen to serve them in ways based not only on sentiment but on thought'.

Barnett always viewed the settlement as an instrument of education. He thought that the social problem was at root an educational one, that those who strove to raise the standard of living were powerless without knowledge, while no position of security could be achieved until people were educated to win it for themselves. Moreover no happiness was satisfactory except that which came from the 'inward eye'.[1] He therefore hoped that a long succession of 'colleges' would grow up naturally to meet a felt need, just as colleges sprang up in the Middle Ages at Oxford and Cambridge. This education should have two main aims: knowledge of the nature of the social problem must be gained, involving research by educated men, usually graduates or undergraduates, who came into friendly intercourse with the people themselves, and who learnt of social problems with the active help of those who suffered. The other should be to share the culture of those who had been privileged with those who had not. This took the form of formal classes for adults at the settlement, such as the University Extension

[1] H. Barnett, *op. cit.*, p. 340.

Classes, which were available to all at a small fee, and of general neighbourliness in cultural activities, as in the art exhibitions, concerts, visits to places of interest, the organization of games, and hospitality to meals. As Mrs. Stocks reminded us of the Manchester settlement,[1] 'the Ancoats Hall piano was trundled down into the courts and alleys of Manchester and Salford and concerts given at street corners'. One has to remember, however, there was no competition for the cultural and recreative interest of the poorer neighbourhoods. The alternative was the public house. As the Hammonds suggested (The Bleak Age), the spiritual poverty of the people was worse even than their physical poverty. In Barnett's mind education was not something for mutual edification and pleasure alone; it had a social and political purpose. Barnett fully appreciated, as had Denison, the need both for leadership in the community and for awakening the conscience of England to its responsibilities for the existence of chronic poverty in the midst of prosperity. The settlement encouraged the neighbours and expected the residents to take their full part in the life of the community, whether it was on management committees, at election times, or as a vigilance committee to patrol the streets at night during and after the period of the Jack the Ripper murders! A much quoted paragraph of the Toynbee Hall Report of 1889 stated that of the residents six were school-managers, six were committee members promoting evening classes, four C.O.S. committee members, two were almoners of the Society for the Relief of Distress, one was a guardian of the poor, nine were club members and five organized children's holiday funds.

But more was needed: the whole country, especially those in the seats of power, must be made aware both of the needs of the poor and the possible ways of helping them. This necessity, thought Barnett, could be achieved in several ways. First, propaganda was to be used, which might take the form of publishing monographs analyzing the problem and suggesting cures; hence the part they played in the Booth Survey of 'London Life and Labour' 1887-9, the scheme for contributory insurance against unemployment they published in 1890, their investigation in 1892 into the causes of unemployment, and their memoranda on such questions as *Emigration, Boys in Industry*, and *The Homeless*. Secondly, young men of public spirit, especially undergraduates, were to be encouraged to

[1] M. D. Stocks, *Fifty Years in Every Street* (1945), p. 19.

spend some time at a settlement, either during their vacations or after they had qualified. Their experience would then be used by them later when they entered public life and achieved positions of responsibility. In this he was undoubtedly right, as a glance at the list of residents in any settlement will show. Many of the foremost social reformers and political leaders of the last half century have had some connexion with settlement life.

The prestige of the warden was always a key to the value of a settlement. Barnett stated categorically[1] that he should be a University graduate, and a personality of authority trusted by all parties, qualified by character to guide men, and by education to teach. Experience has shown the difficulties of finding the right person for wardenship, and the dangers of appointing the wrong one. Some settlements, notably Oxford House, have faced a different problem in the selection of their Head. Founded by the Church of England, Oxford House at least twice appointed as Head a man who was also a functioning priest of a parish, but each time they found it necessary to revert to a situation where the Head had no other office. For though there were many advantages in combining the work of the parish with that of the settlement, the excessive load of the two offices and the danger that the settlement would lose its identity and become an adjunct to the parish, outweighed the advantages. On the whole Barnett did not favour the personal participation of the warden in the social work of the settlement. This did not mean he should be divorced from it. On the contrary, he held that every settler must be responsible for the social work he had in hand and should spend not less than half an hour each week discussing with the warden his aims and methods, and the result of the work he had done. In this way the warden could co-ordinate all that was going on, and give advice to each worker.

Mention must be made in this context of the religious issue. We have seen how Canon Barnett, himself a clergyman, came to the settlement idea from his experience in a slum parish, and how it was largely to University men of deep spiritual conviction with a desire to express their religious urge for social betterment, that he appealed in furtherance of his ideas. Yet he was anxious to avoid confusion with the missions, nor did he want to limit the scope, either of his work or his helpers, by attachments to any church or sect. He wanted to keep the work religious but religious in the

[1] J. A. R. Pimlott, *Toynbee Hall* (1935), p. 31.

widest sense.[1] 'If,' as he said, 'there is any truth in the saying that "Everyone that loveth, knoweth God", then it must be that the work of the settlers, inspired and guided by love, will be religious.'

This apparently did not satisfy all the Oxford friends of the settlement idea. For some, notably the Warden of Keble College and Canon Scott-Holland, preferred to think of a settlement as part of an existing ecclesiastical organization and attached if possible to a definite parish. So, while plans for Toynbee Hall were being made, alternative plans for what became Oxford House were also going forward, both with the active support of the Oxford and Cambridge colleges. As it happened the Oxford House arrangements were completed first, and by October 1884 it was opened with accommodation for three residents, while it was not until January 1885 that Toynbee Hall was opened. It is doubtful if the initial difference of purpose has had very much effect on the way each settlement has worked. Oxford House, and others like Cambridge House, have seldom been attached to a parish, and when they were, as in the brief periods when the Warden was also priest of the parish, they have not pressed the connexion. Moreover, as the Warden of Keble said when Oxford House was founded, 'though the basis of the scheme was to be religion and Christianity, anyone would be welcome to join in the work, including those who could scarcely define their attitude to Christianity or the Church of England'.[2] Allowing for this toleration, Oxford House, and some of the other settlements, have felt much of their strength to lie in their acceptance not only of Christianity as a basis, but of their association with the established Church, and have felt unhappy, as a search through their records reveals, whenever they have found the link weakened. The need for such close ties with the established Church did not seem to worry Barnett.

Though Canon Barnett was a pioneer of group work, particularly in education, he had little appreciation of the formative influence group life can have upon the individual. His motto was 'One by one'; and by that he meant that the greatest good was done individually.[3]

Unless the friendless are befriended, unless the boy is considered and put in circumstances fitted for his character; unless his teacher or school

---

[1] Anon., *Oxford House*, p. 8.   [2] *Ibid.*, p. 10.
[3] H. Barnett, *op. cit.*, Vol. II, p. 71.

manager or a visitor act as his friend, he will hardly consider himself a member of society. Hooliganism is the protest against treating the poor in a lump.

His attitude to clubs therefore was restrained. He did not think, as many were thinking at that time, that clubs were a method of combating hooliganism. They would only do that, he thought, if they offered something better, the influence and love of a friend. He was not therefore in favour of clubs just for pleasure or amusement. He countenanced them if they inculcated discipline built on self-respect and friendship. In consequence he gave little support to the building of extensive premises, or the gathering of large numbers of boys together. All the same he encouraged camping as being healthy and likely to promote good citizenship, and approved of club managers, if they were likely to make friends with the boys.

If Barnett did not think of clubs as a major part of settlement work, others, notably 'Oxford House', did. From the beginning this settlement developed its club life, not only for boys, but for adults too, and in this it has been copied by settlements all over the world. For they believed that one of the services they could offer most effectively was the provision of a centre of political and religious neutrality where all living in the neighbourhood might find warmth and friendship, and might therefore have the opportunity for personal development through group life that most human beings need.

While settlements were not started as places of social service in the narrower sense, the site on which they were built demanded the establishment of these services, and often the pioneering of new ones. In Manchester, settlement work extended into readings to the blind, penny banks, social evenings, poor man's lawyers, clubs for boys, for girls, for cripples and for the casuals from the common lodging houses. Other settlements have sought to render service in different ways, women's settlements particularly have pioneered child welfare clinics, play centres, or nursery schools.

Spread of the Movement

If Canon Barnett were disappointed towards the end of his life at the way things were going in the settlement movement, he must equally have been surprised at the way his ideas spread not only in this country but all over the world. Within the same decade as the foundation of Toynbee Hall no fewer than eleven settlements were started, including Oxford House (1884), the Women's University Settlement, Southwark (1886); and by the 1890's twenty-two more came into being, including those at Manchester (1895), Liverpool (1898) and Birmingham (1899). In the United States at least four were started by persons who had their direct inspiration from English Settlements (e.g. Hull House, established by Jane Addams in Chicago, the Neighbourhood Guild in New York started by Stanton Coit in 1886, North Western University Settlement in Chicago, and South End House founded by Robert A. Woods in 1892). By the end of the century the settlement movement had been introduced into all the Dominions of the British Empire, the Western European countries and in China and India.

Criticisms

Some critics felt that Toynbee Hall had no ecclesiastical connexion and stood for no particular religious doctrine. Barnett replied that the only secure foundation for a settlement was [1] 'love; love strong enough to stand the strain of working with little or no apparent results; broad enough to take in sectarians and secularists; deep enough to sink differences in the one common purpose of raising the low, the sad and the poor to their true life which is now with God'.

A second difficulty concerned the recruitment and quality of the residents in settlements. Barnett said there should be at least twelve men of education with broad interests and loyalties in every settlement. Apparently Toynbee Hall had no difficulty in recruiting as many as it wanted, but some settlements (e.g. Oxford House) found great difficulty in attracting a sufficient number of suitable residents. Moreover, many of those who did come were often unable for financial or other reasons to gain as much benefit as they might, because they could not stay long enough. In spite of this, on the whole, settlements in the nineteenth century succeeded in attracting enough people of the right calibre to make an immense impression on the neighbourhood.

Octavia Hill's criticism was of a different kind. She doubted the wisdom of settlements because the strain of living in the worst places would be too trying for educated people. To live constantly in the squalid parts of our great towns would, she thought, diminish their strength and so their usefulness, and it would be better

[1] Anon., *Oxford House*, p. 9.

therefore that they should begin in a limited way by spending a number of hours each week in these areas. Her fears, though not groundless, did not deter all the earnest spirits who sought so sincerely to do this work.

The other main criticism centred round the nature of Barnett's programme. He was accused of priggishness, and was asked if the inhabitants of East London were to be regenerated by the efforts of undergraduates, and the sight of 'aesthetic furniture and Japanese fans'. And again he was asked if he hoped to save starving souls by pictures, parties and pianos. To his expenditure on entertainment he rejoined that it [1] 'belongs to our whole system of dealing with the poor. The religion of amusement has been greatly lost sight of. If we refuse a coal ticket because we wish to treat people with respect, it is only right that we should ask them to meet us as friends.' Even so the elevation of the poor by entertainment in a middle class environment might be the subject of criticism in any modern society.

Conclusion

In considering the contribution to social work made by the settlements, we have to recognize two factors: first, they came as part of the new awareness about poverty and misery in our large towns; secondly, they were designed to appeal especially to the educated classes, whereas earlier the philanthropic had been drawn from the upper and middle classes. Where Barnett showed his greatest insight was in focusing attention on barriers to social change, and in recognizing that it was only educated men of good will who could tackle them. His teaching, which was accepted by all settlements of Barnett's day, was that exact knowledge of the true needs of an area must be gained before anything can be done; and that the deep suspicions by the poor of the motives and lives of the better off and educated leaders who came to live amongst them must be overcome. His first emphasis therefore was equally on research, and love; research in the sense of studying the social structure of the neighbourhood and understanding the needs of the individuals in it; love in the sense of loving one's neighbours as oneself, giving them a helping hand when they needed it and sharing in their hopes and aspirations—a very different conception from that of the case-worker sharing the lives of his clients only in their

[1] H. Barnett, *op. cit.*, p. 152.

difficulties. His second emphasis was on the need to educate the poor to rise out of their material poverty and spiritual drabness. This he thought the poor could not do unaided. It was the duty of settlements to keep the world informed not only of the need itself, but of possible solutions. A further emphasis implicit in the whole settlement idea was on the spirit of human equality. For 'settling' by the educated in areas of great need was always intended as a two-way arrangement. It meant that the inhabitants taught the residents about the way of life of the poor, and the educated were able to share, with no sense of patronage, the culture that upbringing and education had given them. Thus for the first time equality between social worker and client was regarded as a principle of social work. It is doubtful whether the aim was ever within their grasp, for the hierarchical divisions of nineteenth-century society precluded it. But the ideal was stated, and has had its influence on subsequent generations.

CHAPTER 13

GROUP WORK—II

YOUTH WORK

MODERN attitudes to young people are different from those of the nineteenth century, and the social work that reflects these attitudes must of necessity be different too. In a century struggling towards prosperity the bulk of the young were used as workers in the factories, while only the few could be trained for leadership in government, commerce and learning. Though there was sound reason for such a dichotomy the problems that arose out of it were different from those of today when the nation is not only wealthier but has a low birth-rate. The country now can afford to regard children as a scarce and precious commodity whose capabilities must be developed wherever they are found. For these reasons as well as the increased leisure which higher productivity has made possible, this generation has naturally a different perspective, and youth work is a fairly well-defined sphere of social work, with a definite and recognized place in modern British society. Since the publication of the Government Circular on *The Service of Youth* in 1939,[1] the 'service' is said to be concerned with the leisure-time activities of boys and girls between fourteen and twenty years. Youth work in the nineteenth century, on the other hand, was not so clear-cut. The young were numerous compared with the number of jobs available, and in consequence wages were low; and their legal and social status was low. Knowledge, moreover, of child development was only beginning, and it was thought that training in habits of obedience, industry and reverence were the most suitable ways of bringing up the child. The well-known maxims, 'Spare the rod and spoil the child', and 'Children should be seen and not heard', while not to be taken too literally of the nineteenth-century practice, had a sufficient acceptance to provide the clue to adult-child attitudes.

[1] Board of Education, *Circular 1486*, November 1939.

In the last century youth work was envisaged as having a two-fold purpose. It set out: (*a*) to train young people in habits of industry and piety, so that on reaching maturity they could take their place as good and satisfied workers; (*b*) to deal with those young people who were in potential danger, or had already fallen from the socially accepted standards of care or rectitude. The fulfilment of these purposes impinged on the pioneering enterprises of education on the one hand, and institutional work for the neglected or delinquent child on the other. Institutional care involving a separation of children either permanent or temporary, from their homes, is dealt with in Chapters 8 and 9, while full-time education does not come strictly within the scope of this work. We are left therefore with a field of part-time, mostly leisure-time, service involving voluntary attendance on the part of the young people. Few of the organizations providing for youth were clubs in the modern sense. Many, such as the Y.W.C.A. or the Metropolitan Association for Befriending Young Servants, had hostels, employment exchanges and other services attached. Age groups were not as clearly defined as they are today. Some clubs had a minimum age of entry but seldom was there an upper age limit. On the whole 'the young' was a fairly elastic term, though when the death-rate was so high that the expectation of life at birth was no more than forty years, and children could be employed full-time in the mills, 'youth' was not prolonged unduly.

It is appropriate to think of the development of youth work in two phases. The earlier one was closely concerned with teaching, and found its affinity with the educational movements of the day; while the latter part of the century saw the development of youth movements similar in many ways to the clubs of today.

In the early part of the nineteenth century the most influential youth organizations were the Sunday Schools and the Ragged Schools. Sunday schools were perhaps the earlier and can be traced back to the seventeenth century or even before. Robert Raikes and Hannah More had begun their work years before the turn of the nineteenth century. In 1780 Robert Raikes, proprietor of *The Gloucester Journal*, in co-operation with a local curate, decided to open four Sunday schools in Gloucester. His paper publicized the project, and others in different parts of the country, reading of his schemes, soon followed his example. By 1785 the 'Society for the Establishment and Support of Sunday Schools throughout the Kingdom' had been formed, and it was on the crest of this wave of interest that Mrs. Hannah More and her sister were swept into their work in the Mendips. It is not therefore as a pioneer that Mrs. More claims our attention, but as one who worked in the Sunday schools she had founded, and wrote extensively about her principles and methods.

Hannah More was born in Gloucester in 1745, fourth of the five daughters of a schoolmaster.[1] She was thus nurtured in an atmosphere of education, and when later some of her sisters opened a fashionable school in Bristol, she taught in it. About 1773 she became engaged to a Mr. Turner, who however put off the marriage repeatedly for six years. Whereupon she turned her back on matrimony, and while adopting the title of 'Mrs. More' decided to devote her life to good works. Her friends, meanwhile, arranged an annuity of £200 per annum from Mr. Turner, who, when he died, left her £1,000 in his will. For though he would 'not marry her, he admired her'. She died in 1833 after a life of hard work and much illness. She wrote no fewer than eleven books after she was sixty.

In 1787 Lord Wilberforce had drawn her attention to the ignorance and brutality of life in the Mendip villages; and two years later her first Sunday school was started in Cheddar. In the next ten years she and her sister had started more than a dozen such schools. In spite of all that had been written about the value of Sunday schools, both in their promotion of piety and their prevention of depravity, she met with intense and often implacable opposition. Notwithstanding the work of Wesley and the Methodists, the people in these rural parts of England were still largely unaware of the teachings of Christianity.

At Cheddar [in 1791, she wrote] we found more than 2,000 people in the parish, almost all very poor—no gentry, a dozen wealthy farmers, hard, brutal and ignorant. . . . We went to every house in the place, and found every house a scene of the greatest vice and ignorance. We saw but one Bible in all the parish, and that was used to prop a flower-pot. No clergyman had resided in it for forty years. One rode over from

[1] H. Thompson, *Life of Hannah More* (1838).

Wells to preach once each Sunday. No sick were visited, and children were often buried without any funeral service.[1]

This state of affairs was apparently accepted by, and acceptable to, the wealthy of the villages, some of whom, she said, 'begged I would not think of bringing any religion into the country. It was the worst thing in the world for the poor, for it made them lazy and useless.'[2]

This sentiment was not however shared by Mrs. More, who believed that the depravity and inertia of the poor were due to their lack of religious knowledge and moral teaching. Though she was oblivious to some of the major social and economic evils of her time, and accepted without question, as did most people in her day, the social stratification of society, she believed it was her calling to 'train up the lower classes to habits of industry and virtue'. 'I know no way of teaching morals', she wrote, 'but by teaching principles, nor of inculcating Christian principles without a good knowledge of scripture.'[3]

Sunday being the day when prospective scholars and teachers would be free, in the Mendip villages, it was appropriate to use that day to run the schools. Evenings were not neglected, for in some villages evening classes, particularly for the mothers, were started and proved fruitful. There was then, as there is in many 'backward' countries today, a mystical belief among many that literacy would open the doors to freedom and ease; and the response therefore to Mrs. More's efforts was remarkably encouraging. Not that all parents accepted her offer. Some feared she would 'get an influence over their children after a time, and waft them across the seas'!

The schools were of two kinds: for children, and for parents and adolescents; and the teaching consisted mainly of reading, knitting and sewing. Writing and cyphering she did not teach, maintaining that such accomplishments would breed sedition, and give the lower orders ideas above their station. At first even the reading was of the Scriptures only, though later she began herself to write stories, homilies and poems with a moral purpose, for she believed as John Wesley did, that it was no use to teach people reading, if all there was to read was the 'seditious or pornographic literature of commercialism'. The object of the schools was also to make honest

---

[1] W. Roberts, *Memoirs of Life of Hannah More* (1834), Vol. II, p. 30.
[2] *Ibid.*, pp. 206–7.   [3] H. Thompson, *op. cit.*, pp. 99–100.

and virtuous citizens, and this was furthered by her various savings societies. At each meeting all the members, especially the women, were encouraged to deposit a little, even a penny a week, against the rainy day. This was used as a kind of insurance fund from which a sick contributor was able to draw out 3s. per week, while maternity grants of 7s. 6d. were available. She hoped also to raise the moral standard of the village by refusing membership of her schools to the non-virtuous. Girls found indulging in 'gross living' were to be shunned and excluded!

These early examples of youth work are instructive not only in the aims they sought, but in the methods they used. Hannah More has left a record in her *Hints on how to run a Sunday School*. She set out the need for a programme suited to the level of the members, with plenty of variety and as entertaining as possible. She believed that the best came out of a child if his affections were engaged by kindness, and that terror did not pay. With these impeccable sentiments no club leader today would quarrel, but some eyebrows would be raised at her use of bribery.

I encourage them [she said] by little bribes of a penny a chapter to get by heart certain fundamental parts of Scripture. . . . Those who attend four Sundays without intermission receive a penny. Once in every six to eight weeks I give a little gingerbread. Once a year I distribute little books according to merit. Those who deserve most get a Bible. Second-rate merit gets a Prayer-book—the rest, cheap Repository tracts.[1]

Among many other supporters of Sunday schools was Mrs. Trimmer, who died in 1810 at the age of sixty-nine. Her book *The Oeconomy of Charity*, published in 1786, which described her experience of this kind of work, went through several editions and had a great influence. She had started a Sunday school at Brentford in 1785 and found it beneficial, not only as a means of teaching the Scriptures and the doctrines of the Church of England (she was determined that Dissenters should have separate establishments), but in improving the behaviour and appearance of the children.

It is clear that Sunday schools, of which there were 1,516 in 1801, catering for 156,490 children, were only a little like to the clubs of today. But to some extent, they met the need of youth and were conducted by humanitarians who, though their vision was limited, were interested in young people for their own sakes.

[1] W. Roberts, *op. cit.*, Vol. II, p. 150.

2 RAGGED SCHOOLS

At the same time as Sunday schools were developing and providing the answer to one of the needs of the ordinary boy and girl, a different movement was trying to rescue children in danger. Thus came the Ragged Schools which, as their title implies, were concerned with only a small section of the young and that the poorest and most deprived children. The objects, like those of the Sunday schools, were partly educational in the narrower sense of education, and partly the moral regeneration of a section of society, which by its physical condition, was thought to be in special need of it.

We have suggested that perhaps Sunday schools were chronologically the elder, but no-one knows exactly when ragged schools first began. They existed long before 1835, when the London City Mission was founded, long before the writings of Dr. Guthrie of Edinburgh, or the school of John Pounds in Portsmouth. Yet it was to the inspiration of these two men that the nineteenth century owes many of its Ragged Schools. For about the middle of the century Dr. Guthrie's books on John Pounds and his work were almost best sellers and many, fired by what they had read, set out to emulate the example so vividly described. Wrote Dr. Guthrie:[1]

My first interest in the cause of Ragged Schools was awakened by a picture which I saw in Anstruther, on the shores of the Firth of Forth. It represented a cobbler's room; he was there himself, spectacles on nose, an old shoe between his knees, that massive forehead and firm mouth indicating great determination of character; and from between his bushy eyebrows benevolence gleamed out on a group of poor children, some sitting, some standing, but all busy at their lessons around him.

From this he went on to describe how John Pounds, by trade a cobbler in Portsmouth, had taken pity on the ragged children, whom ministers and magistrates, ladies and gentlemen, were leaving to run wild, and go to ruin on their streets, how he had gathered in these outcasts; had trained them up in virtue and knowledge, and how single-handed, while earning his daily bread by the sweat of his brow, had rescued from ruin and saved to society no fewer than five hundred children. If Pounds could not catch a poor boy in any other way, like St. Paul he would win him with

[1] Quoted by C. J. Montague, *Sixty Years of Waifdom*, pp. 37-43.

guile. He was sometimes seen hunting down a ragged urchin on the quay of Portsmouth, and compelling him to come to school, not by the power of a policeman, but by a potato. He knew the love of an Irishman for a potato, and might be seen running alongside an unwilling boy with one held under his nose! 'Nearly everything', wrote Montague in 1904, 'in the operations of the Ragged School Union existed in germ in that wonderful little shop, 6 ft. × 16 ft.'[1] The fresh air movement had its counterpart, for the scholars took turns at sitting on the step and the form outside. The clothing department was represented by the garments Pounds loaned to the children to enable them to attend Sunday school. The cripples department was foreshadowed by that curious contrivance of leather he made for his crippled nephew in the imitation of an orthopaedic instrument he had seen, and which apparently cured the distortion. When there was competition for places in his little academy, he always gave the preference to the 'little blackguards', thus forestalling in practice Lord Shaftesbury's advice 'stick to the gutter'. When he went out upon the Portsmouth quays at night, he put in his pockets baked potatoes for the 'drifts'. Not only so, but he taught his girl scholars to cook simple foods, so that the ragged school cookery class had its origin in the shoemaker's room. To the lads he taught his own trade, while the reading, writing and arithmetic stood for general education. Being doctor and nurse to his young charges, he may be said to have had his medical department as well. As a maker of hats, shuttlecocks and crossbows for the youngest he exhibited an interest in recreation. Even the 'robin dinner' was anticipated by the good old man in the plum pudding feast he held every Christmas Day. He was not an ascetic, but lived simply. He died suddenly on 1st January 1839 in the very act of asking a favour for a poor child.

The ragged schools which followed in London and elsewhere, were opened in barns, stables, covered-in railway arches or disused store-rooms. Few had less than twenty-five scholars, and none more than two hundred and fifty. The teachers were voluntary, and in the main the expenses were met by them and their friends. The main purpose of the schools was to teach reading with a view to subsequent Bible study. The time of opening was usually limited to Sundays, but some opened on week-nights too. It was soon realized that unpaid, untrained workers were not achieving the desired

[1] Quoted by C. J. Montague, *Sixty Years of Waifdom*, pp. 37–43.

end as quickly as was hoped, and by 1846 four schools in London were opened with full-time paid workers, and were kept open all day and every day. Naturally there were many troubles, especially as the scholars were so rough and undisciplined. One superintendent in great trouble came to Lord Shaftesbury and said 'The neighbours are alarmed, the landlord will close the doors, the teachers will flee.' 'Well,' said the Earl, 'you cannot have a ragged school without the preliminaries!'[1]

It has sometimes been stated that Sheriff Watson's scheme in Aberdeen was also a model for subsequent ragged schools, but his evidence before the Select Committee on the *Education of Destitute and Neglected Children* in 1861, did not bear this out.[2] There he described how he established a society in Aberdeen to educate destitute children. He appointed district visitors to give tickets to the children of the poor, entitling them to attend any ordinary day school in the town, the tickets being renewed every three months, if attendance and behaviour were good. Objections came from the teachers, who did not like having in their classes children so dirty, ragged and poor, and from the visitors, who found the children so hungry, that offering a ticket seemed like offering a stone instead of bread. Mr. Watson was driven therefore to revise his plans, and to establish the first industrial school in Aberdeen in 1840, to feed, educate and train all the vagrant children of the town. In this he was helped by the police, who arrested all vagrant children and put them in the school! Some 280 children of the town had lived by begging, vagrancy, and stealing, but the number was considerably reduced after the establishment of four of these industrial schools. Interesting though these methods of compulsion were, it is difficult to connect them with the essentially voluntary day classes of the ragged schools.

By 1844 about twenty schools all over England had been founded,[3] with about 200 voluntary teachers trying to instruct nearly 2,000 children. Because each was an isolated unit, a few interested men decided to form the 'Ragged School Union', to supply a unity of purpose and to share experience. At first there was some opposition to this kind of association, particularly from the incumbents of some parishes who objected to their schools

---

[1] W. Besant, *The Jubilee of the Ragged School Union* (1894), p. 18.
[2] 1861 (460), vii. Education of Destitute and Neglected Children. Select Committee. *Report, Minutes of Evidence*, etc.   [3] W. Besant, *op. cit.*, p. 21.

being associated with schools run by other denominations, or the laity only. This opposition soon passed away however and by 1851 new schools had been started in every part of the United Kingdom, nearly forty were in existence outside London, and about a score in the Metropolis. Each school was completely independent, and, though most were members of the Ragged School Union, many had developed their own special characteristics such as industrial schools, refuges, seaside camps, emigration training homes and the like.

The condition of the big towns was certainly a challenge to all humane people who realized what was going on. Sir Walter Besant wrote:

> Children of the gutter were sent out by their mothers, as soon as they could walk, to pick up their living somehow in the streets. They sang ballads, they sold matches; they picked up coals on the river bank, they pilfered from the open shops and stalls. Whatever else they did or pretended to do they always pilfered.

And Lord Shaftesbury, speaking in Parliament in June 1848, said,

> Of 1,600 children in fifteen ragged schools, 162 had been in prison, 116 had run away from home because of ill-treatment, 170 slept in lodging houses, 253 lived by begging, 216 had no shoes or stockings, 68 were children of convicts, 101 had no under-linen, 219 never slept in beds, 125 had stepmothers, 306 had lost one or both parents.'[1]

THE AIMS OF THE RAGGED SCHOOL MOVEMENT

The pioneers in ragged schools were careful not to compete or conflict with the 'British and Foreign' or the 'National' Schools, which had been founded to teach the three R's to the 'lower orders', or the industrial schools, which were intended as places of industrial training. They claimed to cater for a special class of children only, namely children who were sons and daughters of convicts, thieves in custody, drunkards and profligates; children already vagrants, orphans, deserted; children whose clothes were poor and whose habits were low; in other words, to quote Mary Carpenter, 'Children who for whatever cause cannot attend the ordinary day schools.'[2] The children attending ragged schools were as a rule

[1] *Ibid.*
[2] 1861 (460), vii. Education of Destitute and Neglected Children. Select Committee. *Report, Minutes of Evidence*, etc.

poor, mentally as well as physically, and for many reasons, such as poverty or the need to earn, their attendance was often irregular.

Secondly, they aimed at siting a school where the children were. This meant the abandonment of any hopes of ideal buildings, or even good buildings, but rather the taking of an old shed into which could crowd fifty to sixty children and perhaps a dozen teachers. Such buildings were seldom water-proof or even wind-proof but they served well enough, never through over-grandness repelling these forlorn and neglected children.

The education was designed to meet the needs of the children, and their first requirement was a standard of morals. Here they followed the doctrine of Hannah More, who had stated that moral standards were obtainable only through religious instruction. Indeed, as Sir Walter Besant went on to say,

to propose the education of these children would have alarmed people; education is more dangerous, they thought, than ignorance. But none can dispute they have souls. Thus it was to teach religious tenets that ragged schools were started in the most degraded quarters. The children at first behaved like little savages, and the teachers were pelted with mud and stones.[1]

But this could never be the whole content of ragged school work. For with this class of children, the teachers had to contend with an almost complete absence of parental control. Thus Mary Carpenter described an ideal ragged school as one 'where habits of obedience, cleanliness and order are enforced, and where the ability and character of the teachers are satisfactory, and where they must have the opportunity to carry out their ideas. If they want to develop industrial training, help them. If they want to install a bath for compulsory cleansing, help them.'[2] She was, in this, making a plea for Treasury grant-in-aid, a hope never achieved. In her view, industrial training was an essential part of all ragged school work, but it was not every school that included it. The three R's were also taught to a greater or less extent. But the main purpose of the schools was not academic-learning, it was child-care. Hence the teacher-pupil ratio was high, as only through personal influence of the master on the few, could children be regenerated. The expenses of the schools were correspondingly high,

[1] W. Besant, *op. cit.*
[2] 1861 (460), vii. Education of Destitute and Neglected Children. Select Committee. *Report, Minutes of Evidence,* etc.

in spite of the voluntary service given by the teachers. In 1857 it was reckoned as a pound a year per child, compared with five shillings in the 'British Schools'.[1]

The fourth aim of the schools developed out of experience, which demonstrated the need for the care and after-care of the children. If these children were to have any hope of a decent useful life as adults they needed to be looked after, as they were in the night shelters and medical units associated with many of the schools. They needed food and clothes; few of the schools could resist the need for some canteen arrangements, and most started a clothing club. But above all the children needed a start in life, and some supervision till they became established. One method used was that of teaching a skilled trade, but the cost of raw materials on which to practise was often more than the charitable resources of the schools would allow, and many had to fall back on unskilled work, such as stick-chopping, whose products could be sold to defray expenses. But the youngsters were taught to work, and that was no mean achievement. Other schools experimented in emigration schemes, and found them well suited to some temperaments. In 1851, the 'Shoeblack Brigade' was started at the Great Exhibition, by John Macgregor, and the idea spread all over London, where shoeblacks could be seen in their distinctive dress. Other jobs such as broomers (crossing sweepers), rag-collecting, messengers, were organized to provide an honest living for some ragged school children.

These aims carried the schools along unaided until 1870. In a sense the prime need for them had already passed. Boards of guardians were taking their responsibilities for the 'deprived' child more humanely than before. Orphanages started by volunteers were making their appearance, and when schooling became available and compulsory, the role of the full-time or part-time ragged schools was over. They quickly adapted to the new circumstances and attention was devoted to other work for children. 'Invalid Children's Aid' and other charities for children which have now become separate organizations, owed their origin and inspiration to the ragged school movement.

It is doubtful whether the methods used in the ragged schools have anything specific to offer to the study of modern group work

[1] National Association for the Promotion of the Social Sciences. *Transactions*, 1857.

method as such. They did however show three things. The first was that the building need not be ideal, so long as it was easily accessible to the haunts of the young. Another was that everything depended on the character and quality of the leader. Mary Carpenter, as far back as 1861, recognized that the aims of the ordinary day schools of her day were diametrically opposite to those of the ragged schools, and that the good teacher in the former was less likely to make a good one in the freer, less-ordered regime of the latter. A third contribution was the importance they attached to the whole person of the child, physical, mental, moral, to his family and his future. For it was common practice among ragged school teachers to visit what homes the children had, in the hope of creating a better understanding, and of giving help and advice if possible.

Their greatest contribution however was the experience of social conditions they gave to the men and women who taught in and worked for them. As many of these people became leaders of social work and social reform during the nineteenth century, the experience was destined to have far-reaching results. Best known of these was William Ashley, Lord Shaftesbury. But there were others like Mary Carpenter of Bristol, whose work on penal methods with juvenile delinquents is described elsewhere; Professor Leoni Levi, founder of the Liverpool Chamber of Commerce and statistician to Mr. Gladstone; General Gordon—hero of Khartoum; Mrs. Barker Harrison (née Miss Adeline Cooper) an intimate personal friend of Baroness Burdett-Coutts; Dr. Barnardo; Miss Charlesworth, author of 'Ministering Children', whose profits she devoted to the Bermondsey ragged school; Charles Dickens; Dr. Guthrie; and Mr. Quinton Hogg.

3 MODERN YOUTH ORGANIZATIONS

While these educational and social movements were catering for the needs of one class of young people in the early part of the century, youth clubs, similar to those of modern times, began to make their appearance. An admirable account of these developments may be found in Miss Percival's book *Youth will be led*,[1] and in Mr. Eager's study *Making Men*,[2] and it is not proposed here to do more than summarize the main features there described.

[1] A. C. Percival, *Youth will be led* (1951).
[2] W. McG. Eager, *Making Men* (1953).

MAIN BRANCHES OF SOCIAL WORK

military organizations like the army cadets and the boys' brigades, who tackled disorderliness and slackness by military discipline; the playing fields movement, which developed athletics and provided open spaces; and the temperance movement, which tried through coffee houses and the like to find alternatives to beer houses and gin palaces. These four influences were clearly seen in the variety of clubs established, though the formal education of the school-room and mechanics institute type had often been discarded in favour of the more informal education based on recreation, and though the military discipline of the boys' brigade was found to suit the temperament of many lads but to be anathema to others. Boys' clubs grew up precisely because the needs of boys were so varied. They were the answer to those who required the freer atmosphere of the recreational club where sport, handicrafts, and other elements of a balanced programme could be accepted or re-jected at will. Clubs of this kind seem to have appeared spon-taneously in many of the largest towns throughout the last forty years of the century. In Nottingham and Birmingham in the 'eighties, in Liverpool, Bristol and Manchester in the 'seventies, clubs were flourishing, and men were giving their services either because they felt it was God's work, or because it was the only way they knew of helping their fellow men. In London possibly the first boys' club, to be so called, was started in 1858 in Bayswater by Mr. Charles Baker, though others, sometimes called 'Youths' Institutes', were founded soon after. On the whole the institutes tended to stress the educational side of the programme, but some became so concerned about the working boys' need for character-training, and for recreation after a hard day's work that they began to lay stress on the evening classes. Thus a split occurred, some institutes remaining purely educational and others becoming boys' clubs.

By the 'eighties, when the settlements were beginning to develop, the need for clubs for working boys was more generally appreci-ated, and many settlements, led by Oxford House, began to run them, though Canon Barnett himself was not really convinced of their value. By 1888, so far had working boys' clubs and institutes developed in London that a federation was founded to promote interchange of opinion among those interested and to help each club by arranging sports competitions, by encouraging lec and the other activities of a club programme. The settl

1 *The Young Men's Christian Association.* The first in time was prob-ably the Y.M.C.A., started in 1844 by George Williams, a young drapery employee of Messrs. Hitchcock and Rogers, London. Having invited some of his contemporaries to a Bible Class and Prayer Meeting in his bedroom, they conceived the idea of regular meetings, and of forming other groups for the same purpose else-where. The movement spread, partly through the business con-nexions of the firm, though Mr. Hitchcock himself took no more than a benevolent interest in it, and partly because it obviously answered a real need of this type of young man. Its purpose was to create an active Christian missionary organization among young men, and to build their Christian character. The religious motive was therefore uppermost. Later literary and scientific lectures were organized; and by 1845 T. H. Tarlton, a city missioner and Williams' friend, had become the first salaried secretary and missionary of what had now come to be called the Y.M.C.A. Within ten years the movement had spread in this country and abroad to such an ex-tent that an international conference was called in Paris, and a 'World Alliance' formed (1855). It is curious that an international organization, however loosely formed, should have appeared be-fore a national constitution, with a council and divisional com-mittees, had been hammered out in the parent country. Yet such a constitution was not finally achieved in Britain until 1882. By 1894, when George Williams was knighted, no fewer than 405 local associations existed in England, Wales and Ireland, with nearly 34,000 full members and 26,000 associates.

The age group included boys and men of fourteen to forty years, though quite early (1857) a 'Youths' Section' was mentioned, and by 1880 a 'Boys' Department' established. The programmes soon developed from the early religious meetings and Exeter Hall lec-tures, to providing opportunities for games, both indoor and out, and to social gathering of all kinds.

2 *Young Women's Christian Association.* Quite separate in origin was Miss Robart's 'Prayer Union', which this daughter of a retired merchant founded in Barnet in 1855. Her object was to unite all young women, wherever they were, in prayer. But she soon real-ized that women had bodies as well as souls, and some provision for the general needs of girls began to be made. Lively social even-ings, with refreshments, became just as important as the prayers themselves. In the same year as the 'Prayer Union' was formed, the

Hon. Mrs. Arthur Kinnaird opened a Home in London for nurses en route to or from Florence Nightingale's hospitals in the Crimea. That need over, the house was used for girls coming up from the Provinces who were unable to pay more than moderate charges, the object being to provide a happy home life under Christian guidance. Out of this grew the women's hostels, so important a part of the Y.W.C.A. today. These two were the origin of what became the Y.W.C.A. in 1877. For a little before Miss Robart's death the two associations united under that title and developed rapidly during the rest of the century. Though the work has always extended beyond the provision of clubs, the various branches and institutes had social evenings for their members, with occasional open evenings for non-members. A club night once a week was considered quite often enough to bring girls out of their homes, and the every-night-in-the-week club was not only unheard of, but would have been severely frowned upon. The objects of the Y.W.C.A. were not unlike those of the Y.M.C.A., with whom it has always co-operated. In the 'Basis and Objects', printed in 1877, it declared itself both a missionary movement, aiming at the spread of Christianity among all women, and a Union for prayer. The movement was always inter-denominational, but full members were required to be practising Christians.

3   *The Girls' Friendly Society*. It is said the idea for a G.F.S. came to its founder Mrs. Townsend in 1871 as she was listening in Winchester to an address on rescue work. 'If', she thought, 'the power of rescue work will be increased by organization, why should not work be organized to save girls from falling.' Mrs. Townsend was born the daughter of a clergyman in Kilkenny in 1841, and married a clergyman, who was subsequently called to a living in Winchester. Turning the idea over in her mind, she prepared a pamphlet in which she pleaded for the girl who leaves her native town, and is then lost to view.

Far different it would be, if the moment a girl went out into the world, she could be furnished with a letter to another friend, who by kind interest and loving words would keep her in the right path, one also who would make her known to the clergyman of the parish, and thus obtain for her his guidance and spiritual instruction.[1]

The matter was discussed at a meeting at Lambeth Palace, and the Girls' Friendly Society was duly started on 1st January 1875.

[1] E. A. Pratt, *Pioneer Women* (1897).

The organization developed as the idea was accept branch was based on the parish, membership being thirteen to twenty-five years of age, of any denom associates were the interested ladies of the parish were the basis of a hierarchy which culminated council. In 1897 there were over 150,000 full memb 17,000 working associates in England and the spread all over the world. The work was partly lonely girl, but partly also to develop recreatio tional facilities for young girls, whether they wer or in a strange town.

4   *The Boys' Brigade*. William Alexander Smith v and on his father's death moved from the nort Glasgow, where he entered his uncle's business. A twenty, after attending a Moody and Sankey M the Free Church, and in the following year, the Volunteers. His interest in both religion and r never left him, and he made them the basis of th tion he was to found.

He became a Sunday school teacher at the N attended, and soon saw that though the young cause they were sent by their parents, the olde 'ran wild' and became a nuisance to their neigh that such high spirits should be directed and th thing they could be proud to work for. With thi few friends laid before the Mission a plan to twelve years old into a brigade where they wou drill, punctuality, cleanliness, and obedience mand. The brigade would be an object of tha *esprit de corps* which public school boys were matter of course. The success of his idea was in movement spread, the two principles of militar Sunday bible class being common to every bri time William Smith, following the example o the Y.M.C.A., gave up his own work in busir full-time to the boys' brigade.

5   *Boys' Clubs*. It is Mr. Eager's opinion[1] tha which shaped the origins of 'boys' clubs' institutes, whose desire was to impart u

[1] W. McG. Eager, *op. cit.*

1   *The Young Men's Christian Association.* The first in time was probably the Y.M.C.A., started in 1844 by George Williams, a young drapery employee of Messrs. Hitchcock and Rogers, London. Having invited some of his contemporaries to a Bible Class and Prayer Meeting in his bedroom, they conceived the idea of regular meetings, and of forming other groups for the same purpose elsewhere. The movement spread, partly through the business connexions of the firm, though Mr. Hitchcock himself took no more than a benevolent interest in it, and partly because it obviously answered a real need of this type of young man. Its purpose was to create an active Christian missionary organization among young men, and to build their Christian character. The religious motive was therefore uppermost. Later literary and scientific lectures were organized; and by 1845 T. H. Tarlton, a city missioner and Williams' friend, had become the first salaried secretary and missionary of what had now come to be called the Y.M.C.A. Within ten years the movement had spread in this country and abroad to such an extent that an international conference was called in Paris, and a 'World Alliance' formed (1855). It is curious that an international organization, however loosely formed, should have appeared before a national constitution, with a council and divisional committees, had been hammered out in the parent country. Yet such a constitution was not finally achieved in Britain until 1882. By 1894, when George Williams was knighted, no fewer than 405 local associations existed in England, Wales and Ireland, with nearly 34,000 full members and 26,000 associates.

The age group included boys and men of fourteen to forty years, though quite early (1857) a 'Youths' Section' was mentioned, and by 1880 a 'Boys' Department' established. The programmes soon developed from the early religious meetings and Exeter Hall lectures, to providing opportunities for games, both indoor and out, and to social gathering of all kinds.

2   *Young Women's Christian Association.* Quite separate in origin was Miss Robart's 'Prayer Union', which this daughter of a retired merchant founded in Barnet in 1855. Her object was to unite all young women, wherever they were, in prayer. But she soon realized that women had bodies as well as souls, and some provision for the general needs of girls began to be made. Lively social evenings, with refreshments, became just as important as the prayers themselves. In the same year as the 'Prayer Union' was formed, the

Hon. Mrs. Arthur Kinnaird opened a Home in London for nurses en route to or from Florence Nightingale's hospitals in the Crimea. That need over, the house was used for girls coming up from the Provinces who were unable to pay more than moderate charges, the object being to provide a happy home life under Christian guidance. Out of this grew the women's hostels, so important a part of the Y.W.C.A. today. These two were the origin of what became the Y.W.C.A. in 1877. For a little before Miss Robart's death the two associations united under that title and developed rapidly during the rest of the century. Though the work has always extended beyond the provision of clubs, the various branches and institutes had social evenings for their members, with occasional open evenings for non-members. A club night once a week was considered quite often enough to bring girls out of their homes, and the every-night-in-the-week club was not only unheard of, but would have been severely frowned upon. The objects of the Y.W.C.A. were not unlike those of the Y.M.C.A., with whom it has always co-operated. In the 'Basis and Objects', printed in 1877, it declared itself both a missionary movement, aiming at the spread of Christianity among all women, and a Union for prayer. The movement was always inter-denominational, but full members were required to be practising Christians.

3   *The Girls' Friendly Society.* It is said the idea for a G.F.S. came to its founder Mrs. Townsend in 1871 as she was listening in Winchester to an address on rescue work. 'If', she thought, 'the power of rescue work will be increased by organization, why should not work be organized to save girls from falling.' Mrs. Townsend was born the daughter of a clergyman in Kilkenny in 1841, and married a clergyman, who was subsequently called to a living in Winchester. Turning the idea over in her mind, she prepared a pamphlet in which she pleaded for the girl who leaves her native town, and is then lost to view.

Far different it would be, if the moment a girl went out into the world, she could be furnished with a letter to another friend, who by kind interest and loving words would keep her in the right path, one also who would make her known to the clergyman of the parish, and thus obtain for her his guidance and spiritual instruction.[1]

The matter was discussed at a meeting at Lambeth Palace, and the Girls' Friendly Society was duly started on 1st January 1875.

[1] E. A. Pratt, *Pioneer Women* (1897).

The organization developed as the idea was accepted. Each local branch was based on the parish, membership being open to girls of thirteen to twenty-five years of age, of any denomination, while associates were the interested ladies of the parish. The branches were the basis of a hierarchy which culminated in the central council. In 1897 there were over 150,000 full members, and nearly 17,000 working associates in England and the movement had spread all over the world. The work was partly to befriend the lonely girl, but partly also to develop recreational and instructional facilities for young girls, whether they were living at home or in a strange town.

4 *The Boys' Brigade.* William Alexander Smith was born in 1854, and on his father's death moved from the north of Scotland to Glasgow, where he entered his uncle's business. At the age of about twenty, after attending a Moody and Sankey Mission, he joined the Free Church, and in the following year, the Lanarkshire Rifle Volunteers. His interest in both religion and military discipline never left him, and he made them the basis of the great organization he was to found.

He became a Sunday school teacher at the Mission Church he attended, and soon saw that though the younger boys came because they were sent by their parents, the older ones did not, but 'ran wild' and became a nuisance to their neighbourhood. He felt that such high spirits should be directed and the boys given something they could be proud to work for. With this in mind, he and a few friends laid before the Mission a plan to organize boys over twelve years old into a brigade where they would learn elementary drill, punctuality, cleanliness, and obedience to the word of command. The brigade would be an object of that loyalty, pride and *esprit de corps* which public school boys were said to acquire as a matter of course. The success of his idea was instantaneous, and the movement spread, the two principles of military inspection, and the Sunday bible class being common to every brigade. Within a short time William Smith, following the example of George Williams of the Y.M.C.A., gave up his own work in business to devote himself full-time to the boys' brigade.

5 *Boys' Clubs.* It is Mr. Eager's opinion[1] that the four movements which shaped the origins of 'boys' clubs' were: the mechanics' institutes, whose desire was to impart useful knowledge; the

[1] W. McG. Eager, *op. cit.*

military organizations like the army cadets and the boys' brigades, who tackled disorderliness and slackness by military discipline; the playing fields movement, which developed athletics and provided open spaces; and the temperance movement, which tried through coffee houses and the like to find alternatives to beer houses and gin palaces. These four influences were clearly seen in the variety of clubs established, though the formal education of the school-room and mechanics institute type had often been discarded in favour of the more informal education based on recreation, and though the military discipline of the boys' brigade was found to suit the temperament of many lads but to be anathema to others.

Boys' clubs grew up precisely because the needs of boys were so varied. They were the answer to those who required the freer atmosphere of the recreational club where sport, handicrafts, and other elements of a balanced programme could be accepted or re-jected at will. Clubs of this kind seem to have appeared spon-taneously in many of the largest towns throughout the last forty years of the century. In Nottingham and Birmingham in the 'seventies, in Liverpool, Bristol and Manchester in the 'eighties, clubs were flourishing, and men were giving their services either because they felt it was God's work, or because it was the only way they knew of helping their fellow men. In London possibly the first boys' club, to be so called, was started in 1858 in Bayswater by Mr. Charles Baker, though others, sometimes called 'Youths' Institutes', were founded soon after. On the whole the institutes tended to stress the educational side of the programme, but some became so concerned about the working boys' need for character-training, and for recreation after a hard day's work that they began to lay less stress on the evening classes. Thus a split occurred, some institutes remaining purely educational and others becoming boys' clubs.

By the 'eighties, when the settlements were beginning to develop, the need for clubs for working boys was more generally appreci-ated, and many settlements, led by Oxford House, began to run them, though Canon Barnett himself was not really convinced of their value. By 1888, so far had working boys' clubs and institutes developed in London that a federation was founded to promote the interchange of opinion among those interested and to help each club by arranging sports competitions, by encouraging lec-tures and the other activities of a club programme. The settlements played an important role in this, and for many years Oxford House contrived to find a secretary for the federation.

Meanwhile two men in different parts of England were obtaining experience and crystallizing their thoughts about boys' clubs. They were the Hon. T. W. H. Pelham, Chairman of the London Federation, who in 1889 published a *Handbook to Youths' Institutes and Working Boys' Clubs*, and C. E. B. Russell, a man of great efficiency and purpose who became honorary secretary of the Manchester boys' brigade while pursuing an exacting job in a railway company. The fruits of his experience were published in 1908 in his manual on *Working Lads' Clubs*, which set out what was probably typical of the methods and principles of club work in Manchester during the latter part of the nineteenth century.

Both men agreed on the need for a varied programme, and for premises to be as attractive as possible. Both agreed on the need for night schools attached to the club. But in spite of a similarity of outlook on these points these two men, who were to have so deep an impact on clubs not only of their own generation but of the subsequent one, were poles apart on some fundamental questions. Pelham preached the doctrine of personal influence, Russell discounted it; Pelham argued that a club should be small, and never outgrow the personal influence of the leader, that attractions in themselves soon cease to be effective and that only personal friendship was lasting. He was in favour of the boys helping to run their own club, claiming that members' committees for simple projects like the running of a concert should be created as a start, and that with experience the boys would grow up to undertake committee work for the whole club. To this Russell was completely opposed. An efficient business man himself, he wanted to see the large club elaborately organized by men who knew what they wanted, and saw that they got it. Management, he thought, should be a 'benevolent despotism . . . a common cause of failure in clubs is want of discipline'.

Thus while both men stressed the importance of education and religion, and wished to build up boys' characters and bodies so that they became good citizens, they differed completely on how it should be done.

6 *Girls' Clubs.* The nineteenth century does not present us a picture of growing effort for girls comparable to that for boys. Perhaps this was because girls were more closely guarded than boys, and a

town full of working girls wandering the streets in the evening because they had nowhere else to go, was unheard of. If girls were about in this way, it was commonly believed they had already succumbed to temptation, or would soon do so. It is known that girls' clubs had been started in the early 'sixties during the cotton famine, especially for mill girls in Lancashire, but there is apparently no record, to indicate that they persisted. In 1883 Miss Maude Stanley had founded in London the 'Girls' Club Union' to which, by 1890, some twenty-eight London and Provincial clubs were federated. So there must have been a number of clubs in existence, though little is known of them today. In her book *Clubs for Working Girls*, written in 1890, Miss Stanley suggested that her aim was to keep girls off the streets, and to provide for their leisure hours 'healthy and safe recreation' which parents would not, or could not provide at home. She was careful, however, to deny any wish to 'raise girls out of their class, but rather to see them ennoble the class to which they belong'.

AN ASSESSMENT OF THE NINETEENTH-CENTURY CONTRIBUTION TO YOUTH WORK

While work for youth in the present generation has different emphasis, the elements of the modern arrangements in both principle and method can be distinctly seen in the nineteenth-century activities. These elements may be summarized as those concerned with religion and morals; with education in the broadest sense; and with the physical and recreational activities.

1 *Religion and Morals*

With one or two exceptions, youth movements were the direct outcome of the religious motive, and were started with the express purpose of promoting Christian knowledge, and inculcating Christian principles. There was no reluctance, as there is occasionally now, to speak openly of religion, and youth leaders would not then have excused themselves from so doing on grounds of their own incompetence. For in the main, clubs were started either to keep the members on the 'straight and narrow path', or to bring them back to it should they have strayed, and the only method regarded as sure was a study of the scriptures, and the direct teaching of moral principles. Nor were the members expected to assume a purely passive role. For in many an organization they were encouraged to be active missionaries of the Christian faith among their fellows. Whatever the methods, or under whatever auspices the organizations were founded, the principles were rooted in religion: to quote the boys' brigade literature, 'The object is to advance Christ's Kingdom'.

Only two organizations, which have persisted, were founded without the principal motive being religious. They were the Co-operative Youth Clubs, and the Army Cadets, and even these were never indifferent to Christianity. Consumers' co-operative societies, begun in 1844 as part of the working class movement to improve the status and condition of working people, were always interested in their young people, and from the beginning spent a certain proportion of the surplus funds on education and recreational activities. Thus while their elders found social nourishment in men's and women's guilds, the young people had joined junior circles or comrades' classes whose object was to keep the aims and principles of co-operation before their minds and train them to participate in community affairs.[1] Indeed, apart from the Catholic Young Men's Society, and some of the London boys' clubs, the co-operative societies were alone in seeking to prepare youth specifically to take their place in a developing democratic society. In the days before the Forster Education Act of 1870 this was a useful service and though it was mainly concerned with the furtherance of co-operative principles, these principles were interpreted in the widest sense.

The 'Army Cadet Force' was founded on a very different motive. During the Napoleonic Wars 'Volunteer Forces' were established in England to guard against invasion, and some were formed among the elder boys of the public schools. The volunteers, however, persisted after the war was over, and gradually began to raise their own 'Cadet Corps'. In 1860 the Queen's Westminster Rifle Volunteers allowed some thirty-five cadets to lead them as they marched past Queen Victoria. After this the development of the Cadet Corps was rapid. The cadets wore the uniform of the parent battalion, which provided the officers and the administration. Though the military discipline contributed to standards in dress, behaviour, and morale, those responsible could not remain unaware of the other needs of the young people. Within twenty years a 'strong movement started to use cadet organization as a means

[1] Co-operative Youth Movement Literature.

253

of rescuing boys from the squalor of bad housing, cheap liquor, wrong feeding and bad working conditions'.[1] The first to state these aims was the First Manchester Cadet Regiment, R.A., raised in 1884. Another was the East London Cadet Corps, 1885, based on Toynbee Hall. Octavia Hill encouraged their formation on her housing estates.

2 Education

Religion, then, as a means to the development of adults of good character and industrious life, was in most cases the openly preached and principal method of nineteenth-century youth work. The emphasis in the twentieth century has moved away from the purely religious and moral to education in the broad sense. For, though the basic techniques of reading and writing and the main body of transmissible knowledge are now passed on in the schools, helping youth to find serious human relationships in a free community is one of the objects of the modern club. Participation in the government of the club, with all the self-discipline and mutual forbearance this involves, practice in toleration, and the social education involved in choosing one's life partner—it is the provision of opportunities for all these activities which today is regarded as the justification of a club. A club with these attributes is a training ground for democratic living in adult life. How far did these aims exist in the nineteenth century? The answer is not easy to find owing to the different climate of thought. For instance, class distinctions were both more rigid and more widely accepted than they are today, and youth did not yet expect to practise the freedoms and responsibilities of its elders. We can perhaps answer the question better by looking more closely at the place given in the clubs to individual initiative, responsibility, preparation for voluntary service in public life, and experience in human relationships.

(a) *Initiative.* Initiative to start clubs or organizations came mainly from adults, and the initiative in the clubs did not as a rule lie with the young people themselves. Yet the first of the modern youth movements, the Y.M.C.A., was started through the initiative of a few youths who felt the need to join with other youths for prayer and Bible study, and who wanted other young men to find what they themselves had discovered. In its initiation nothing could have

[1] Official Handbook of Army Cadet Force Association, Cap. II.

been more democratic, and if later, the Y.M.C.A. became an organization for youth rather than by them, it but followed the general experience of the time. With this notable exception, most organizations for youth in the nineteenth century (as in the twentieth) were begun by adults, who were the leaders, and who appointed or recognized other leaders who were also adult. But where the leader of the nineteenth century differed so much from his most modern counterpart was in his conception of leadership. Then, in the main, the leader set the stage, arranged what was to be done, and who should do it. The club member received the orders, accepted the policy, and enjoyed a programme made for him, his own initiative was seldom encouraged in any important way, and he remained passively rather than creatively active. In a sense, the position both of leader, as the general controller, and of member, was simpler, more clearly definable, and the relationship easier to work than the more complex one in the modern club. And in its avowed purpose of making honest and industrious individuals who had cultivated habits of obedience to their superiors, the nineteenth century method was undoubtedly successful.

To this generalization, the one outstanding exception (though there were probably others) as far as can be ascertained, is found in the London boys' clubs at the end of the century. Here, if the leaders followed Pelham's advice, practice in self-government by the boys was an important part of club life. How far the leader, who was to be a close friend of the boys, influenced them in the decisions they took, we have no means of knowing, and how far the method would have been successful in the large club, where the leader's influence was more dispersed, we do not know. But it is significant that Russell, who advocated the very large club, believed in the benevolent dictatorship by the leader, and would have none of these experiments in self-government by the boys.

(b) *Responsibility*. Some glimmerings of the need to give responsibility to youth is evident in the methods of some of the organizations, such as the boys' brigade, and those other uniformed organizations, which divided the brigade into smaller sections, as in the Army, and put boys in charge of them. While undoubtedly responsibility of this kind was valuable and extremely educative, it was responsibility exercised in a known framework, and accepted as such by the younger members. This is different in both kind and quality from that expected of committee and council members in the freer atmosphere of a modern mixed youth club, or from the responsibility that was beginning to be given in the London boys' clubs of the later part of the century.

(c) *Work in Public Life.* The two bodies that set out deliberately to train their members for work in organizations outside the club were the co-operative societies and the 'Catholic Young Men's Society'. The latter, an avowedly proselytizing organization, hoped to achieve the return of the Roman Catholic Church to its original place in Britain, by training its young men to enter every walk of public life open to them. The Co-operative Societies have always had a social purpose, to promote working-class emancipation and extend the ideal of co-operation. It was logical for them, therefore, as one of the aims of their youth work, to train young people and encourage them to enter in due course those fields of public life that were beginning to open to them. Otherwise in the nineteenth century youth movements were not notably interested in this aim.

(d) *Experience in human relationships.* In a sense all club activities must consider human relationships. But because the modern club is so conscious of this element it is useful to examine earlier experience to find how they tackled it. On the whole the problem to youth workers then was not complex. They encouraged regular attendance at the club so that friendships could be made. They set out to attract strangers (this, for instance, was part of the G.F.S.'s *raison d'être*) to give them the solace of human companionship. They realized that the crowded housing conditions in which the young lived were often a bar to much that was necessary in human growth; and they understood all too well that alternative ways of cultivating human relationships, like the street or the public house, were dangerous. They tried therefore to provide premises and a programme of activities that would 'keep the young off the streets' and would attract them regularly to make their friendships within a framework of club rules and customs. There is no evidence however that nineteenth-century youth workers thought deeply about the question. The differing needs of children and adolescents, the problem of club discipline, the importance of encouraging or withholding responsibility—the freedom to join in the club programme or to do nothing—all these questions so difficult and complex in the modern club to them had fairly simple and straightforward answers. Above all the controversial question of mixed sex clubs had not raised its head, and though many of the church week-night meetings and the Bible classes included both sexes, it was not until the twentieth century that this matter became an issue of policy.

3 *Physical and Recreational Activities*

Youth work is inconceivable without its physical activities. The young are too conscious of their bodies for them to be long ignored. Thus the experience of all organizations was to provide sooner rather than later for some bodily activity whether it be drill or games. The programme of the Y.M.C.A., though not typical of all provides an example of the changes in thought on this matter. It started by cultivating religious activities but soon extended these into the literary and then into the social and physical fields. Physical exercise, either through games, or drill, or walking, became part of the plan, while amusements of other types were added as well. It was not long before some began to look upon sport and entertainment as a good thing in itself, and this for a time produced a hardening of attitude, for we find Mr. Edwyn Shipton, the assistant general secretary under George Williams, warning his committee that 'the Association must not be considered as places of amusement for young people'. It was not long before he had to alter his view and recognize the value physical training had in youth work. These heart-searchings were not shared by all organizations; the uniformed ones, for instance, recognized the value of physical exercise frankly from the beginning. In the girls' organizations, hampered as the members were by the kind of clothes they wore, and tired by long hours of work, sport and drill were not so appropriate. Instead they concentrated on the care of the body, and learnt something of hygiene and home nursing. However, by the end of the century, they too were beginning to drill in the new uniformed organizations for girls such as 'Girls' Guildry' and 'Girls' Life Brigade'.

CONCLUSION

Both the principles and methods of youth work showed a gradual change as the century advanced. At first the need was to provide some basis of knowledge for an otherwise ignorant proletariat. This knowledge and the basic skills for its acquisition were required, not only because an industrial system needed them, but because it was thought that habits of obedience and piety were more difficult to instil if the individual had no access to the written word. In the earliest forms of youth work, it was therefore necessary to concentrate on the scholastic side, so that both normal children and delinquents might be given the means to help themselves, and find a socially accepted place. When the schools had become so numerous (even before 1870) that most children had access to one, youth work took on a broader and less easily defined form. It is doubtful whether in general the twin aims postulated earlier, were departed from in any material degree, but preparation of the boy and girl for their place in society, and helping to save them from the sins and temptations of this world, took a different form.

EPILOGUE

THIS survey of the principal trends in social work during the nineteenth century has disclosed the profound effect the culture and public opinion of a society can have upon the men and women who try to assist those in distress, or attempt to promote the welfare of those unsuccessful in promoting their own. The culture of the last century, in its acceptance of class divisions, and its growing belief in the rectitude of the ideals attributed to the middle classes, imposed an attitude towards human frailty that was bound to affect the principles and methods upon which social work was based. The limitations in fundamental knowledge were also profound in their influence. When most men lacked deep acquaintance with psychology, anthropology, or sociology, and the scientific researches into social phenomena were in their infancy, it is understandable that social workers went forward, mainly on an intuitive basis, in their work of help and guidance.

But what they achieved with the resources they had has been a challenge to those whose equipment has been different. For the principles they evolved and the methods they developed deserve the closest study by the practitioners of a later day. The twentieth century is seeking to solve its cruder ills of poverty, ill-health and bad housing by state and community effort, and to tackle its subtler problems of personal inadequacy and disharmony by the use of modern knowledge and a changing concept of individual worth. And in so doing a study of the struggles of the pioneers and the hard experience they won are both a lesson and a hope.

INDEX

Able-bodied men, 44, 48, 49

Absenteeism in Church, 31

Accommodation societies, 84–5

Ackworth Quaker school, 39

Adoption, 148

After-care, children, 141–6; drunk-ards, 178; moral welfare homes, 221; prisoners, 158–63; ragged schools, 245; reformatories, 171

Age of consent, 210

Agricultural wages committee, 1824, 44

Allen, Wm., 37, 39, 40

Almsgiving, 71, 72, 78, 87, 93, 94, 100, 188

American social work, 93, 108, 149, 166, 171, 172, 174, 200, 232

Anti-Corn law league, 36, 41

Apprenticeship, 131, 146, 186, 195, 205

Archer, Mrs., 136, 137, 143

Army cadets, 253–4

Arnold of Rugby, 30

Baptists, 33

Barlee, E., 51

Barnardo, T. J., 102, 129–31, 148

Barnett, S. A., 2, 53, 54, 94, 101, 112, 224–34, 250

Bath society, 86–7

Bedford, P., 37, 39, 40

Bedford institute, 39, 81

Bentham, J., 9, 17, 19, 20–2, 25, 54

Blackley, Canon, 61

Blind, 183–90

Blue-coat schools, 126

Boarding-out, 130, 131, 134–8; supervision, 138–41; after-care, 141–6; private, 146–8

Booth, Bramwell and Florence, 208, 219

Booth, Charles, 27, 36, 61

Booth, William and Catherine, 213, 217

Bosanquet, C. B. P., 97

Boys' brigade, 249'

Braidwood, T., 192

Bright, Joseph, 9, 41

British society, 13

Bull, G. S., 31

Burdett-Coutts, Baroness, 150

Burgoyne, M., 13

Burial clubs, 23

Butler, Josephine, 207–10, 212, 217, 219

Carlile, Wilson, 214–15, 217

Carlyle, T., 7, 10, 22, 41

Carpenter, Mary, 133, 144, 163–72, 181, 243, 244, 246

Case committee, 82, 88, 89, 103

Case work, 1, Chaps. IV, V, VI, 98, 124–5, 162, 172, 179, 197

Catholic young men's society, 256

Chadwick, Edwin, 12, 20, 26, 46, 47, 54, 55, 59, 127

Chalmers, Thomas, 2, 3, 7, 50, 67–78, 88, 113, 155

Chamberlain, J., 26, 61

Champney, W., 30

Charity, 96, 175

Charity organization society, 2, 27, 60, 85, 90, 92–114, 119, 145, 183, 186, 188, 200, 214

Chartism, 10, 14, 21, 22, 32, 35, 49, 50, 62

Children in factories, 11

Children in mills, 11, 12

Children's agent, 171, 173
Children's homes, 130, 133
Children's officer, 126, 152
Christian socialists, 22, 32, 33, 116, 122
Church army, 179, 214–15
Church of England, sisterhoods, 218; temperance society, 173, 175, 178, 214
Cobbe, Frances Power, 56
Cobbett, Wm., 7, 10, 15
Colquhoun, 8, 10, 16, 18, 19, 67–8, 74
Community organization, 1
Contagious diseases acts, 207–8
Co-operative movement, 23, 36
Co-operative youth work, 253
Cottage homes, 130, 132–4
Cripples, 199–205

Davies, D., 43
Deaf, 190–7
de l'Epée, 191
Democracy, 34, 41, 60
Denison, Edward, 90, 100, 223–4
Deserving, 68, 91, 98–9
Dickens, C., 7, 36, 55
Discharged prisoners' aid societies, 158–63
Disraeli, B., 7, 14, 22
District schools, 128
Dresden institute for blind, 185

Eden, F. M., 43, 67, 74
Education, 13, 14, 24, 37, 60, 155–6, 157, 171, 185–6, 194, 198, 202, 203, 224, 227, 228, 233, 236, 241, 244, 254–7
Elberfeld system, 78, 79–80
Emigration, 158, 171
Employment, 178, 187, 195, 205, 220, 245
Epileptics, 198–9
Evangelical movement, 16, 28, 29, 31, 32

Fabian society, 60
'Fallen' women, 207–22

Fox, Rev. W. G., 36
French revolution, 9, 14, 34, 41
French social work, 93, 135, 167
Friendly societies, 2, 10, 18, 23, 51
Fry, Elizabeth, 37, 38, 153–8

Gaskell, Mrs., 22
George, D., 11
Gilbert, Elizabeth, 184
Gilbert's act, 44
Girls' friendly society, 145, 248–9
Girls' guildry, 257
Girls' life brigade, 257
Godwin, 20
Goschen minute, 50, 58, 96
Graham, Sir J., 48
Grellet, Stephen, 154–5
Group work, 1, 156, 223–58
Guardians of the poor, 48, 51, 54, 56, 58, 61, 62, 73, 83, 95, 96, 113, 126, 127, 128, 132, 134, 136, 183, 196, 198
Guthrie, Dr., 240

Handloom weavers, 10, 47
Health of towns association, 36
Heinicke, S., 191
Hill, Florence, 134
Hill, Matthew D., 173
Hill, Octavia, 53, 115–25, 142, 226, 232, 254
Hopkins, Ellice, 211–12, 219
Hospital almoner, 108–9
Housing, 12, 13, 33, 53, 115–25
Hunt, Dame A., 201

Improvement societies, 85
Indigence, 68, 76
Industrial and reformatory schools, 40, 133, 163–72, 242; Kingswood, 168
Industrial revolution, 10, 11, 14, 17, 23, 25, 27, 43
Insanity, 197–9
Inspectors, 26, 60, 62

Jebb, Lt.-Col., 159, 160
Jevons, 26, 36

Jones, Agnes, E., 57
Jones, Sir R., 201

Kingsley, C., 22, 33

Labour homes, 163, 178
Labour test, 51
Labour yards, 178, 215
Ladies' diocesan association, 58
Lancaster, J., 40
Less eligibility, 46
Levy, W. H., 184
Libraries, 24, 37
Life insurance companies, 23
Little, W. J., 200
Local government board, 26, 58, 59, 60, 61, 62, 139
Loch, Charles, 2, 78, 79, 97
London, condition of, 12, 26, 61, 62
Lowther, 10
Luddites, 10, 34

Magdalen hospital, 217
Malthus, 16, 17, 19, 45
Manchester refuges, 201-2
Martin, M., 7
Martin, Sarah, 159
Maurice, 32
Mechanics' institutes, 14
Mendicity, 7, 8, 13, 86
Mentally defective, 197-9
Merrington, Martha, 57
Methodists, 28, 31, 34-5
Metropolitan association for befriending young servants, 143, 145-6, 236
Metropolitan common poor fund, 61
Metropolitan poor amendment act, 59
Metropolitan visiting and relief association, 89, 96
Mettray colony, 167
Mildmay deaconesses' home, 81, 90
Mill, J. S., 19
More, Hannah, 13, 154, 236-9, 244
Municipalities, 26, 29, 51

Napoleonic war, 38, 43, 45
National children's homes, 131-2
National society for the prevention of cruelty to children, 149-52
National society (Education), 13
Newman, 32
Nonconformists, 14, 29, 32, 33

Oastler, R., 11, 31
Oddfellows, 23
Old age pension, 1, 61
Otherworldliness, 31, 34
Owen, R., 7, 12, 20, 39, 40
Oxford movement, 32

Paine, Tom, 9, 34
Pauper education act, 1862, 143, 186, 198
Pauperism, 71, 75
Payment of social workers, 107, 242
Pelham, T. W. H., 251
Penitentiaries and homes, 218, 219
Philanthropic society, 163
'Philanthropist', The, 39
Philanthropy, 29, 30
Police court mission, 174-80, 182, 216
Poor relief in England, 7, 12, 21, 43-63, 73, 83, 95, 96, 113, 126, 127, 128, 132, 134, 136, 183, 196, 198
Poor relief in Scotland, 70, 77
Poor relief—Jewish, 1, 82-4
Population, 9, 12, 19
Poverty, 68, 74, 81, 196
Pounds, John, 240-1
Preventatories, 142
Probation, 172-80
Probation in America, 172, 174-5
Public parks, 24, 37

Quakers, 37

Ragged schools, 40, 116, 129, 166, 202, 203, 205, 236, 240-6; union, 242
Raikes, Robert, 236-7
Rainer, Frederick, 174, 176

Rathbone, William, 57, 79, 80, 95
Rauhe Haus, Hamburg, 131, 132, 167, 169, 171
Records, 89, 103-4, 140-1
Refuges and shelters, 51, 84-5, 217, 220
Register, 109-10, 189, 204
Religion, 13, 14, 16, 28-42, 129, 131, 154, 171, 180, 190, 196, 202, 211, 213, 214, 229, 230, 238, 247, 248, 249, 252-4
Rescue work, 212, 216
Retreat (York), 38
Revenue, 8, 26
Ricardo, 18, 19, 20
Robbins, L., 17, 19
Royal commissions, 26
Royal national orthopaedic hospital, 200, 203
Ruskin, John, 116-18, 120, 224
Russell, C. E. B., 251

Sabbatarian movement, 29
Salvation army, 208-10, 213, 214, 217
Savings banks, 23, 36, 40, 52, 90, 122
Schools, 131, 133; cripple, 203; prison, 164; ragged, 240-6; Sunday, 236-9
Senior, Mrs. Nassau, 139, 142, 144
Settlement laws, 44, 52
Settlements, 61, 225-34; Toynbee Hall, 226, 228, 230, 232; Oxford House, 229-31, 250; Manchester, 228, 231
Shaftesbury, 7, 9, 31, 36, 160, 246
Sims, G. R., 27
Smith, Adam, 18, 19
Smith, Southwood, 36
Social democratic federation, 60
Social science association, 53, 58, 93, 147, 168
Socialism, 9, 20, 22
Society for bettering the condition of the poor, 8
Spitalfields soup society, 39
Speenhamland, 44-7
Stanley, Maude, 252

Stead, W. T., 208-210
Stephenson, T. B., 131-2
Stepney, 58, 59
Strangers' friend societies, 81, 92
Sunday schools, 13, 30, 236-9
Suppression societies, 85-6

Temperance movement, 24
Ten hours act, 23, 34
Thomas, H. O., 201
Thrift movement, 23, 36, 40, 52, 90, 122
Tidd-Pratt, 23
Tolpuddle martyrs, 34
Toynbee, Arnold, 224-5
Tractarians, 32
Trade unions, 9, 14, 25, 37
Training of social workers, 78, 105-7, 124, 179, 206, 213-15, 221
Treloar, William, 204
Trevelyan, 7, 45
Trimmer, Mrs., 239
Twining, Louisa, 55-8, 134, 142-4

Unitarians, 36
Utilitarians, 16, 18-21, 25, 50

Vipond, E., 37
Visiting, 104, 113
Visiting societies, 88-90, 166, 188, 200

Wages, 24, 47
Ward, Mrs. Humphrey, 203
Waters, Esther, 27
Way, Hon. Mrs., 142-3
Wesley, J., 28, 34
White cross league, 211-12
White slavery, 208-11
Whitechapel, 59
Wilberforce, 29
Workhouse, 44, 47-9, 54-9, 61, 127, 144, 146, 208, 215; apprenticeship, 146; District schools, 128, Norwich preventatories, 142; schools, 128, 134; test, 47; visiting society, 56

Working men's clubs, 40

Working men's college, 33, 117

Young men's Christian association, 247, 254-5, 257

Young women's Christian association, 236, 247-8

Youth clubs, 231, 236, 249-52

Youth work, 235-58

Youths' institutes, 250